ECONOMIC METHODOLOGY AND FREEDOM TO CHOOSE

ECONOMIC METHODOLOGY AND FREEDOM TO CHOOSE

Patrick J. O'Sullivan

UWIST, Cardiff

London
ALLEN & UNWIN
Boston   Sydney   Wellington

Allen & Unwin, the academic imprint of
Unwin Hyman Ltd
PO Box 18, Park Lane, Hemel Hempstead, Herts HP2 4TE, UK
40 Museum Street, London WC1A 1LU, UK
37/39 Queen Elizabeth Street, London SE1 2QB, UK

Allen & Unwin Inc.,
8 Winchester Place, Winchester, Mass. 01890, USA

Allen & Unwin (Australia) Ltd,
8 Napier Street, North Sydney, NSW 2060, Australia

Allen & Unwin (New Zealand) Ltd in association with the
Port Nicholson Press Ltd,
60 Cambridge Terrace, Wellington, New Zealand

First published in 1987

British Library Cataloguing in Publication Data

O'Sullivan, Patrick J.
  Economic methodology and freedom to choose.
1. Economics—Methodology
I. Title
330'.01'8   HB131
ISBN 0–04–330375–7

Library of Congress Cataloging-in-Publication Data

O'Sullivan, Patrick J., 1951–
  Economic methodology and freedom to choose.
Based on the author's thesis (doctoral—European
University Institute of Florence, 1981)
Bibliography: p.
Includes index.
1. Economics—Philosophy.   2. Economics—Methodology.
I. Title.
HB72.O78   1987   330.1   86–22247
ISBN 0–04–330375–7 (alk. paper)

Set in Trump Medieval by Grove Graphics
and printed in Great Britain by
Biddles Limited, Guildford, Surrey

To

My Mother and Father

Contents

Foreword

MARK BLAUG

The last few years have seen a simply amazing renewal of interest in the methodology of economics, amazing, that is, in the light of the traditional antipathy of economists to any and all questions of methodology. Apart from six major books – Bruce Caldwell (1982), *Beyond Positivism: Economic Methodology in the Twentieth Century*; Lawrence Boland (1982), *The Foundations of Economic Method*; A. W. Coats (ed.) (1983), *Methodological Controversy in Economics: Historical Essays in Honor of T. W. Hutchinson*; Johannes Klant (1984), *The Rules of the Game: The Logical Structure of Economic Theories*; T. Lawson and H. Pesaran (eds) (1985), *Keynes' Economics: Methodological Issues*; and E. Roy Weintraub (1985), *General Equilibrium Analysis. Studies in Appraisal* – and three anthologies – W. L. Marr and B. Raj (eds) (1983), *How Economists Explain. A Reader in Methodology*; B. Caldwell (ed.) (1984), *Appraisal and Criticism in Economics. A Book of Readings*; and D. M. Hausman (ed.) (1984), *The Philosophy of Economics. An Anthology* – the journals have of late been full of articles on methodological issues, culminating in the appearance of the first issue of a new journal in *Economics and Philosophy* in April, 1985.

Patrick O'Sullivan's book is a welcome addition to this growing body of literature. It stands out from other books of the genre not only because of its greater concern with the philosophical foundations of alternative methodological positions but also because of its singular thesis. It argues that economists have consistently failed to appreciate the profoundly subjectivist character of their own theories, employing a mode of explanation of human action that has more in common with the hermeneutic preoccupations of nineteenth-century German philosophers than with the positivist-empiricist tradition of British philosophy. Economists have prided themselves on following the mechanical-causal mode of explanation of the natural sciences, whereas in fact they have always utilized what he calls the 'teleological' mode of explanation, according to which economic behaviour is explained as the effect of the deliberate and purposive intentions of individual economic agents. Economists have sat at the feet of Thomas Hobbes, David Hume and John Stuart Mill but have actually marched with Max Weber and Alfred Schutz. (It is indeed Alfred Schutz, the late Austrian-American philosopher and sociologist, who emerges as O'Sullivan's hero of economic methodology.)

O'Sullivan has a simple explanation of the surprising misunderstanding on the part of mainstream economists of their own style of reasoning: the German style of teleological explanation was thought to be grounded in '*a priorism*', that is, the belief that there is valid knowledge of reality which does not depend for its justification on sense experience, thus ruling out the empirical testing of hypotheses, which alone was said to distinguish science from non-science. But O'Sullivan argues that there is little philosophical basis for this positivist prejudice against the teleological mode of explanation: a subjectivist interpretation of human action does not entail a commitment to *a priorism* and does not obviate the necessity of checking every substantive proposition about human behaviour against the observable evidence of that behaviour. This much was made clear by Max Weber and Alfred Schutz but even O'Sullivan is forced to concede that the Austrian economists, and particularly the neo-Austrian followers of Ludwig Von Mises, who *did* espouse the teleological brand of causal explanation in economics, were partly to blame for the orthodox prejudice against subjectivism because of their studious insistence on an extreme brand of *a priorism*.

Enough has now been said to suggest the thought-provoking flavour of O'Sullivan's book, which can hardly fail to set the cat among the methodological pigeons. There is much detail in this book with which I personally disagree – the interpretation of the ideas of Imre Lakatos, the fundamental argument for methodological monism, the distinction between the applicability and the truth-value of scientific theories, and so on – but even as I disagreed, I was made to think again. For my part, I prefer books that rouse the mind rather than those that lull it into agreement and that is the sort of book this is.

London

Acknowledgements

This book has grown out of the doctoral thesis which I presented at the European University Institute of Florence in January 1981. The original thesis was prepared between 1977 and 1980 in the pleasant surroundings of the European University Institute of the Badia Fiesolana in the Tuscan hills just outside Florence. Subsequent work on developing the thesis into the form of this book has been carried out in Cardiff, London and the Irish seaside village of Rosslare Strand. This is an array of locations almost as varied as the range of topics in economics, the human sciences and pure philosophy which I have sought to cover in the book and I may note in particular that the often wild maritime atmosphere of Rosslare Strand proved highly conducive to creative philosophical reflection, even if at times encouraging solipsistic thoughts.

Since the book is an interdisciplinary exercise in the fields of philosophy and the human sciences I have incurred a wide range of debts of gratitude of which I shall now try to record the most important. Professors Patrick Masterson of Dublin, Louis Duquesne de la Vinelle of Louvain and Mark Blaug of London have given me persistent encouragement, advice and help, and I have had many long discussions with them on questions that have arisen in the book. Above all, perhaps, I should thank them for never having lost faith in the enterprise, in particular when I was a rather eccentric doctoral student at Florence. (Some other members of staff at the Institute were not quite sure what I was doing, I suspect.)

I also owe a debt of gratitude to the late Lord Vaizey of London, to Professor Raymond Boudon of Paris and to Professor Pierre Salmon of Dijon, all of whom read patiently through drafts of this work, giving advice and constructive criticism, during the years when it was being prepared as a doctoral thesis. My thanks are also due to Professor Glyn Davies of University of Wales Institute of Science and Technology, Cardiff who secured for me a permanent academic post against all the odds (given the financial climate in the Universities in Britain) in 1982: it was the acquisition of this permanent post which allowed me at last to settle down and get on with completion of the book. I should also mention that the Department of Economics and Banking at UWIST has proved to be a most congenial atmosphere in which to develop my ideas. Those lively students who attend my regular philosophy symposia have contributed enormously by their constant outpouring of radical new ideas and perspectives, while my staff colleagues, in particular Nigel Allington, have demonstrated considerable interest in my work.

There are others to whom I owe academic debts of gratitude for the manner in which they have contributed towards the eventual position I have put forward in this book: Professors Desmond Connell and Patrick Lynch of Dublin and Professor David O'Mahony of Cork. But more than any other I should mention Tony Barlow of Cork who throughout the past seven years has never ceased to be a source not only of encouragement but also of the most incisive criticism – often carried out in the course of delightful Italian dinners accompanied by excellent Chianti. In relation to all of the above, I hasten to add of course the usual disclaimer that in the end I alone am responsible for the views expressed in the book.

In addition to these many academic acknowledgements I should also like to record my sincere gratitude to the Bank of Ireland whose scholarship award made my three-year sojourn in Florence, as a doctoral student, possible. Mr J. F. M. Rudd, Secretary of the Bank, administered the scholarship in an efficient and highly sympathetic manner, while Mr R. J. Quilty of the Bank of Ireland in Wexford was always prepared to help out in the labyrinthine maze of financial headaches which are liable to surround any long stay in Italy. I should also like to thank my sister, Mrs Kate O'Sullivan-Gallagher, who patiently and efficiently typed up my doctoral thesis; and Mrs Margaret Aven and Mrs Juliette Thomas of Cardiff for the long hours of typing and photocopying of the present manuscript which they have carried out.

If anybody has tolerated my eccentricities over long periods it has surely been my parents. I should therefore like to express my sincere gratitude to them both for that long-standing tolerance and also for the way in which they have always encouraged and helped in every way my education and intellectual development. Since this book, growing out of my doctoral thesis, could be regarded as a culmination of that process I have dedicated it to them.

Lastly, I should like to express my thanks to my beautiful companion, Cecile. Herself also a philosopher, she has contributed immeasurably to this book both through our unending but always fascinating discussion of matters philosophical and above all by loving me and encouraging me when I needed it most.

Rosslare Strand, July 1985   Patrick J. O'Sullivan

Introduction

In the course of this book I shall be roaming far and wide in the realms of knowledge, visiting many exotic places whose significance to the work as a whole may not at first be obvious. Accordingly, in this brief introduction I shall attempt to give a sketch or flight plan of my proposed journey which may help the reader to grasp the overall strategy of the argument.

The main goal of the book is to make a definitive contribution to one aspect of the debates in the methodology of human science. I have examined the long-standing controversy between the subjectivist or interpretive approach to the methodology of human science with its teleological mode of explanation and (consequent) insistence on a radical differentiation of method between the natural and human sciences (methodological dualism), and the objectivist or behaviourist approach with its efficient causal mode of explanation of human action and (consequent) insistence that there is *no* crucial or essential difference of method between the natural and human sciences (methodological monism). I have sought to resolve that long-standing controversy once and for all by putting forward a hopefully decisive defence of the subjectivist-interpretive approach and an equally decisive rebuttal of the claims of the objectivist-behaviourist approach.

I should hasten to add that I have dealt here with *only one aspect* of the methodological debate in the human sciences. For in addition to the controversy between the subjectivist and objectivist approaches, which I have sought to resolve, there is a third major alternative approach to methodology of human science, opposed to both of these but about which I have said nothing at all in this work. This third approach may be broadly labelled as the 'social holistic' approach and like each of the above two approaches it comes in various versions, such as structuralism, historicism, or Marxism. In recent times the foremost proponents of the social holistic approach have been those from the neo-Marxist Frankfurt School of so-called 'critical social theory'.[1]

It is *not* because I regard this third approach as unimportant or as being on the lunatic fringe that I have said nothing at all about it in this work. Rather it is simply because an exhaustive treatment of the claims of the social holistic approach in relation to the subjectivist-interpretive approach (and the objectivist approach), similar to the treatment of the controversy between the subjectivist and objectivist approaches presented here, would have been far beyond the scope of this book and would merit another of the same scope and size. That is why I shall be emphasizing, in Chapter 16, that one of the major issues left outstanding by this book has been precisely the appraisal of the claims of the social holistic approach to methodology of human science. Having clarified this point at the outset I may perhaps be excused for having said nothing at all about the claims of the social holistic approach against the other two alternatives, a situation which might otherwise have seemed to be a glaring omission or oversight to many commentators on methodology.

The proposed defence of a subjectivist-interpretive approach against the claims of an objectivist-behaviourist approach will be carried out along two main lines of attack.

(1) Having argued in Part 1 that issues of methodology can only be dealt with and resolved decisively on the plane of philosophy, in Part 3 I propose a hopefully decisive philosophical defence of the subjectivist-interpretive approach with its teleological mode of explanation. This defence is carried out by deducing the central principles of a subjectivist-interpretive methodology from a foundation of absolute philosophical clarity in existentialist phenomenology, or more specifically, in the existentialist phenomenological analysis of human subjectivity. I shall also show how the same rock-solid philosophical considerations equally rebut decisively the claims of the objectivist-behaviourist approach to human science with its efficient causal mode of explanation.

(2) In order to bring the abstract philosophical discussion to life, I have also carried out in Part 2 a case study of the methodology in practice of a leading human science: economics. I show that in spite of what most mainstream economists have said or understood about their methodology, in practice the corpus of mainstream economic theory is an outstanding exemplification of the subjectivist-interpretive methodology at work in a leading human science. However, since methodological questions can only be adequately dealt with on the plane of philosophy, and not simply by describing what scientists actually do for that would beg the whole question involved in a critical appraisal of methods,[2] this case study cannot constitute conclusive evidence in favour of the subjectivist-interpretive approach. I should emphasize, therefore, that its purpose is purely illustrative.

As the work unfolds it will become clear that a comprehensive critical treatment of the methodology of human science will require that a variety of tricky or unusual side issues will have to be faced squarely. Consequently I shall have occasion at a number of points to travel up branch lines through some rarefied and exotic terrain which may seem to some to digress far from the main themes. In view of this I have provided a detailed retrospective summary of the central arguments of the book in Section 16.1.

From what has just been said it will be clear that the book as a whole has a decidedly interdisciplinary flavour. In fact I have presumed throughout a fairly deep appreciation of both philosophy and the human sciences, especially economics. Given the argument of Part 1, where

I show that any genuinely critical methodology of science must be based on philosophy, this interdisciplinary character of the work is inevitable and essential. For my own part, I was lucky enough to work in the purposively interdisciplinary atmosphere of the European University Institute of Florence when developing the germinal ideas of the book.

Notes

1 As expounded, for example, in the works of J. Habermas or H. Marcuse (cf. Chapter 16, pp. 251–257 for further elaboration on this approach and some references).
2 Cf. my rejection of 'descriptivism' as an approach to methodological questions in Chapter 2, p. 18.

PART 1

Philosophical Prolegomena

Introduction to Part 1

In this book I shall be carrying out a sustained and critical philosophical examination of the methods of the human sciences. The work is therefore essentially interdisciplinary in character since in addition to drawing on the human sciences and especially on economics (of which I present a methodological case study in Part 2), it also draws heavily on pure philosophy. The bulk of the purely philosophical argument will be found in Part 3, but because there are certain very fundamental philosophical positions and presuppositions which will pervade the work as a whole I have thought it advisable to outline these philosophical fundamentals at the outset. In doing so I would hope to give the reader a clearer idea of whither I am aiming and the springboard or point of philosophical departure whence I am setting out. I should add that far from being boring preliminaries, the contents of the four chapters contained in Part 1 are vital to an adequate understanding of the discussions which follow in Parts 2 and 3.

Of the various philosophical prolegomena which I outline in Part 1 by far the most important is my defence of a critical philosophically-based approach to the methodology of science guided by the regulative criterion of truth and which will stand in a normative relation to the practices of science. This notion of methodology pervades the work from beginning to end and is indispensable to it. I have sought to defend it by adopting a loosely dialectical form of argument – a form of argument which I have also adopted in Part 3 when I undertake the defence of the subjectivist-interpretive methodology of human science (cf. Chapters 12–14). The inspiration of dialectical modes or forms of argumentation comes both from Hegel's logic and from Plato's dialogues. A dialectical argument consists of three phases:

(1) The *thesis* phase, in which a position is asserted and positive arguments in its favour are laid out.

(2) The *anti-thesis* phase, in which positions contrary to (and so involving denial of) the thesis position are outlined. We then proceed to subject these antithesis positions to further criticism and refutation, that is, we 'negate the negation' of the thesis and so arrive at

(3) the *synthesis* phase, in which either (a) the thesis position is reaffirmed, but now in a manner in which a much deeper appreciation of its rational underpinning will have been achieved and in the light of which it may have been significantly modified or (b) a synthesis phase, in which both the thesis and the antithesis

phases have been largely surpassed and a new thesis has emerged from the critique of both earlier thesis and antithesis.

It is because the dialectical form of argumentation offers such a powerful and systematic way of presenting a rationally argued case that I have adopted it here in my defence of a philosphically-based approach to methodology, and will adopt it again in defending the subjectivist-interpretive methodology of human science in Part 3. The thesis phase of this argumentation in Part 1 occurs in Chapter 1 where I present the positive arguments in defence of a critical philosophically-based methodology of science. I invoke and defend the spirit of critical rationalism, arguing that it lies at the foundation of all human inquiry and in particular that it has been the very spirit of open-minded critique of received opinion and dogma which has made possible the spectacular advances in our understanding of the world achieved by the various sciences. I then go on to show that this spirit of critical rationalism must require the sciences to submit their methods to a critical-rational scrutiny guided by the criterion of quest for truth, which is the ultimate goal of all rational critique and inquiry. Since such a critique of methods of science cannot be carried out by any one of the sciences without becoming involved in vicious circularity and since any such critique raises ultimate questions concerning the conditions for the possibility of valid knowledge which belong to the field of pure philosophy, and specifically of a philosophy which is capable of grounding its own methods, I argue that it can only be based on a philosophy which is reflexively self-justifying.

Chapter 2 moves on to the antithesis phase of the dialectical argumentation by considering the main positions which have sought to deny that methodology of science should be based on philosophy and stand in a normative relation to scientific practices. I consider first and briefly the descriptivist position which simply holds that methodology ought to be nothing more than a description of what scientists do. I then go on to consider the much more serious challenge to my thesis of Chapter 1, which is presented by the anti-philosophies of positivism and of relativism, both of which hold that philosophy is a meaningless exercise; hence, *inter alia* it will follow that a philosophically-based approach to methodology is a pointless, nonsensical exercise. I have devoted some time to a decisive refutation both of positivism, and especially of relativism, because not only is such a refutation a crucial element in my dialectical defence of a philosophically-based approach to methodology of science, but I shall also have occasion to draw on these refutations at a number of other crucial junctures in the course of the book.

Finally, at the end of Chapter 3, I present the synthesis stage of my dialectical argumentation. Having 'negated the negation' by refuting the anti-philosophies of positivism and relativism I return to reassert the thesis that any science which is inspired by the critical rationalist spirit must carry out a rational critique of its methods and that such a genuine critique can only be carried out on the plane of philosophy and will, *qua* critique, stand in a normative relation to the practices of science. In the course of the argumentation our appreciation of just how vital such a critical philosophical approach to methodology is will have been considerably deepened; and in particular the indispensable character of truth as the ultimate regulative criterion of all inquiry will have been brought home by the refutation of the relativist anti-philosophy.

This dialectical defence of the critical philosophically-based approach to methodology is by far the most important of the philosophical prolegomena with which I deal in Part 1; for that conception of methodology is of the very essence of the work as a whole. I have also dealt with a number of less pivotal philosophical positions and presuppositions which I deemed it useful to clarify at an early stage: the so-called 'realist' conception of scientific theories (which might more appropriately be labelled as 'rationalist') and the whole question of the Popperian logic of falsification in regard to empirical testing of scientific theories.

Finally, in Chapter 4, I have given a sketch of the main features of the two methodological positions which constitute the terms of the debate and discussion carried out in the book, before proceeding in Part 2 to the detailed case study of economic methodology. I have indicated the main features both of the objectivist-behaviourist approach to the human sciences with its assertion of an efficient causal mode of explanation for human science and a unity of method between natural and human sciences; and of the subjectivist-interpretive methodology with its assertion of a teleological mode of explanation for human science and consequent differentiation of method between the natural and human sciences. In both cases I have also indicated the purely philosophical inspiration and underpinning of these opposing approaches to the methodology of the human sciences.

A comprehensive philosophical discussion of the issues at stake between these two opposing methodologies of human science will be presented in Part 3. I have introduced this preliminary sketch of the approaches and of their philosophical linkages in Chapter 4 in order to give some clear bearings to the methodological case study of economics which follows in Part 2 and which is carried out with one eye always on the overall goal of the work: the provision of a conclusive defence of the subjectivist-interpretive approach to methodology of human science against the objectivist-behaviourist approach.

1

A Critical Philosophical Methodology of Science

In this first chapter I will deal with the thesis stage of the overall dialectical argument of Part 1 of the book; that is to say, I will outline the positive arguments in defence of a critical and philosophically-based methodology of science that will stand in a normative relation to the practices of the various sciences.

1.1   The Spirit of Critical Reason

The central driving force of Western thought and civilization in general can fairly be said to be the *spirit of critical rationalism*. By this I mean the willingness to call every received opinion into question in the quest for *truth*. It should be emphasized at the outset that the spirit of rational critique is inextricably bound up with the quest for truth. Truth is the goal, or *telos*, of the activity of critical reasoning.

It has been precisely this spirit of critical rationalism which has underpinned the spectacular achievements of all Western thought and civilization if not indeed of all human civilization. In the fields of the specific sciences, natural and human, the amazing advances in our understanding of the world and of man (if not in our uses of that understanding)[1] have been made possible because scientists have been prepared ruthlessly to call into question received conventional wisdom and shibboleths in the quest for a more adequate insight into the workings of the natural world and of human society. Equally in the field of the arts, it has been the willingness to call into question and depart from the prevailing conventions and received opinions, both as to form and content of the work of art, which has given us the incredibly rich diversity of the Western artistic heritage with its various great movements and expressions.

The highest form of expression of this critical rational spirit in its quest for truth is found in the field of philosophy, for while all of the other forms of human inquiry and expression of civilization take at least some propositions for granted as axioms without calling them into question, in philosophy every proposition is thrown open to question and nothing at all may be taken for granted. Philosophy, therefore, is concerned with the ultimate questions that man can raise about himself and the world. It must of course be admitted that philosophy has been a great deal better at posing the ultimate questions than it has been at answering them; more than one philosopher has spoken of the scandal of the great heap of discarded metaphysical systems of the past.[2] That fact does not detract one jot from the significance and importance of philosophy as the ultimate expression of the critical-rational spirit: it testifies only to the extreme difficulty of philosophical inquiries.[3] It still remains true that in a sense, *qua* ultimate expression of the spirit of critical rationalism, philosophy is the fountain-head of the whole of Western civilization.

Although the spirit of critical rationalism has been defended throughout the long history of Western civilization there is perhaps no defence of it more eloquent and powerful than one of its earliest expressions; that by Plato in ancient Greece. In various works, but most powerfully in the Republic,[4] Plato draws up a radical contrast between *doxa* and *episteme*. As the similes of the Divided Line and the Cave[5] make very clear, *doxa* is simply received common sense opinion, conventional wisdom of the masses. Such mere opinion is an amalgam of superstition, prejudice, convention and 'long-defunct theory', and its hallmark is precisely (or above all) that it is unquestioned and so rationally unfounded and uncritical opinion. Plato contrasts this *doxa* with *episteme*, by which he meant propositions which are rationally well founded, that is to say propositions which have been proven true after a process of critical rational reflection. For Plato, only *episteme* is knowledge properly speaking and the growth of knowledge requires that we should call into question, and indeed turn our backs upon, unfounded common sense opinion (the state of prisoners in the cave) and should seek and accept only those propositions which upon critical rational reflection can be said to be true, or at least acceptable until further notice for practical purposes (as well-corroborated scientific theories, for example). Moreover, for Plato the highest form of expression of this quest for rationally-founded truths was philosophy, precisely because in philosophy[6] 'no axiom whatever is taken for granted'.

Throughout the ages, Plato's insistence that the spirit of reason in pursuit of truth lies at the heart of all human inquiry and knowledge has been re-echoed by a long line of rationalist thinkers. Descartes, for example, resolved in the pursuit of genuine knowledge to call every received opinion and theory into question until he could find some proposition or set of propositions which he could not possibly doubt and which could thus serve as a basis of rock-solid certainty on which human knowledge could be built. Husserl, in more recent times, has argued that the spirit of Reason in its quest for truth has been central to Western civilization and has followed Descartes in looking for a rock-solid basis of absolutely true propositions from which a rationally founded body of human cognitions can be built up.[7]

Following Plato and others, I would argue, therefore, that the critical activity of Reason lies at the root of all Western thought and civilization, if not of all civilization in general: the activity of critical reasoning is the very basis of all human cognition and knowledge properly speaking. Furthermore, the goal to which this fundamental critical activity of Reason is directed, the *telos* which provides the criterion of critique is the quest for truth, or to be more precise, for conclusively proven truths.

Thus far I have not, strictly speaking, proved that the spirit of critical rationalism must be our starting point or must lie at the root of all human knowledge. I have only put forward suasive points concerning the spectacular achievements which the spirit of critical rationalism has made possible. It has sometimes been suggested that one cannot go any further than this in defending critical rationalism and that ultimately when we adopt such a fundamental stance we are involved somehow in an 'act of faith in Reason' (to use Popper's words). I should now like to indicate how a conclusive demonstration of the ultimacy of Reason in relation to all human cognition can be made, although the treatment of the point must, perforce, be cursory here and would merit a whole chapter if this were a work of pure metaphysics.

If it is denied that the critical activity of Reason in its search for absolute truths is the foundation of all human cognition this may be because either (a) it is held that the activity of reasoning is not an ultimate or the ultimate element in cognition and inquiry, or (b) it is held that the goal or *telos* of Reason, the attainment of conclusively proven truth, is in fact unattainable and so the critical activity of Reason is pointless and cannot be the foundation of all human knowledge. Taking the first of these alternatives, that the activity of critical reasoning is not an ultimate basis of cognition, the very attempt to put forward such a view, at least in the course of any discussion or academic work, involves a direct contradiction. For in the very act of putting forward the view in academic work or discussion, the proponent of the view will himself be reasoning. Put another way, the whole academic enterprise as well as the whole field of dialogue and reasoned discussion is inconceivable without the critical activity of Reason at its foundation; critical reasoning is of the very essence of the search for knowledge, at least where that search is carried out through dialogue or through academic channels rather than through black magic or other occult channels. Hence in any attempt to doubt or to deny that the activity of critical Reason lies at the basis of all human knowledge, the doubter, at least if he is engaged in any kind of academically acceptable work, must already be involved in reasoning and so the attempted denial founders hopelessly and immediately on the rocks of performative self-contradiction.[8] Any person who seriously and genuinely doubts that the critical activity of Reason does not lie at the very root of all human inquiry and cognition should in all honesty *give up all academic pursuits and all reasoned arguments*, both in regard to his denial of Reason and in regard to all other matters.

An alternative way of rejecting the fundamental role of critical reason in its quest for truth as the basis of all human knowledge is to hold that absolutely proven truths are unattainable, hence that to make the activity of Reason the key or basis of all human cognition is futile and can lead nowhere. This viewpoint, which denies that there are any absolute truths, or at least denies that there are any absolute truths discoverable by man, is known as 'epistemological relativism' or sometimes as 'conceptual relativism'. In Chapter 2 (pp. 23–30) I shall be discussing epistemological relativism at some length, and seeking to refute it by a line of argument very similar to that which I have just offered in regard to the ultimacy of the activity of Reason: I shall attempt to show that epistemological relativism is either self-contradictory or else involves hopelessly nihilistic consequences in regard to all reasoned discussion and academic work.

In the light of these rather briefly sketched considerations it may be seen that in invoking the spirit of critical rationalism with its quest for absolute truth at the very outset of the work I am not simply making an 'act of faith in Reason' or suggesting that it is a plausible starting point in the light of its past achievements. Rather I would argue that the critical activity of Reason must lie at the basis of all human cognition. For I have shown that in any reasoned discussion or academic inquiry, such as this is, there can be no other ultimate starting point than the critical activity of reasoning in its pursuit of truth. The attempt to assert otherwise becomes involved in a variety of hopelessly untenable absurdities.

I should perhaps hasten to add one crucially important but all too often forgotten qualification to my declared critical rationalist intent. It cannot be said often enough that the rationalist spirit is above all a spirit of open-minded critique, of *quest* for truth. Thus when the rationalist spirit is invoked it should not be imagined that a parade of absolute truths, or conclusively proven truths, is about to be offered. Many rationalist thinkers have succumbed to the temptation of constructing supposedly 'absolute' speculative systems in the past but it is not by these excesses that the ideal of the critical rationalist spirit should be judged. Rationalist thinkers would do well to remember always that most important of Socrates' remarks: that the only thing of which he was absolutely certain was the severe limitations of his own knowledge, the daunting extent of his ignorance.

In what follows, therefore, I shall seek to heed the Socratic maxim: although I shall put forward a small set of propositions as absolutely true I shall refrain from the construction of any new speculative system of supposedly absolute truths.

1.2   The Philosophical Basis of Methodology of Science

Having thus invoked the spirit of critical rationalism let us now turn to examine its implications in regard to the subject matter of this work; the methodology of the human sciences. Any science at all which is to retain any claim to having a critical rational foundation must at some stage subject its methods to a critical rational scrutiny before the court of

Reason guided by the goal of truth. When the methods of science are thus subjected to a critical rational scrutiny this will involve raising questions (a) concerning the conditions for the possible achievement of valid knowledge in that scientific field, and (b) arising out of the above, some questions regarding the nature of the objects studied by the science may have to be answered in order correctly to specify the conditions for valid knowledge of such objects.

No one specific science, however, can ever hope to provide such a critical methodology of science. In the first place, no specific science can ever hope to provide a critique of its own methods. If, for example, psychology were used to carry out a methodological critique of psychology that would involve using and so presuming the validity of the methods of psychology in order to carry out a critique of psychological methods. Since the whole purpose of the methodological exercise is to try to establish just what are valid methods in psychology it would therefore be viciously circular to assume the methods of psychology in carrying out a methodological critique of psychology. Exactly the same argument would apply to the attempt by any other specific science to provide a critique of its own methods.

If a science cannot turn to itself as a basis when carrying out a methodological critique because of the vicious circularity involved, what may we say of the possibility of turning to some other specific science. Now there is no reason of logic why psychology or sociology, for example, should not be used in carrying through a critique of the methods of economics or physics, except to the extent that exactly the same methods are involved in these various sciences. In that case the vicious circularity of assuming the validity of the methods whose validity we are trying to prove would appear again. In fact, there are many methods which are shared by all of the sciences and so once again the procedure is viciously circular, at least to some significant extent. In any case, even if the sciences had wholly different methods we would still be faced with the problem of providing a non-circular critique of the methods of whatever specific science we were taking as ultimate. Thus, for example, if sociology were being used as the basis for a critique of the methods of physics or economics, to the extent that the methods of the latter were very different from those of sociology, there would still remain the problem of providing a methodological critique of the procedures of sociology. Since no other specific science could be used without involving vicious circularity (for sociology has already been used to carry out a critique of their various methods), and since sociology cannot provide a critique of itself without becoming involved in vicious circularity, we reach the conclusion that no specific science, human or natural, can be used as a basis for carrying out a methodological critique of itself or of any other science without becoming involved in vicious circularity.

Having established that no one of the specific sciences may be invoked when carrying out a critical rational appraisal of the methods of the sciences we may wonder where to turn in developing such a methodological critique. If we examine the sorts of question which will be raised in a critical appraisal (inspired by the spirit of critical rationalism) we shall find that these are essentially philosophical questions, and so it is to philosophy rather than to any one of the specific sciences that we must turn when developing a critical methodology of science. As we have seen, a critical methodology will raise questions concerning the conditions for the possibility of valid cognition in various fields – an ultimate question which has been the classic problem area of epistemology – and questions concerning the ultimate nature or character of the objects studied by a science, which have been the classic concern of ontology or of metaphysics. Thus on a closer examination it appears that a critical appraisal of the methods of the sciences before the court of Reason will raise a set of ultimate questions which have been the classic concerns of philosophy, and so it is surely to philosophy rather than to any specific science that we should turn in developing our critical rational appraisal of scientific methods, that is to say, our critical methodology of science.

In the light of what has been said in the preceding pages about the process of methodological appraisal it must be added that in turning to philosophy as a source or basis for methodological critique of the sciences, it must be capable of living up to a very special requirement: it must be capable of providing its own ground, its own critical rational foundation. In the case of the various sciences we saw that no one science could ever hope to provide a critical methodological grounding of itself or of any other science without becoming involved in vicious circularity. Hence I argued that to carry out a methodological critique of the sciences we must look to another, more ultimate, discipline – philosophy. But the spirit of critical rationalism would require that we should subject the methods of philosophy itself to a critical-rational appraisal: yet since it is in philosophy that all of the ultimate questions are posed by Reason there can be no question of looking to some discipline lying beyond philosophy which can in turn be used to criticize and ground the methods of philosophy. (In any case, if we were to search for such a discipline we would be off on an infinite regress of critical appraisal which would result in our failing to ground any cognition at all.)

It is incumbent on philosophy, therefore, as the ultimate discipline to provide a critical-rational foundation of its own methods without becoming involved in a vicious circularity of the kind that arises if a specific science, such as psychology or physics, tries to provide its own methodological ground. It is in principle possible for philosophy to live up to this tough requirement. To do so, philosophy must be capable of producing a set of *reflexively self-justifying propositions* as its first principles. A reflexively self-justifying proposition is one which, in the very moment of being called into question or doubted, is seen immediately and indubitably to be true because the attempted denial of the proposition would involve the thinker or speaker in a performative contradiction. By a performative contradiction I mean a contradiction between the words spoken or proposition thought and the activity or activities in which the agent is engaged. To take the classic example of a reflexively self-justifying proposition consider the Cartesian'*cogito*'. If when I am reflecting or thinking I seek to assert the proposition 'I am not thinking', this involves a performative contradiction since in order to assert or to think that 'I am not thinking', I must think. Hence in a critical reflection on the proposition 'I am thinking' I can know with absolute certainty that the proposition is true since if I were to try to deny it I would still be thinking. Descartes went on to point out that if I reflect on my activity of thinking, not only can I know with certainty that I am thinking, I can also know that I actually exist, since once again if I try to deny that I actually exist I would still be thinking and so the attempted denial of my actual existence would again involve the nonsense of a performative contradiction.

Such propositions which can, upon reflection, be known to be absolutely true because the attempted doubt or denial of them would involve the nonsense of performative contradiction I shall call reflexively self-justifying propositions.[9] If a set of such propositions can be found (and the Cartesion 'cogito' is already an example) they will make possible a philosophy which is capable of providing its own critical grounding without vicious circularity. For if philosophy takes as its starting point or set of first principles the set of such reflexively self-justifying propositions, then since these propositions can in reflection be known to be absolutely true (that is they provide their own justification) it follows that philosophy by basing itself on these propositions as its springboard will have its own ground and will not stand in need of any further critical appraisal by any more ultimate discipline. Put another way, the set of reflexively self-justifying propositions provides philosophy with just that core of absolute truths which it requires in order to live up to its classical task of answering the most ultimate questions which can be posed by Reason in its quest for truth.

Although the terminology and manner of presentation I have adopted in arguing that philosophy must be built up from a set of reflexively self-justifying propositions is perhaps novel, what I am driving at here has been a long-standing theme in rationalist thought. Plato, in the simile of the divided line, insisted that since philosophy is the most ultimate discipline of all in Reason's quest for truth it must take nothing for granted and be based on first principles which, as he put it, will be 'self-sufficient' and so in need of no further justification.[10] Equally, Descartes sought as the starting point of his philosophy a proposition or set of propositions which could not possibly be doubted. I have already shown that the proposition which he chose as the absolutely indubitable starting point of his philosophy, the famous 'Cogito, ergo sum' ('I think, therefore I am'),[11] is a classic example of a reflexively self-justifying proposition, even though Descartes himself did not see it in quite those terms. He spoke instead of an 'absolutely clear and distinct idea'. Finally, I may remark that in more recent times Husserl clearly saw the necessity for philosophy to have at its core a set of absolutely indubitable propositions if it was to be capable of living up to its task of providing an ultimate critique of human cognition in various fields. Husserl felt that such

indubitable truths could be found in the realm of self-consciousness
and he argued that there were a great many more propositions of a
reflexively self-justifying, and so indubitable, kind than simply the
Cartesian 'cogito', which could be found in this sphere of consciousness
reflecting upon itself. These propositions are to be the foundation of all
philosophy and to be elucidated by the 'phenomenological method'.[12]
Again Husserl does not use the term 'reflexively self-justifying' to describe
the propositions which are to be the core of philosophy; rather he speaks
of the 'absolute givenness' or 'immediacy' of such propositions, but it is
quite clear from his work that by this absolute givenness of certain
propositions Husserl had in mind something similar to my notion of the
reflexively self-justifying proposition.

Thus while my terminology and presentation may be seen as somewhat
novel, what I have been arguing here in regard to the need for philosophy
to adopt as its starting point a core of reflexively self-justifying
propositions is very much in accord with a long line of rationalist thinking
in philosophy and at most gives an ancient and often implicit theme a
forceful new presentation.

In the light of these various considerations regarding the critical
appraisal of the methods of the sciences, we have now arrived at a clear
characterization of what is involved in 'methodology' of science. It is
perhaps worth remarking in the first place that methodology always
involves the adoption of a critical stance in relation to the practices of
sciences. It is not merely a description of the methods which scientists
adopt as might be imagined from the use of the term in many quarters,
especially in journal articles in the human sciences. This exercise of
describing methods actually used should properly speaking be called
'methodography' since 'methodology' denotes (from the Greek word
logos) a 'reasoning about methods' and so, in effect, a critical appraisal of
the methods used by a science.[13]

From the spirit of critical rationalism which I have invoked at the
outset it follows, *inter alia*, that the methods of the sciences should be
subjected to a careful critical scrutiny before the court of Reason, in other
words that it is of crucial importance to develop a genuinely critical
methodology of science as well as methodography of science. We have
seen that a genuinely critical and rational appraisal of methods cannot be
carried out by any of the specific sciences and that, therefore, the
methodology of science must be based on philosophy, in particular on
a philosophy whose first principles are reflexively self-justifying and
which thereby provides its own ground. Furthermore, since the impulse
towards methodological critique comes from the spirit of critical
rationalism – the activity of Reason whose *telos* is truth – it also
follows that the fundamental regulative criterion of a rational critique
of methods of the sciences must be the quest for truth. In other words,
when we are seeking to pass judgement on the validity or otherwise
of various procedures of science we are to be guided by the efficacy or
otherwise of those procedures in leading us towards the truth in science.
Finally, since methodology is a critique of scientific methods it will,

when complete, stand in a normative relation to the actual practices of science.

The conception of methodology outlined in this chapter, although widely held by various exponents of methodology of science throughout the ages, has been challenged, in particular in this century both by thinkers who have held that philosophy cannot or ought not to be the ultimate basis for scientific method, and by some others who have denied that methodology should stand in a normative relation to the practices of science. In the next chapter I shall review these 'anti-philosophical' approaches to methodology and by seeking to refute them conclusively I shall, in effect, be reinforcing powerfully the positive arguments in defence of a philosophically-based methodology which have been put forward in this chapter. Put in terms of the overall dialectical strategy of argument in Part 1, I have completed my statement of the 'thesis' phase of the argument in Chapter 1 and shall move on in the next chapter to the 'antithesis' phase of the argument.

Notes

1   Many of the technological uses to which advances in science have been put could hardly be called 'advances'. One does not have to be an ecologist to see that the use of nuclear physics to construct weapons of horrific destructive power is no advance of civilization.
2   Descartes, Hume, Husserl to name but a few.
3   Indeed, Sir Karl Popper has taught us that the supposed contrast between philosophy and the sciences on this score is bogus. Once we adopt the falsificationist approach to science we shall not be surprised at all to find the history of science equally littered with discarded old theories (cf. Aristotelian and, later, Newtonian physics).
4   Plato (1970), *The Republic* (Harmondsworth: Penguin Classics), bks 6, 7.
5   Plato, *The Republic*, pp. 275–86.
6   Plato, *The Republic*, p. 277.
7   E. Husserl (1965), 'Philosophy as rigorous science', 'Philosophy and the crisis of European man', in Q. Lauer (ed.), *Phenomenology and the Crisis of Philosophy* (New York: Harper). See also his more extended work (1970) *The Crisis of the European Sciences and Transcendental Phenomenology* (Evanston, Ill.: North Western University Press).
8   The proof I have offered here is an instance of the notion of a reflexively self-justifying proposition which I shall introduce later in this chapter (p. 12). The attempted denial involves a contradiction between a person's assertion and/or thought and his or her actions.
9   Because, when reflected upon, they are immediately seen to be true without appeal to other propositions.
10 Plato, *The Republic*, p. 277.
11 R. Descartes (1979), *Discourse on Method and the Meditations*, Discourse 4, p. 53 and also Second Meditation, pp. 102–12.
12 Husserl's philosophy is discussed at greater length in Chapter 12, pp. 176–79. On the specific theme here, cf. E. Husserl (1973), *The Idea of Phenomenology* (The Hague: Martinus Nijhoff), pp. 13–32.

13 There is a view that methodology should be completely replaced by
    methodography, arising from the assertion that the sciences are the very
    paradigm of valid cognition and so their methods, at least in principle, are
    beyond criticism. Such a view of methods and methodology is known as
    'descriptivism' and I shall deal with it, and refute it, in Chapter 2, p. 18.

2

The Challenge of the
Anti-Philosophies

In the last chapter I put forward a range of positive arguments in defence
of the notion that a genuinely critical methodology of science must be
based upon philosophy and will stand in a normative relation to the
practices of scientists. In this chapter I shall turn to examine the main
arguments which have been put forward against such a position, and by
disposing of those counter-arguments I shall thereby seek to buttress,
by a negative path, the positive arguments in favour of a critical
philosophically-based methodology already put forward.[1] I shall identify
three main approaches to scientific methodology which have rejected the
notion that it should be based upon a normative philosophical critique of
the methods of science: first, crude descriptivism and, secondly, and also,
thirdly, the 'anti-philosophies'[2] of positivism and of relativism. In the
course of the discussion which follows, it will become clear that while
'descriptivism' is a rather naïve position which simply ignores the
possibility of carrying out ‚a philosophical critique of the sciences,
positivism and relativism reject a philosophically-based methodology as a
direct result of a wider rejection of all speculative philosophy. Since this
latter is a much more serious charge to bring I shall devote most of my
attention in this chapter to an attempted refutation of positivism and
relativism.

2.1   The Descriptivist Approach to Methodology

The first position I shall consider is that of crude descriptivism. This
viewpoint holds that methodology is to be nothing more than a
description of the methods which are or have been actually employed by
leading scientists. In seeking inspiration in methodology, we should turn
therefore to the history of science rather than to philosophy, and any
notion of evolving a normative philosophical critique of the sciences is
simply ignored or else rejected outright without further ado. Clear-cut
elements of such a descriptivist approach are present, for example, in the

work of Thomas Kuhn[3] who has based such methodological conclusions as he does reach on an examination of the history of revolutions in scientific theory.

The most basic criticism of any such crudely descriptivist approach to methodology is that it adopts a naïvely uncritical approach to the practices of scientists. It puts the methods of the sciences in effect beyond the pale of rational criticism and thus involves a dogmatic assertion of, or act of faith in, those methods which puts them beyond question. Not only is such a blind faith in the merits of any line of human inquiry unwarranted, this reluctance or failure to call the methods of the sciences themselves into question betrays that very spirit of rational probing, of calling everything into question before the court of critical reason, which I have shown in the last chapter to be the kernel of the Western intellectual tradition. Without that spirit of rational inquiry the sciences as we now know them would never have emerged in the first place and so crude descriptivism involves an attitude to the methods of science which is directly at variance with the spirit of all genuine scientific inquiry.

Since crude descriptivism involves such a transparently uncritical and indeed 'unscientific' attitude to the practices of science it is not surprising to find that it has not secured widespread adherence among methodological commentators. It is worth remarking, for purposes of clarity, however, that since both positivists and relativists also hold that there cannot be a philosophically-based critical methodology of science they must also end up with an effectively descriptivist approach to methodology. If a philosophical critique is impossible, then methodology can only be some kind of description of the practices of the best or most successful scientists.[4] The difference between the crude descriptivist and the positivist or relativist lies in the manner in which they each reach this conclusion. Where the crude descriptivist reaches it simply by ignoring philosophy and adopting a blind dogmatic faith in the sciences, the positivist and the relativist reach the same conclusion only after a sustained and serious consideration of the possibility of philosophy, which culminates in a rejection of philosophy and hence, a fortiori, in the notion of a philosophically-based criticism of the methods of science. Not surprisingly, therefore, positivism and relativism have had many more adherents than crude descriptivism and it is these anti-philosophies which pose by far the greatest challenge to the notion of a critical methodology based on philosophy.

2.2 Positivism

We shall consider in the first place the 'anti-philosophy' of positivism. There have, of course, been a number of variations upon the basic positivist theme over the past century and a half, but the main features common to all positivists are our concern here. These common features are succinctly and powerfully summarized in A. J. Ayer's seminal work *Language, Truth and Logic*[5] and I shall pay particular attention to his presentation of the positivist position.

Postivism may, perhaps, be seen as an inevitable development or outgrowth of the broader empiricist tradition which has dominated Anglo-Saxon philosophy at least since the time of Locke and even since Hobbes. Empiricism is the view that all valid human knowledge must be based upon sense experience, on what can be perceived, and any knowledge claim not so based is 'sophistry and illusion'.[6] Ayer's positivism is an even more forthright statement of such a view in the form of the famous 'verification principle' of meaning. According to this principle, for a statement to have any meaning at all it must either be:

(1) A tautology, that is a proposition which simply stipulates how words are to be used in a particular language: a statement of definition of words, or
(2) an empirically verifiable proposition (at least in principle, that is a proposition which has some basis in sense experience).

Any proposition which is neither a tautology nor empirically verifiable is dismissed as meaningless and hence as incapable of having a claim to be a valid cognition.

Two points emerge straight away from this positivist viewpoint. First, since the bulk of philosophy (and certainly all speculative philosophy) is neither a mere set of tautologies nor a set of empirically verifiable propositions, it follows that most traditional philosophy is quite meaningless. Ayer actually speaks of the complete 'Elimination of Metaphysics'[7] and for the positivist the only possible role left for philosophy is in elucidating the meaning of words – an exercise which will consist entirely in the elaboration of various tautologies. Indeed, such a subordinate role for philosophy in the field of human inquiry has been envisaged by Anglo-Saxon thinkers ever since Locke, who spoke of philosophy as being 'employed as an underlabourer in clearing the ground a little and removing some of the rubbish that lies in the way to knowledge'.[8]

At the same time as philosophy is eliminated or accorded a very subordinate role, the modern sciences, and especially physics, are hailed as the paradigm of valid human cognition since they are based squarely on empirical evidence and are always verifiable in principle. Since philosophy has been denied any role other than that of clarifying linguistic usages, it follows, *inter alia*, that the positivist must reject any notion of philosophy developing a critique of the methods of science which would result in the issuing of norms for the methods which scientists ought to use. The positivist thus rejects any notion of a philosophically-founded methodology of the sciences and as a result he must end up with an effectively descriptivist attitude to the methods of science. Indeed, since to positivists the sciences constitute the paradigm of valid cognition such an attitude to methodology is fully consistent with their overall position.

A second point arising from the verification principle also deserves some emphasis. Although enunciated in the first place as a principle of meaning, that is of the conditions which a proposition must fulfil in order to have any meaning at all, the verification principle also covertly embodies a theory of knowledge; it contains an implicit epistemology. For it is quite clear that Ayer and other positivists, in seeking to show that certain types of (philosophical) proposition are meaningless, are in effect putting forward a theory of what precisely constitutes a valid human cognition. Indeed, it is obvious that they hail the sciences as the paradigm not so much of a meaningful set of propositions as of a body of valid human knowledge claims. Hence the 'verification principle' of modern positivism contains an implicit but ill-disguised theory of knowledge which is in a direct line of descent from the empiricist tradition.

Turning to offer a refutation of the positivist attempt to eliminate a philosophically-founded critical methodology of the sciences it will not be sufficient to point to the fact that it ends up with an effectively descriptivist attitude and that such an attitude is hopelessly uncritical and crude. For the positivist has reached this conclusion *faute de mieux*: it is not through ignorance of philosophy and its role but rather as the result of a carefully developed critical conclusion that all philosophy is nonsense that the positivist holds that a philosophically-based normative methodology of science is impossible. Hence a more elaborate argument on the plane of pure philosophy will have to be presented in order to dispose of this positivist challenge.

We have already noted that although put forward as a theory of meaning the verification principle enunciates in effect a generalized theory of what constitutes a valid human cognition in any field. It is, or involves necessarily, an epistemology, and it is *qua* theory of knowledge that I propose to criticize this fundamental principle of positivism and its anti-philosophical implications. Put succinctly, the positivist theory of knowledge which is embodied in the verification principle asserts that 'all valid human cognitions must either be tautologies or empirically verifiable propositions'. This assertion could be put forward in two possible ways, and in what follows I shall deal with each of these in turn.

(1) It could be proposed as a universally true proposition about human cognitions, as an absolute requirement for any genuine knowledge. This is quite clearly how the positivists have intended it to be taken.

(2) Alternatively, if the above interpretation gives trouble, the assertion could be construed as merely a plausible opinion or conjecture devoid of any absolutely binding assertions or claims.

The verification principle of positivism has almost always been put forward as a universally true proposition about human cognitions in general. Construed in this way the principle must, on pain of avoiding self-contradiction, be itself either a tautology or an empirically verifiable proposition. This in fact is a particular instance of a more general point which I made in Chapter 1 concerning any adequate theory of knowledge, namely that any such theory must be reflexively self-justifying and so consistent with itself. If we proceed to examine the verification principle in this light we can say immediately that it certainly is not simply a tautology. In laying down the principle, the positivists have not intended simply to stipulate the meaning of certain words in the language – an exercise which even by their own lights would be largely a trivial one.

If the verification principle is not a tautology then it must be an empirically verifiable proposition. However, upon closer examination, it will be seen that there are insurmountable obstacles in the way of seeking an empirical verification of the verification principle. To see this let us recall that the positivist principle amounts to the bold assertion that 'all valid human cognitions must either be tautologies or empirically verifiable propositions'. There are serious difficulties of principle involved in the notion of testing this assertion empirically.

(1)   First, any attempt to assert a strictly universal proposition – that is, a proposition whose range of possible empirical instances is infinite – on the basis of the necessarily finite sets of empirical evidence for it which men may hope to collect, involves the fallacy of induction. Consequently, the truth of the verification principle could never be established on the basis of empirical tests.

(2)   There are, in any case, some serious confusions involved in the whole idea of trying to verify the verification principle on the basis of empirical evidence. Since what we are trying to test is the assertion that 'all valid human cognitions are either tautologies or empirically verifiable propositions', what we require is to find some instances of valid theories in the various fields of human inquiry and to show that these valid theories are either tautologous or testable empirically.

The trouble here is simply this: how are we to identify a valid theory in any particular field of inquiry?

The positivist certainly cannot allow each field of inquiry to propose its own standards of validity since in that case each one of the fields which he has sought to denigrate as pseudo-science would have to be reinstated as valid knowledge: on their own terms serious philosophers and sorcerers make a contribution to human knowledge. Thus the positivist must evidently introduce some general or overriding criterion whereby a valid theory in any field of cognition can be identified. If he invokes the verification principle to establish what theories in any field are valid then he is begging the question, he is assuming what he wanted to prove, namely that all valid cognitions are tautologies or empirically verifiable. If, on the other hand, he invokes some other different criterion for recognizing the validity of theories in various fields he will be automatically denying the principle which he is trying to prove, which is that all valid cognitions are tautologies or empirically verifiable propositions and nothing else.

From these considerations it follows that the positivist theory of knowledge enunciated in the verification principle cannot be regarded itself as an empirically verifiable proposition: any attempt to test it empirically must encounter contradictions and other insurmountable logical difficulties. Since the verification principle is not a tautology either we may conclude that the principle is self-contradictory: it makes a purportedly universal assertion about valid human cognition which is neither a tautology nor an empirically verifiable proposition. Indeed, the verification principle, which I have already suggested is effectively a positivist epistemology, turns out to be a speculative philosophical proposition of the very type which positivists have sought to eliminate as meaningless. I conclude, therefore, that construed as a universally true proposition about valid human cognition the verification principle is self-contradictory and hence completely untenable.[9]

It might be thought that if we were to construe the verification principle as a mere plausible opinion rather than as a universally true proposition we could rescue it from the above logical difficulties. However, not only would the principle lose its power if so construed it would still encounter the problem of self-contradiction. For even if construed as a possible opinion rather than as an absolute truth, that opinion will embody the view that 'all valid cognitions are either tautologous or empirically verifiable' and will therefore be self-contradictory qua opinion[10] just as much as qua absolute truth.

In any case, if we construe the verification principle merely as a possible opinion regarding valid human cognitions it loses most of its power. It fails, for example, to eliminate philosophy (and hence fails to eliminate a philosophically-based critical methodology of science) since being only one possible opinion among others it cannot exclude the possibility that many thinkers may hold philosophy to be a discipline that is just as valid in its own field as the sciences are in theirs. Moreover, construed as an opinion, the positivist view which implies (as we saw) that the natural sciences are the paradigm of valid human cognition, and philosophy by contrast a load of nonsense, is not even plausible. For while it is true that the natural sciences have yielded up enormous tangible benefits to mankind in the material field through technology (trains, boats, planes and rockets to the moon), it is equally true that technology has also brought with it the agonizing over the appropriate use of nuclear power, the blight of pollution and the spiritual vacuum associated with affluence. On the other hand, philosophy itself has made vital contributions to the advance of human consciousness notably in the ethical field, but also by providing in its abstract speculations the inspiration for many of the most spectacular advances of the sciences (cf. Einstein's reflections on the philosophical problems of space and time led him towards relativity theory).

Hence we may conclude that even when construed as an opinion of the positivist rather than as the assertion of an absolute truth the verification principle is not only still self-contradictory, it is not even a plausible opinion upon examination and would certainly not be sufficient to eliminate philosophy.

The upshot of this sustained criticism of positivism is that I have shown that no matter how we construe the central principle of positivist thought – the verification principle – it turns out to be self-contradictory and so untenable. In particular, I have shown that positivism which embodies an implicit theory of knowledge fails to eliminate philosophy from the field of valid human cognitions, and so *a fortiori* fails to undermine the notion of a critical philosophically-based methodology of science.

2.3   *Relativism*

The third and final approach to scientific methodology which rejects the notion of a critical philosophically-based methodology is the anti-philosophy of relativism. As in the case of positivism the relativist does not simply reject the need for a philosophical critique of the sciences out of hand. Rather he reaches the conclusion that such a critique is impossible because of a wider conviction that all philosophy is impossible or nonsensical.

In introducing the anti-philosophy of relativism it will be useful to recall briefly the central tasks of philosophy such as were outlined in Chapter 1. Philosophy is that discipline which seeks to grapple with and to answer the most fundamental questions which man can pose for himself. In philosophy human reason probes relentlessly: it seeks to call everything uncertain into question until such time as a basis of absolutely certain cognitions which can put a terminus to further critical questioning is achieved. Put another way, philosophy is the quest for a kernel of absolutely true propositions which can form the basis of all rationally-founded human cognition, of knowledge properly so called. As I remarked in Chapter 1, this search for a core of absolute truth is ineluctable: man cannot renounce it unless he is prepared to renounce his rational powers.

Following from this conception of philosophy and the critical role of Reason we saw that any methodology of science which attempts a genuine critical appraisal of its methods will raise essentially philosophical questions about the conditions for the possibility of valid knowledge in various fields of scientific inquiry. Such a critical methodology will stand in a normative relation to the practices of the sciences and it will be guided by the overriding regulative criterion of truth : it will, in other words, be an outline of how scientists ought to proceed if they are to further the quest for truth; the quest for knowledge, properly speaking, in the field of the sciences.

I have recalled rationalist philosophical themes of the first chapter in order to throw up in relief their sharp contrast with the relativist anti-philosophy. Relativism is a progeny of positivism but it attempts an even more complete elimination of the philosophical approach than does positivism. We saw in the previous section that when the positivist puts forward his position as a universally valid − that is to say, as an absolutely true − theory of valid human cognition he is involved in self-contradiction.[11] Recognizing this serious shortcoming of positivism, relativists assert as their fundamental position that 'there are no absolute truths at all'. From this it follows immediately that philosophy as the quest for a basis of absolute truth which could ground all human knowledge is an entirely pointless search and so once again philosophy is eliminated. There is no truth and the quest for it in philosophy or elsewhere is immature if not stupid. Theories or beliefs are to be appraised not in terms of their truth value but solely in terms of such pragmatic criteria as their social usefulness, simplicity or predictive power, and so on.

From this elimination of philosophy it follows immediately (a fortiori) that the relativist will reject outright the notion of a critical philosophically-based methodology of science which would seek to lay down absolute rules of method and theory appraisal in science guided by the pursuit of truth as an overriding regulative criterion. Any such notion of a methodology of science derived from an (absolute) epistemology, that is from a philosophical theory of the conditions for the possibility of valid knowledge in any field, is complete anathema to the relativist. There are no absolute criteria for the appraisal of theories; and beliefs may be appraised only in terms of their usefulness, simplicity or other pragmatic criteria.[12] It may perhaps be added that most leading relativists, in a distinct echo of their positivist inheritance, regard the sciences and especially the natural sciences as the exemplar of a pragmatic and useful set of cognitions and hence as the paradigm of all valid human cognition.

Relativist approaches to scientific method have been widely upheld in recent times and this has been largely due to the widespread influence of Imre Lakatos and Thomas Kuhn on methodologists. Lakatos argues[13] that it is neither possible to prove a scientific theory true nor to prove it conclusively false, hence that truth value has no role to play as a criterion of appraisal of scientific theories. Lakatos, therefore, goes on to reject any kind of a critical philosophically-based methodology of science since any such approach would involve appraising the methods of science in the light of the quest for truth as the overriding regulative criterion (of appraisal). Indeed, it is quite clear from certain passages in his work that Lakatos adopts a wider relativist position since he holds that the pursuit of 'proven truth', i.e. absolutely grounded truth, in any field is pointless and involves what he calls the 'justificationist fallacy': the search for an absolutely conclusive proof of a proposition when no such proof is to be found. This espousal of a thorough-going relativism only underpins and strengthens Lakatos' rejection of a critical philosophically-based methodology of science. Instead of such an approach, Lakatos argues that methodology can only be based on the history of science: it is to be a rational reconstruction or redescription of the methods actually used by the best or most successful scientists.[14] Far from being derived from an epistemological critique, the rules of scientific method are simply conventions for procedure adopted by fiat by practising scientists.

There is a close resemblance between these views and the theory of scientific method which has been foward by Thomas Kuhn. For Kuhn the rules of scientific procedure are also a mere matter of prevailing convention and indeed Kuhn makes a violent frontal assault on the notion of a critical philosophically-based methodology which would lay down absolute standards of procedure and of theory appraisal guided by the regulative criterion of truth. Rules of method are for Kuhn part and parcel of the prevailing paradigmatic theory or 'research programme' and when paradigms conflict it follows that there are no absolute criteria whereby the merits of the competing paradigms may be unambiguously assessed. Whence Kuhn's famous conclusion that in periods of scientific revolution or 'paradigm change' all manner of irrationality breaks out as scientists seek to compel adherence of their fellows to one or the other paradigm theory.

There is little doubt that Kuhn's opposition to a critical philosophically-based methodology derives as with Lakatos from a wider relativist position. For as certain passages of his book[15] suggest, and as subsequent interpretations of Kuhn have made clear, Kuhn holds that there are no absolute truths nor any absolute criteria for the appraisal of theories in any field of human inquiry. All fields of human thought are dominated in any historical period by a prevailing paradigm which prescribes its own rules of method and theory appraisal. Human cognition in any field is thus no more than a matter of ideological fashion.

Furthermore, Kuhn's position, which regards methodology as simply the study of the historically-relative conventions which have been bound up with various paradigms and which rejects outright the possibility of a philosophical critique of method, could only be plausible if underpinned by such a generalized 'epistemological relativism'. Indeed Kuhn must be credited with having brought right out into the open one of the most important implications of relativism: he has argued that in the absence of any absolute set of criteria of theory appraisal the choice between competing paradigm theories in science must be an essentially irrational exercise.

Relativist models of thought have enjoyed widespread popularity in all fields of contemporary thought and culture and it may perhaps be useful to pause here in order to note the variety of different forms in which it has manifested itself. Thus when speaking of relativism in general I have meant what might more accurately be called 'epistemological relativism', the view that 'there are no absolute truths at all'. In addition to this most basic version we might also identify for example:

(1) *Logical relativism*: the view that there are no absolute criteria for the appraisal of validity in argument. There are clear elements of logical relativism present for example in Kuhn[16] alongside his less obvious espousal of epistemological relativism.

(2) *Historical relativism*: the view that while theories or beliefs may be said to be true they are true only for a particular historical epoch and not beyond it.

(3) *Ethical relativism*: the view that there are or can be no absolute moral standards.

(4) *Aesthetic relativism*: the view that there can be no absolute standards of beauty or excellence in the arts.

It will be clear that each of these more specific versions of relativism will have much more cogency when underpinned by the more general 'epistemological relativist' thesis that there are no absolute truths at all and many proponents of these more specific types of relativism have adopted or at least expressed explicit sympathy with epistemological relativism. Both for this reason and also because it is epistemological relativism which, by its elimination of the philosophical quest for truth, poses the most serious and direct challenge to the notion of a critical philosophically-based methodology of science, I shall concentrate my attention in the criticisms which follow on the 'epistemological relativist' thesis. If that thesis can be shown to be untenable then none of the other relativisms have much plausibility.

Before moving on to the detailed criticisms of relativism there is one rather vague and general point which I think should be made against all relativist positions. One of the reasons for the widespread contemporary popularity of relativist ideas is that they seem to strike a highly tolerant attitude to a wide variety of different opinions, whereas the philosopher or seeker after truth is portrayed by the relativist as a dogmatist by comparison. The ethical or cultural relativist, for example, prides himself upon an urbanely open-minded attitude to a range of different moral codes or art forms and suggests that the moral philosopher or art critic in his search for absolute ethical or aesthetic standards has often a closed mind to the values of primitive ethics or art. Without wishing to become involved in such ethical or aesthetic controversies I would suggest that upon a closer examination of any relativist position, but most especially of epistemological relativism we shall find that it is relativism which harbours by far the greater totalitarian potential.

In order to see this, consider the far from hypothetical case of a regime which decides that a certain scientific theory (or moral theory) would be 'socially useful' or would help to promote 'social justice' or the goals of the regime. Invoking epistemological relativism the regime may argue that theories are to be judged only by such pragmatic criteria as their social usefulness and so may adopt and even impose upon the academic community such theories as suit their purposes on the grounds that theories which are not 'socially useful' are 'in error' or are mere quackery. This is precisely what happened under Hitler in Germany (racial theories) and under Stalin in Russia (the famous case of Lysenko's biology).

How is our urbane and tolerant relativist to react to such situations? He may at the most record his distaste and disagreement with the regime's theories but he cannot consistently do any more. In particular, he cannot (as the philosopher can) invoke the pursuit of truth as the overriding goal of all human inquiry and insist that the quest for truth, however unpalatable it may turn out to be, is vastly more important than any consideration of social expediency. The philosopher, or seeker after truth, is engaged upon an enterprise which transcends the practical exigencies of any era or regime and it is only by insisting on the pursuit of truth as the universal and overriding goal of all human cognition that the thinking man can effectively defend and guarantee himself against totalitarian encroachments upon academic life. However abhorrent the relativist may find such encroachments and the 'socially useful' theories they bring with them, he remains largely defenceless against them.

The above considerations are somewhat vague and generalized and I shall now turn to a set of much more precise and, in my view, decisive arguments against epistemological relativism. There is nothing at all novel about these arguments since they follow much the same lines as the classic refutation of epistemological relativism put forward by Plato[17] against Protagoras in ancient Greece, and similar arguments have been put forward by Husserl and by Trigg in modern times against relativism.[18] Indeed in view of the conclusive character of these arguments it is somewhat surprising to find such a widespread recrudescence of relativist ideas today.

The central assertion of epistemological relativism is that 'there are no absolute truths at all'. This proposition may be taken to be a universally binding one, that is to say, as itself an absolute truth, or it may be taken merely as the expression of a possible opinion.

If we take the central assertion of relativism to be itself an absolute truth (we might dub this as 'absolute relativism') then we immediately encounter self-contradiction. For the relativist seeks to enunciate as an absolute truth that there are no absolute truths and so in the very act of enunciating the proposition as an asbolute he is contradicting what he is saying in the proposition. This is an even more blatant self-contradiction than that which we found in the positivist attempt to enunciate the verification principle as universally binding; and the contradiction arises in a very similar manner to that of positivism. For, loosely speaking, we may say that both the positivist and the relativist in their attempts to enunciate a universally binding proposition which would eliminate philosophy are themselves involved in philosophizing.

Since the absolute version of the epistemological relativist thesis encounters a direct self-contradiction analogous to that of positivism many relativists have put forward the thesis as itself only a matter of opinion, as one possible belief among a range of possible opinions. (We may dub this as 'relativist relativism'. They have sought to defend their opinion not on the ground that it is (absolutely) true but rather that it is more useful or fruitful, and so on. While this version of relativism shows a good deal more self-consistency than 'absolute relativism', it too encounters some fatal objections.

(1) In the first place, although a primary aim of relativism is to eliminate philosophy and the quest for absolute truths this version of relativism fails completely in the attempt to do so. For if relativism is just one opinion among many then there is no reason why the philosopher should not also be entitled to his viewpoint, which regards the quest for absolute truth as of paramount importance. Indeed since the philosopher will typically regard his intellectual activity as 'useful' in some sense, the upholder of a relativist relativism must perforce recognize that his opinion is on an exactly equal footing with the

opinion of the philosopher who asserts the importance of the quest for truth.

(2) Most relativists, as we saw, regard the sciences and especially natural sciences as the exemplar of useful and hence valid human cognition, while at the same time they disparage philosophy which seeks after absolute truths. Taken simply as the expression of an opinion about what sorts of inquiry are useful, this is not even a plausible position. As I have already noted in connection with positivism (cf. p. 22) while the sciences have brought enormous practical benefits to mankind in certain areas these have not been unmitigated blessing as the problem of pollution and the agonizing dilemmas over nuclear power amply testify. On the other hand philosophy has made vital contributions to the progress of civilization both in the moral field and as a source of inspiration for many of the most spectacular breakthroughs in the sciences.

(3) It is the third criticism of 'relativist relativism' which deals the decisive death blow however; for this position generates purely nihilistic consequences for the possibility of rational discussion. The relativist (whether absolute or relative) will be committed *inter alia* to the view that there cannot be any absolutely binding set of criteria for the appraisal of arguments, that is to say he must *a fortiori* uphold a 'logical relativism'. For if there were some absolute standards for the appraisal of valid argument then the propositions enunciating these standards would be absolutely true,[19] and so a thorough-going and consistent epistemological relativist cannot admit the possibility of such standards.

But if there are no absolute standards for the appraisal of arguments this eliminates in principle the possibility of a serious rational discussion, that is to say the possibility of learning or growing in knowledge through a rational exchange of views or dialogue. For unless one happens to share much the same set of criteria of appraisal of arguments as another person there will be no standard whereby the merits of competing intellectual positions may be rationally compared or assessed. Hence relativist (and absolute) relativism would mean that over a definite and possibly quite wide area rational discussion of opposing viewpoints would be pointless and impossible; where standards of appraisal differ, there genuine dialogue ends, and the proponents of various positions can only have recourse to sinister techniques of persuasion or to physical force when they seek adherents to their own viewpoint.

Since there are undoubtedly in existence fields of human thought which do not happen to share exactly the same criteria of appraisal of argument and since these are usually the fields among which rational dialogue is most interesting and morally most urgent, this criticism of relativist relativism is a particularly damning one and brings out once again the totalitarian linkages of relativism itself. For as Kuhn had the courage to infer, the consequence of relativism, when there are wide differences of opinion and no absolute set of criteria for their appraisal, is that we are left with irrationalism: you have your opinion, I have mine and there is nothing more to be said about it unless one of us is prepared to use force or techniques of indoctrination.

It may be appropriate to note that faced with a similar situation of widely differing intellectual positions whose criteria of appraisal are not the same, the philosopher or seeker after truth does not cop out or despair in the same way as the relativist must. Rather the appraisal of such widely divergent positions is the greatest challenge to philosophy and the first step in the attempt to mediate will be precisely to evolve and lay down a set of absolute standards whereby the competing positions can be rationally and decisively compared or assessed for truth value. Where, for the relativist, rational discussion terminates and gives way to the use of force, for the philosopher it entails perseverance in the rational quest for truth; to do otherwise is only to degrade and debase humanity.[20]

It must follow as an inescapable consequence of 'relativist relativism' that most academic work and discussion is an empty charade. Rational exchange of views can only occur between those who already happen to be in agreement on a comprehensive set of standards of appraisal and among such people there will typically already be almost universal agreement on substantive issues anyway so that rational discussion of views among them would be largely superfluous. Over any area where precisely the same set of criteria of appraisal are not shared – that is to say, over precisely the area where academic work is most interesting and rewarding – the relativist must conclude that no rational exchange of views or dialogue is at all possible. Hence the vast bulk of academic work is a vain pretence at rational discussion over areas where (for the relativist) no such discussion is possible.

This third line of argument against a 'relativist relativism' thus shows not only that the relativist has annihilated the possibility of rational discussion over a wide and interesting field, but also that he is involved in a 'peformative contradiction'. For we have just seen that most academic work must for the relativist be an empty charade, yet in putting forward his viewpoint in an academic work or debate against the upholder of the search for truth the relativist is by his actions contradicting the viewpoint which he is putting forward. He is by his actions making a fool of himself since he is endeavouring to engage in rational discussion in an area where he must regard such discussion as clearly impossible and pointless. The upholder of 'relativist relativism' and the seeker after truth are after all profoundly at odds with each other over the criteria whereby their positions should be appraised and so for a consistent relativist a rational exchange of views between them must be impossible. Hence the relativist, in putting forward his position in any kind of academic work or debate, is involved in a performative contradiction and he would do well to follow this parody of a famous maxim: 'Worüber man nicht diskutieren kann darüber soll man schweigen.'[21] Put another way, since I would not be writing this work, nor you, the reader, reading it, if either of us took the relativist version of relativism seriously, we may conclude that at least for any academic person or believer in rational discussion the position is literally untenable.

If epistemological relativism has thus been shown to be untenable it follows also *a fortiori* that the relativist attempt to eliminate a critical philosophically-based methodology of science guided by truth as an overriding regulative criterion has been a failure: philosophy and hence a critical philosophically-based methodology of science have withstood the challenge of the anti-philosophy of relativism. Indeed the whole relativist episode may be said to have underlined how vital is the critical philosophical approach to the very rationality of the whole scientific enterprise: Kuhn's relativism led him (inevitably) to the conclusion that the appraisal of competing paradigm theories is an entirely irrational matter.

2.4   The Progeny of Relativism in Philosophy of Science

In this final section, I propose to examine in somewhat more detail a number of particular relativist-inspired approaches to scientific methodology which have been current in recent years. Specifically, I shall be examining Kuhnian irrationalism and instrumentalism. My reasons for pausing further to look at these relativist-inspired positions are, first, that they have enjoyed widespread influence and popularity in recent times and since each of these positions is diametrically opposed to the notion of a critical philosophical-based methodology of science such as I have sought to develop here it will be useful to spell out in more detail why I dissent from each one of them despite their fashionability. A second reason for pausing over them is that at a number of later points in the work these positions will crop up in various guises and rather than engaging in long philosophical digressions later in the work to indicate why I reject the positions, I have included the discussion of them here in this first part of the book which deals with philosophical prolegomena.

The first type of relativist-inspired position which I propose to examine is that which I have called 'Kuhnian irrationalism'. As we have already seen briefly, Kuhn launched a full-scale attack on the whole notion of a critical philosophically-based methodology guided by the goal of truth and which would lay down absolutely binding criteria for the appraisal of scientific theories. Against this notion he held that methodological rules are simply a set of conventions adopted by scientists: and in particular he held that these conventions are historico-relative – they are part and parcel of the prevailing paradigm theory or research programme and so alter when the paradigm changes.[22]

Following from the conviction that methodology is a set of historico-relative conventions Kuhn evolved his well-known account of the history of science as a process of normal science punctuated by occasional periods of scientific revolution. Normal science refers to periods when there is a widespread consensus among practitioners of a science on the appropriate corpus of theory which should be used and all of the work of the science is carried out within the presuppositions of this prevailing 'paradigm'. Kuhn held that methodological rules, far from being absolute standards externally imposed on a science by philosophy are but one element of the prevailing paradigm corpus of theory in a science. It is precisely for this reason that Kuhn regarded periods of scientific revolution, when one paradigm is replaced by a new set of theories, as essentially irrational episodes.

Inevitably, any paradigm will encounter some falsifying evidence and Kuhn argues that while such anomalies are of limited significance they will simply be glossed over by the science. When anomalies begin to pile up, however, dissatisfaction with the old paradigm and pressure for its replacement build up and thus a period of scientific revolution is ushered in. The central feature of these revolutions in Kuhn's view is their irrationality. For the introduction of a new paradigm brings with it a complete change of world view and in particular a new set of rules of methodological appraisal. The adoption of a new paradigm does not therefore come about by means of a careful rational appraisal of the merits of competing paradigms with the aid of some set of absolute standards; in the absence of any agreed or absolute set of rules of method, paradigm change is more a kind of religious conversion or change of world view and hence an ultimately irrational exercise.[23] As a recent commentator on Kuhn's views put it: 'There is no appropriate scale available with which to weigh the merits of alternative paradigms: they are incommensurable.'[24]

It will be evident that Kuhn's position relies heavily on a broader commitment to an epistemological relativism. He has argued that methodology can only be a set of historico-relative conventions and from his work as a whole it is clear that Kuhn would reject the notion that there can be absolute truths or absolute standards of appraisal in any field of human inquiry. As a recent commentator has remarked, for Kuhn 'It is never possible . . . to produce any context-independent rational justification for preferring the new to the old, any indefeasible proof of ''advance'' or ''progress''.'[25]

Thus, although Kuhn has never said so in any aggressively forthright manner, it is evident that he espouses a thorough-going epistemological relativist position, and certainly he has never sought to repudiate the 'relativist' label attached to his thoughts. Indeed Kuhn's account of scientific revolutions may be credited with having brought right out into the open the inescapable irrationalist implications of any logical or epistemological relativism, the implication that relativism subverts the possibility of rational discussion of differing viewpoints (cf. pp. 24–25). It is because of the centrality of this implication in Kuhn's account of science and its philosophical significance as an implication of relativism that I have chosen the label 'Kuhnian irrationalism' for Kuhn's position.

Although 'Kuhnian irrationalism' has enjoyed widespread popularity, especially among human scientists, it is subject to a number of damning criticisms in addition to the fundamental flaw of espousing an epistemological relativism.

(1) First, Kuhn adopts in the end a wholly uncritical attitude to the methods of science since methodology is to be simply a redescription of the rules of method which are currently used by practising scientists and which are part of the prevailing paradigm. Indeed since for Kuhn the rules of method are historico-relative and change when there is a shift of paradigm it follows that he will have to acknowledge that witch doctoring and voodoo were once fully-fledged sciences. Maybe Kuhn would be prepared to draw such a conclusion but many modern scientists would be somewhat embarrassed by it.

(2) A further implication of his position, which Kuhn fully acknowledges, is that of the essential irrationality of the process of shifting from one paradigm to another in a scientific revolution, given that methodological rules are themselves a component part of paradigms. However, to introduce such an outright irrationality into one of the most crucial phases of the development of any science is to betray the very spirit of a relentless rational probing of the world, which I have suggested in Chapter 1, is of the very essence of Western thought and civilization and without which spirit the sciences as systematic bodies of inquiry could never have emerged.

(3) Kuhn claims to base his theory of science on a careful examination of the history of science. However, a number of astute commentators have pointed out that even as an account of the history of science Kuhn's theory is involved in serious distortion and exaggeration. For while various pieces of irrationality have from time to time crept into science, especially in periods of turmoil, the processes of science and, in particular, the process of paradigm switching are carried out in a largely rational and disciplined manner.

(4) Finally, Kuhn's position is in any case shown to be completely untenable (in the light of the arguments of Section 2.3) in so far as it is based upon an explicitly epistemological relativist position.

The final relativist-inspired position with which I shall deal is instrumentalism. I should point out that instrumentalism is a much more limited thesis than the Kuhnian position which has just been outlined. It is, strictly speaking, only a thesis regarding the nature of scientific theories rather than a complete methodology of science. To be precise, instrumentalism is the view that all scientific theories are mere fictions devoid of truth value and to be assessed, therefore, solely on their predictive merits; that is, theories are regarded as instruments of prediction and as nothing else.

Instrumentalism does not explicitly invoke an epistemological relativism but for reasons which will become clear below it could not be plausible as a view of scientific theory unless underpinned by a wider relativist conviction. For this reason, and also because instrumentalism will crop up on a number of occasions throughout this work, I have included it, together with my reasons for disagreeing with it, in this chapter.

In order to understand the instrumentalist conception of scientific theory we must appreciate how it emerges from a broader inductivist conception of science. According to the inductivist, science must begin and end with facts. Scientific theories or laws are merely extrapolations from experience, from a wide variety of observations and hence theory is simply 'codified general fact'. These generalizations from experience are then tested by comparing their implied predictions against further experience and if a generalization predicts well it is accepted and regarded as well established by science.

However, this inductivist account of science inevitably encounters a certain difficulty. If the task of science is simply to fit generalized hypotheses or theories to sets of empirical data (facts), the problem arises that to any finite set of data an infinite set of hypotheses, all of which can equally well predict the set of data in question, can be fitted. This is the very same point as the mathematician makes when he indicates that through any finite set of points an infinite set of curves could be drawn, or that the logician makes when he points out that a specific true conclusion can easily be deduced validly from false premises. It is also intimately bound up with the logical problem of induction. The reason why a finite set of corroborating instances can never prove a general theory true is precisely because the same set of observations could be fully consistent with a range of other general theories also and so cannot offer a basis for establishing one or another general theory as true.[26]

Since the sciences can never have at their disposal any more than a finite set of observations (facts) and since the inductivist conceives of the task of science as the fitting of generalizations which will suitably codify these facts it follows that the inductivist will be led inexorably towards an instrumentalist conception of scientific theories. For any theoretical generalization which he may fit to the data he must recognize as only one among a potentially infinite set of hypotheses which could equally have been fitted to the same data. Hence he can only regard his theory as a fiction since the chance of having hit upon the theory which is a true account of the phenomena under study is quite remote given the infinite variety of rationalizations of the data which he could have attempted. An inductivist conception of science, therefore, leads inevitably towards an instrumentalist conception of scientific theory according to which theories are mere fictions which are to be appraised not in terms of their truth value (since the truth of theories cannot be established) but rather in terms of such pragmatic criteria as simplicity, usefulness or predictive power.

One of the most forthright expositions of an instrumentalist position in recent times may be found in Milton Friedman's essay on 'The Methodology of Positive Economics'.[27] A central theme of that essay is that the assumptions of a scientific theory may be quite at variance with reality provided the theory predicts well. In other words, theories are mere fictions into whose truth or falsity it is vain to inquire. What is important for Friedman is to examine how well the theory (fiction) predicts events. In order to leave us in no doubt at all that on his conception theories are mere fictions Friedman says that we may prefix a blatantly unrealistic theory with the words 'as if'. When the 'as if' prefix is added to a theory we are quite clearly in the presence of a fiction and any serious attempt to provide a true account of how the world really is or operates has been given up.

Turning now to some criticisms of instrumentalism the first point to be made is that it has a definite affinity with relativism, if not actually being necessarily connected with such a position. For the instrumentalist, through the notion of theory as mere fiction, has in effect abjured the quest for truth in science. He has argued that to investigate the truth value of theories is pointless since all theories are mere fictions. Such a renunciation of the goal of seeking truth in science can only be plausible or tenable for a thinker who believes that the search for truth is in general pointless, that is an epistemological relativist. By contrast, a philosopher who believes that the goal of all inquiry must be the pursuit of truth cannot possibly accept the instrumentalist banishment of truth from science and will argue that to the extent that the instrumentalist conception of scientific theory presupposes epistemological relativism, that whole approach to, and conception of, science is seriously flawed.

In addition to involving in effect an epistemological relativism there are a number of more specific criticisms of instrumentalism which I shall mention here for completeness. Some further comments on these will be found in Chapter 3 and also in an article of mine devoted specifically to a treatment of Friedman's instrumentalism.[28]

(1)   The first of these more specific criticisms is that in retreating into fictions the instrumentalist has somehow given up the attempt at genuine explanation in science. The full import of this criticism will become clear in the next chapter where I shall deal with the question of what constitutes a genuine scientific explanation and show that the demand for genuine explanation (as opposed to mere fictions) is intimately bound up with the quest for truth in science.

(2)   Because instrumentalist fictions do not offer genuine explanations a serious question mark must hang over their usefulness for policy purposes. In radically new sorts of practical situations a fiction which has predicted well in the past may turn out to be a treacherous policy guide and we should feel more confident with a 'genuine explanation'. Again this point will be elaborated in more detail in the next chapter.

(3)   Finally, there is once again the awkward implication, already found clearly in Kuhn, that an instrumentalist will be unable to make any distinction between science and sorcery. For if good scientific theories are mere fictions with a successful record of accurate predictions then since serious astrology and black magic, for example, will both have a good predictive record (at least on their own terms) it follows that they are sciences on a par with physics or

economics. Although most scientists would be extremely loath to draw this conclusion and would probably support their embarrassment by looking askance at the content of astrological and other theories and suggesting them to be far-fetched, yet since to the instrumentalist theories are mere fictions into whose truth value or realism it is vain to inquire, he cannot escape the conclusion that serious astrology and black magic must be regarded as fully-fledged sciences.[29]

These various criticisms of instrumentalism, which I shall be supplementing in the next chapter, amount to a decisive refutation of the position. This refutation we shall find to be of considerable relevance at a number of later points in the work where I have disposed of certain objections or positions in the philosophy of the human sciences simply on the ground that they involve, implicitly or explicitly, an instrumentalist conception of theory.

Notes

1 This chapter thus represents the second, or 'antithesis' stage, in what I have already suggested in Chapter 1 is a Hegelian dialectical strategy of argument in defence of a philosophically-founded methodology (cf. p. 3).

2 The reasons for this label will become clear below.

3 T. S. Kuhn, (1970) *The Structure of Scientific Revolutions* (Chicago: University of Chicago Press), *passim*, but note especially Ch.1, pp. 8–9.

4 Cf. for example, Lakatos who, having rejected the possibility of a philosophical justification of the sciences argues that methodology should be a rational reconstruction of the methods actually used by the best scientists. Lakatos' approach will be further discussed on pp. 45–48.

5 A. J. Ayer (1972), *Language, Truth and Logic* (Harmondsworth: Pelican).

6 Of any book making knowledge claims not based on sense experience, Hume asserted that it should be 'committed to the flames' since it was only 'sophistry and illusion'. Cf. D. Hume (1975), *Enquiry Concerning Human Understanding* (Oxford: Clarendon Press), p. 165.

7 A. J. Ayer, *Language, Truth and Logic*.

8 J. Locke (1960), *Essay Concerning Human Understanding* (ed. P. Laslett), (Cambridge: Cambridge University Press), preface.

9 It may be remarked that while showing the verification principle to be inconsistent with itself implies untenability, to show that it is self-consistent would not be sufficient to show it to be true. It would show only that it *could* be true. To demonstrate its truth would require the development of a rational epistemological critique of the possibility of human cognition such as no positivist has ever attempted, since any such attempt is regarded by positivists as unfounded metaphysical speculation.

10 Since the opinion cannot by its own rights be a valid cognition, being neither tautologous nor empirically verifiable.

11 This is the case since the 'verification principle', which summarizes the theory, is itself neither a tautology nor an empirically verifiable proposition.

12 Interestingly, most relativists would be happy to add the requirement of 'consistency' or 'coherence' to this list. But to require beliefs to be logically consistent looks remarkably like a covert reintroduction of an absolute criterion of appraisal – validity or 'logical truth'. After all, if there are no truths, why bother to be consistent?

13 I. Lakatos (1970), 'The methodology of scientific research programmes', in I. Lakatos and A. Musgrave (eds.), *Criticism and the Growth of Knowledge* (Cambridge: Cambridge University Press), pp. 93–132.

14 It will be remarked that while Lakatos ends up with an effectively descriptivist position, he arrives at it only as a result of his rejection of the possibility of philosophy rather than in the uncritical manner of the crude descriptivist.

15 T. Kuhn (1970), *The Structure of Scientific Revolution* (Chicago: Chicago University Press; 2nd edn), pp. 8–9.

16 Cf. Kuhn's view that rules of method are part of a paradigm theory.

17 Plato (1970), 'Theaetetus' 168c–179d gives the classic case against relativism. See especially F. M. Cornford (1970), *Plato's Theory of Knowledge* (London: Routledge & Kegan Paul).

18 E. Husserl (1965), *Phenomenology and the Crisis of Philosophy*, Q. Lauer (ed. and trans), (New York: Harper), pp. 88–9. See also R. Trigg (1973), *Reason and Commitment* (Cambridge: Cambridge University Press) for a sustained critique showing the absurdities to which relativism leads. This is an interesting work since it refutes relativism from within the broadly empiricist position of Anglo-Saxon thought.

19 Note that although they would be propositions about correct human reasoning they would still be absolutely true. Indeed, the laws of logic prescribe how we must proceed in the pursuit of truth.

20 It will be recalled that in Chapter 1 I suggested the driving force of philosophy is a conviction that man must pursue the use of reason relentlessly in the search for truth.

21 The parody is on Wittgenstein's (1961) closing sentence in the *Tractatus Logico–Philosophicus* (London: Routledge and Kegan Paul). Interestingly enough, the *Tractatus*, although seeking to eliminate metaphysics, is replete with metaphysics and Wittgenstein, like our relativist, would therefore have been better off never to have written it since the whole work is a performative contradiction.

22 For Kuhn's rejection of a critical philosophically-based methodology and his insistence that methodological rules are historico-relative conventions, see T. Kuhn, *Structure of Scientific Revolutions*, pp. 8–9.

23 Kuhn also describes paradigm change as a kind of *Gestalt* switch.

24 B. Barnes (1982), *T. S. Kuhn and Social Science* (London: Macmillan), p. 65.

25 B. Barnes, *T. S. Kuhn and Social Science*, p. 11.

26 We might refer to this by saying that the problem whereby an infinite number of hypotheses can be fitted to any finite set of data is the 'other face of the problem of induction'.

27 M. Friedman (1953), 'The methodology of positive economics', in *Essays in Positive Economics* (Chicago: University of Chicago Press). For an even clearer exposition of instrumentalism, see Boland's article in exegesis of Friedman (L. Boland (1979)), 'A critique of Friedman's critics', *Journal of Economic Literature*, vol. 17, no. 2, pp. 503–22.

28 P. J. O'Sullivan (1984), 'Friedman's methodology revisited: a proposal for a definite resolution of the F-twist', *Explorations in Knowledge*, vol. 1, no. 2.

29 That instrumentalism should lead to this conclusion is not really surprising.

If we consider much of the modern econometric work carried out by economists under the inspiration of Friedman's instrumentalism we shall find that it is of such a poor quality that it resembles astrology more than physics. Cf. P. J. O'Sullivan 'Friedman's methodology revisited', also M. Blaug (1980), *The Methodology of Economics* (Cambridge: Cambridge University Press), pp. 256–57, 260–62.

3

Science and the Quest for Truth

In this chapter my aim is to complete the preliminary philosophical scaffolding of the work of offering a further clarification of some important points regarding the nature of scientific theory and tests thereof. Specifically, I wish first to introduce the so-called 'realist' conception of scientific theory as an alternative to the instrumentalist conception and, secondly, to examine the vexed question of what exactly can be established by empirical testing of general theories. The chapter will close with a summary of the position reached so far in the work.

3.1   The Realist Conception of Scientific Theory

Throughout the previous chapters I have argued that the ultimate goal of science as of all human inquiry is the pursuit of truth. Once the truth as the overriding quaesitum of science is adopted the 'realist' conception of scientific theory follows immediately. The implication of seeking the truth in science is that far from remaining content with any kind of mere fiction, science must seek to achieve a *true insight*, that is to say, a true and accurate theoretical account of how the world really is or operates. This is precisely the so-called[1] realist conception of theory. For to the realist the task of a scientific theory is to inquire into the real processes or generative mechanisms which underlie and give rise to the natural phenomena we daily observe, or in the case of the human sciences, to lay bare the real underlying motivations which give rise to human actions.

In addition to following directly from truth as the overriding goal or regulative criterion of science, the realist argues that it is only when we have achieved some such true insight into the mechanisms or motives underlying phenomena that we can be said genuinely to *understand* those phenomena. Hence only a 'realist' type of theory can offer a genuine scientific *explanation* of phenomena by contrast with instrumentalist theories which *qua* mere fictions have given up any serious attempt at understanding and explanation. Indeed, the proponents of realism go on to point out that versatility of predictive power and practical relevance can be guaranteed only by the achievement of a genuine explanation. Having once attained a true insight regarding the mechanisms or motives which underlie and give rise to some set of phenomena we may then be highly confident of future applications of the theory in new but similar practical problem areas. By contrast with the instrumentalist who cannot rely at all on the extension of his fiction beyond the set of data to which it was originally fitted,[2] the realist, in virtue of having understood the underlying generative processes, can have full confidence in the applicability of his theory to new sorts of practical situation. Predictive power (and hence practical relevance) are therefore the fruits or corollaries of successful explanation in science.

The fundamental argument in defence of the realist conception is, therefore, that it follows immediately from adoption of truth as the overriding regulative criterion of scientific inquiry. This means that 'realism' is in close sympathy with the continental European rationalist heritage of thought and in particular with its most modern manifestation, phenomenology, which has (as we saw in Chapter 1) proclaimed the continuing importance for man of the relentless rational pursuit of truth.

The arguments in defence of realism have usually been developed against the background of the instrumentalist conception of theory as a foil or whipping boy especially in the works of Roy Bhaskar[3] and Sir Karl Popper.[4] Consequently it may be useful now to draw up more explicitly the points of contrast between realism and instrumentalism. In so doing I shall also be supplementing and completing the criticisms of instrumentalism outlined in the last chapter.[5]

The realist conception of theory provides the grounds for two specific criticisms which I levelled at instrumentalism in the last chapter. I suggested there[6] that:

(1) Instrumentalist theories fail to offer a genuine explanation of phenomena. Explanation, the realist insists, is not merely predictive power (or prediction written backwards, as has sometimes been suggested) but rather the achievement of a true insight into the real generative mechanisms and motivations which underlie everyday natural and human phenomena respectively.

(2) I also suggested that instrumentalist fictions would provide a treacherous guide to practical policy. The realist points out that while an instrumentalist can have no ground for believing that his fictions will continue to predict well in new, real-world situations somewhat different from those to which they were first fitted, if by contrast we have achieved a real insight we will be able to make a wide range of successful predictions in real situations quite different from those where our insight was first corroborated. Perhaps this point may best be seen by means of a trivial example. Someone who derives considerable confidence in the view ('theory') that kicking a recalcitrant lawnmower will make it start (on the basis of his experiences to date with kicking it) is surely in a much weaker position than a person who has some understanding of how internal

combustion engines really work. After a night exposed to dense seaside fog, for example, the 'instrumentalist' will be seriously disappointed with the performance of his kick-and-start fiction whereas our 'realist', who has achieved a modicum of insight, will proceed directly to open up and carefully dry spark-plug leads, etc., and will doubtless achieve normal mower starting having carried out this elementary mechanical exercise.

There is a further point emerging from this contrast of realism and instrumentalism which deserves emphasis. As far as the realist is concerned the instrumentalist has seriously misconceived the whole relationship which ought to hold between theories and empirical data or evidence. The instrumentalist, following inductivism, sees science as beginning and as ending with facts while theories are merely generalizations which are fitted to sets of data in order simply to codify them; theories are merely codified general facts. Since to any finite set of data an infinite number of such generalizations could be fitted it follows that all theories are mere fictions to be appraised solely in terms of their 'predictive power' for the set of phenomena they were designed to explain and so we turn back to a further collection and examination of facts in order to appraise the fictions.

Realism, by contrast, argues that the primary task with which science must begin is not an examination of facts but rather a conjecture. The aim of science is precisely to achieve a true insight into the hidden processes which underlie observable data, hence to go *beyond* the facts in seeking to explain them. Since the attempt at insight therefore goes beyond the available facts, it will be a conjecture, and it is only thereafter that we turn to the facts in order to examine whether or not the various predictions which we make with the aid of our conjectured insight are corroborated or falsified. If perchance our conjecture has hit upon a true insight then and only then will our theory have a spectacularly successful predictive record. Thus we may conclude that for the realist the instrumentalist has completely misunderstood the appropriate relationship between theory and empirical evidence. To reiterate a key point: versatility of predictive power is not the touchstone or criterion of a good theory but rather the fruit or by-product of a good theory, that is a theory which has achieved some kind of true insight.

Before leaving aside the discussion of realism there are some serious possible misapprehensions of the position which it will be important to dispel. In the first place, although the realist constantly insists on the importance of achieving true insights, he is fully aware of the extreme difficulty of achieving success in this activity. Rather the realist recognizes that a great many attempts to achieve insight will turn out to be a failure. As Popper in particular has stressed, a great many of our conjectured insights will turn out to be falsified by empirical evidence, and indeed no conjecture could ever be demonstrated to be conclusively true on the basis of empirical evidence alone, because of the problem of induction. However, to recognize that there are difficulties in achieving insight is only to say that there are no short-cuts to truth. It most certainly does not rule out the possibility that we may occasionally in the course of science hit upon a true insight, and in any case in the process of conjecture and refutation (of falsified theories) we might be said to be approaching truth by a process of elimination of definite falsehood. Hence the admitted difficulties of achieving true insight do not constitute a ground for abandoning the quest for truth in science.

Having clearly grasped this point, there is another serious misapprehension which should be dispelled, namely that the realist conception of theory somehow involves or is bound up with an essentialist theory of meaning. Although I shall show that these are clearly distinct philosophical theses I find it necessary to clarify the point because of the tendency in modern philosophy of science to throw '-ism' labels around carelessly and, indeed, often as a substitute for attempting a genuine understanding of the position being put forward by a protagonist.[7] There has in particular been some suggestion or insinuation that realism necessarily involves essentialism and Popper especially has sought to defend realism against this charge.[8]

Essentialism is at root a theory of the meaning of universal words, that is to say of all non-proper names. It holds that we can come to know the real essence or nature of things and that we can encapsulate that real essence in a precise 'real definition'. It would, therefore, follow that in the sciences when we make references to things we have already grasped their real essences or natures and so the theories which we put forward on the basis of, and using, real definitions will reveal absolute truths about the real interrelations among things in the world: they will reveal the 'essential structure of the world'.

To our modern way of thinking such a conception of science seems outlandish, but to get to grips with it we must turn back to the essentialist theory of meaning which underpins it and which perhaps does not look quite so implausible. The decisive criticism of the essentialist theory of meaning is the recognition that the meaning of words is the result of a constitutive activity of consciousness, of the human mind. The mind is not a purely passive receiver of sense-data but is rather constantly active in classifying phenomena in various ways. Hence, as Husserl put it, consciousness constitutes essence. This constitutive activity of consciousness is in turn heavily influenced by prevailing scientific and philosophical theories which suggest that the chaotic mass of sense-data should be divided up and classified in certain ways. A constitutive consciousness, therefore, will only succeed in producing a definition of the real essence of phenomena if it is already in possession of a wide-ranging set of absolutely true scientific and philosophical theories. Rather than 'real definitions' being available to found a science of absolute truths we could never hope to frame a 'real definition' unless we had already developed such a science.[9]

Since we have already seen that all of the realists are painfully aware of the extreme difficulty of achieving true insight in science and regard the attainment of a set of absolute truths in science as a goal that is still very far off indeed it follows:

(1) That realism does not generate essentialism as a necessary implication in any way since it asserts only that the sciences should pursue the truth and certainly not that they have already attained a comprehensive set of truths such as would be necessary to frame definitions which would capture the real essence of things.

(2) More generally, I have shown that since realism is a theory about the nature and aims of a good scientific theory, while essentialism is a theory of the meaning of words, they are in any case clearly distinct theories.

We may conclude that any suggestion or insinuation that the realist conception of theory implies or is somehow bound up with essentialism is a serious misapprehension.[10]

I have spent some time in expounding and defending the realist conception of scientific theory because it is a position upon which I shall rely at a number of later places in the work. Just as the rejection of instrumentalist notions carried out in the last chapter will be crucial at a number of stages in the critical examination of the methodology of human science in later chapters, so also will the defence of the realist conception be crucial since it is precisely with its realist foil that I shall seek to replace discarded instrumentalist conceptions of scientific theory.

3.2   Falsification and the Pursuit of Truth

The main focus of this work is on the methodological differentiation which ought to be maintained between the natural and the human sciences. Accordingly, in subsequent chapters I shall have a great deal to say regarding the points of divergence between the methods of natural and human science. Yet since both types of discipline are labelled as 'empirical sciences' they must have some elements in common in order to justify this labelling. Since these points of convergence will be very much in the background in what follows it may be as well to spell out carefully in the course of these philosophical prolegomena what precisely I would hold ought to be the points in common in the methods of the natural and the human sciences.

There are two main points of convergence upon which I wish to focus here: (1) the notion of explanation as subsumption under generalization, and (2) the imperative of empirical testing and its logic. In both cases my sympathy with the views of Sir Karl Popper will be evident.

The first point of convergence between natural and human science is the shared conception of explanation. To explain a particular event is to subsume it under a generalization (or law) of which it is an instance. This notion of explanation has been championed among others by Karl Hempel and Karl Popper and it is often referred to as the hypothetico-deductive approach to science. The aim of the scientist is to put forward generalized theories or 'laws' from which predictions regarding particular actual events may be deduced; and if the predictions turn out to be correct the generalized theory is said to be an explanation of the particular event.

This notion of explanation has been widely current in modern science and so there is no need to dwell upon it here. There is, however, one crucially important amendment to be made to it. Strictly speaking, we should say that explanation is the 'subsumption of particular events under *insightful* generalizations of which the events are a case'. The so-called realist conception of scientific theory has just been discussed and we saw that a merely fictional generalization cannot be said to offer a genuine explanation even if it can predict well. In particular, we saw that there can be no question of regarding the blatantly unrealistic 'as if' fictions such as Friedman defends as genuine explanations. To explain a phenomenon it is not enough to have hit upon a generalization from which the phenomenon may be deduced: we must also have at least made the attempt to give a true account of the real underlying processes (generative mechanisms or motivations) which underpin the generalization and which the generalization will seek to formulate in a systematic manner.

Hence the important amendment to the usual statement of the hypothetico-deductive approach: explanation is the subsumption of particular events under insight-yielding generalizations of which they are an instance.[11] It is worth remarking that although this formulation amends the more usual formulation as put forward by Hempel and Popper it is at least fully consistent with Popper's approach to scientific theory as a whole. For we have seen in the previous section that in certain of his works Popper strongly defends the realist approach to scientific theory. If we bring these realist assertions together with his statement of the basic hypothetico-deductive form of explanation as subsumption under generalization we should reach a formulation such as my amended one above.

The second point of convergence between the methods of natural and human sciences is the imperative of empirical testing. Of course there have been some commentators who have argued for various reasons that the theories of the human sciences do not need to be tested empirically.[12] These have been very much in the minority, however, and in some cases they have actually dropped the label 'sciences' which suggests a convergence on some points at least with the natural sciences.[13] The general view, however, and certainly the view for which I shall be arguing later on in this work, is that empirical testing plays as important a role in the human as in the natural sciences.

The first step in any science is the hazarding of conjectures, that is to say, the attempt to put forward a systematic true insight into the factors which underlie and give rise to some set of observable phenomena. Since this conjecture attempts to get beyond the observable facts in order to understand their real provenance it will always be a creative construct of the scientist's mind and so will stand in need of some kind of independent check. Since the aim of the conjecture is to achieve an insight into how the world really is or operates the obvious test will be to check the predictions which the conjectured theory will yield against actual observations, whence the imperative of empirical testing. This much of the case for empirical testing has not generally been controversial. What has proved to be much more troublesome is the question of what exactly can be established on the basis of empirical tests. The logical fallacy of induction, that is to say the fallacy of drawing inferences from the particular to the general, means that the truth of a strictly generalized hypothesis[14] can never be established on the basis of finite sets of correct predictions. In other words, no amount of confirming evidence will ever be sufficient to prove the truth of a theory under test. Furthermore, there cannot even be any question of assigning a probability value (near to unity, say) to a theory which has been confirmed in a wide range of cases: for one definitely failed text would be sufficient to demonstrate the theory conclusively false and so reduce the probability of its being true to zero. Thus any notion of assigning a probability p_t of being true where

$$p_t = \frac{\text{number of confirming instances}}{\text{total number of tests made}}$$

is simply nonsense.

The complete futility of trying to make rational inferences from the particular to the general has not prevented generations of philosophers and scientists from seeking to develop a 'justification of induction'. It was not until the present century that Popper finally put an end to this nonsense by introducing his principle of falsification. Popper proposes that the only way to resolve the age-old 'problem of induction' is to grasp firmly the nettle of the impossibility of ever proving a general theory true by means of empirical testing. Drawing upon the logic of the *modus tollendo tollens* he shows that while confirming evidence cannot prove a theory true, contrary evidence can prove a theory false. If from some theory, T, I have deduced as a prediction some proposition p, then if I find in fact that p is not the case, that is I find 'not-p', I may infer without more ado that the theory T is false, at least as formulated: I may infer 'not-T'. Stated in terms of formal logic:

> given T, and $T \to p$,
> from truth of p nothing follows,
> but from falsity of p, falsity of T always follows,
> i.e. not-$p \to$ not-T.

This elementary piece of logic is known as the *modus tollendo tollens*.

Building upon the basic insight, Popper argues that scientists should renounce the attempt to demonstrate their theories to be true on the basis of evidence and should turn their attention to attempts to falsify their theories since only the falsifying result is logically conclusive. This 'falsification principle' leads to a revolution in the whole conception of science and its methods. Empirical work is to be geared to falsification rather than verification and so seeks out severe and stringent rather than easy tests for scientific theories. Moreover, scientific progress is achieved above all in the negative moment of falsification, in the moment when an old theory is abandoned; and contrary to the inductivist view whereby science progresses in a cumulative manner to ever wider generalizations the Popperian presents a view of science as learning by its mistakes, as progressing by discarding falsified old theories.

It may perhaps be remarked *en passant* that Popper's conception of scientific progress through the *via negativa* of falsification bears a remarkably close similarity to the notion of progress through rational criticism of received opinion that has been the animating spirit of continental European rationalist philosophy in general. The parallels for example between the falsificationist method in science and Descartes' method of doubt or even the Hegelian dialectic are striking. Here, as also in his espousal of a realist conception of scientific theory guided by the overriding criterion of truth, Popper exhibits a definite sympathy with continental European rationalism even though he is usually thought of as a thinker within the Anglo-Saxon fold.

Imre Lakatos raises some doubts about the possibility of conclusively falsifying scientific theories and if correct these would seriously undermine Popper's falsificationist methodology since it would mean that falsification was just as impossible to achieve as verification (by empirical testing). Lakatos has two reasons for putting forward his view, namely the problem of fallibility and the problem of the theory-impregnation of facts.[15] The first of these simply refers to the fact that human agents may make mistaken observations and so might reject a theory which was not false. It would seem from his work that what Lakatos intends to propose here is a systematic fallibilism, the view that all human cognition is bound to be or at least is liable to be mistaken. But if every human cognition were bound to be mistaken there would be no point whatever in putting forward any theories or in pursuing truth by reason in any field. Moreover, if every human cognition is liable to be, rather than bound to be, mistaken then there can be no criterion (infallible) whereby we can recognize what is a mistaken cognition and what is not, so again every cognition would have to be regarded as mistaken. These nihilistic and absurd consequences for human inquiry which follow from a systematic fallibilism have been illustrated with great perspicacity by David Hume in his *Treatise of Human Nature* in the section on 'Skepticism with regard to Reason'.[16]

If, on the other hand, by drawing our attention to fallibility Lakatos only means to say that individual human beings occasionally make mathematical or observational mistakes in their testing of theories, then while this is indeed obviously the case, it does not undermine Popper's methodology of falsification. For while in one isolated test an individual scientist may make a computational or observational mistake and wrongly declare a theory false, when independent checks by other scientists are made and when the theory is submitted to a range of other similar tests, any slip-ups by individual scientists should be exposed and a definitive verdict regarding the results of the empirical testing of a theory established.

A much more serious difficulty for the Popperian contention that a theory can be definitely shown to be false in empirical tests is posed by the theory-impregnated character of all observations or 'facts'.

The problem referred to as the theory-impregnation of facts is simply this: when we seek to make an observation of fact there can never be any possibility of reporting facts purely, boldly and without any element of interpretation by the observer. Rather the observer is (a) always involved in structuring and construing the facts in some way or other (b) often his observation will depend upon the theories underlying (and guaranteeing the reliability of) some instrument of observation. Thus, for example, microscopic and telescopic observations rely on theories in optics.

Consequently, we must recognize that when a 'theory (say, T_o) is under test what we are testing is not a single hypothesis but rather a central hypothesis (say H_c) in which we are mainly interested and a range of auxiliary hypotheses (say $H_1, H_2 \ldots H_n$), where these auxiliaries refer to the hypotheses involved in the manner in which we construe facts, in the theories that underpin our instruments and in the stipulation of initial conditions. Put very simply, when we speak of testing a theory T_o empirically what we invariably mean is that we are testing a conjunction of hypotheses

$$H_c; H_1 \ldots H_n$$

and we may say that

$$T_o = (H_c; H_1, H_2 \ldots H_n)$$

where H_c = central hypothesis, that is the one in which we are most interested, H_1, H_2, etc. are auxiliary hypotheses and T_o is a conjunction, H_c, H_1, H_2, $H_3 \ldots H_n$.

Now when we submit a theory $T_o = (H_c; H_1, H_2, \ldots H_n)$ to empirical test it follows that a falsification does not necessarily mean that the hypothesis H_c in which we were mainly interested has been falsified. (This I presume is Lakatos' point.) However, it *does* follow that the theory T_o is falsified; and since T_o is simply a conjunction of H_c with a string of auxiliaries it follows that at least one of $(H_c, H_1 \ldots H_n)$ has been falsified. Consequently, the *logic* of the falsification principle still stands. The theory T_o conceived as a complex conjunction of hypotheses has been falsified by the failure of its predictions and so a new theory T_1 must be formulated. This new theory may be a radical reformulation in which some completely new central hypothesis H_c^1 is brought in: or it may be only a minor reformulation in which some auxiliary H_j is replaced by H^1_j. Thus we may have

$$T_1 = (H_c^1; H_1 \ldots H_n)$$

or

$$T_1 = (H_c; H_1 \ldots H_j^1 \ldots H_n).$$

In either case, however, the logic of the falsification principle is preserved;

the failure of predictions of T_o has led to its abandonment and replacement by a new theory, T_1.

Once we have depicted the problem of empirical testing in the above manner the question arises as to which of the component hypotheses we should jettison when a theory is falsified. In answer to this problem Lakatos suggests that whatever else we should not regard the central or 'core' hypothesis as false and should put the blame for failure of prediction on one of the auxiliaries. However, any such attempt to immunize the 'hard core' of a theory or research programme against falsification is completely at variance with the whole spirit of Popper's falsificationist methodology. (Indeed, it can only be plausible to one who, like Lakatos, believes that he has already shown falsification to be impossible.)

A more strictly Popperian falsificationist approach to this problem would recognize that in principle any one of the string of hypotheses H_c, H_1 . . . H_2 . . . H_n could be responsible for the failure of predictions, hence that which is to be singled out for prime suspicion is a matter for the creative genius of the scientist. Furthermore, whatever hypothesis is singled out must then be submitted to separate and independent empirical tests and will be retained only if well corroborated in such independent tests. This process of independent testing must continue until some hypothesis of the original string has been falsified and then a new or at least a reformulated theory (T_1) in which the offending hypothesis has been replaced by some new conjecture should be put forward and tested. It will be clear from this account of the matter that the process of empirical testing of scientific theories is a good deal more complex than the simple formal logic of the *modus tollendo tollens* might suggest, a point upon which Lakatos has insisted. However, what I wish to emphasize against Lakatos and others is that despite the practical complexity of testing there is no ground for losing sight of or for abandoning the basic logical principle of falsification. The above account of how a science ought to proceed when faced with a falsification of one of its theories is a very brief sketch of how we may remain true to the logical principle of falsification having once recognized the theory impregnation of facts and the complexities for the process of empirical testing to which it gives rise.

There is one recommendation which is made by both Popper and Lakatos regarding the proper procedure to follow when formulating a theory whose predictions have failed, namely that the reformulated theory should be at least as wide in scope as the discarded theory and that 'ad hoccery' should be avoided. 'Ad hoccery' is an extreme case of the vice of overcoming a failure of prediction by narrowing down the scope of the generalization embodied in a theory: extreme 'ad hoccery' is simply a reformulation of the old theory together with an *ad hoc* new auxiliary hypothesis saying that the theory holds in all cases *except* that in which its predictions have been shown to fail. Clearly 'ad hoccery' always reduces the scope of a generalization.

Both Popper and Lakatos speak of this rule against 'ad hoccery' as a convention which is introduced and decided upon by scientists themselves in a largely arbitrary manner. However, this rule can be given a perfectly rational and non-arbitrary foundation if we bear in mind that the empirical sciences seek to explain particular phenomena by subsuming them under generalizations of which they are an instance. From this notion of explanation it follows that any reformulation of a theory which reduces the scope of the generalization embodied therein will be reducing the explanatory power of theory and so would be a retrogressive step for any science to take.

In the above account of the logic and problems of empirical testing in any empirical science I have followed or at some points elaborated upon what I take to be Popper's approach to these problems. It will be evident that my interpretation of the full details of a Popperian methodology differ quite sharply from a Lakatosian methodology[17] despite the fact that Lakatos also claimed to be elaborating a Popperian approach. I would argue, however, that the interpretation which I have given, according central importance to the falsification principle and insisting upon the truth as the overall goal of science[18] is very much closer to the spirit of Popper's thought than Lakatosian conventionalism which explicitly abjures the quest for truth in science, denies the possibility of conclusive falsification of theories in empirical tests making falsification merely a matter of convention and introduces the notion of 'hard cores' of theory which are regarded as immune against falsification. Indeed when it is fully elaborated Lakatos' position turns out to be much closer to Kuhn's irrationalist theory of science than to Popper's philosophy of science.[19]

It is not my purpose to become involved here in pointless exegetic dispute over what 'the correct' interpretation of Popper's position might be. Whether or not the interpretation which I have offered is judged to be closer to the spirit of Popper's work than others, it offers in my view the only fully adequate account of the complexities of empirical testing within the logic of the basis principle of falsification, of the *modus tollendo tollens*. Hence the above discussion should be judged entirely on its own logical and philosophical merits rather than on the irrelevant criterion of how closely it accords with Popper's views.

Indeed, it will be appropriate to point out here that, although I have clearly followed Popper on a number of basic methodological issues, I most certainly have not wanted to follow Popperian methodology of science in all its details. In fact on the very issue which is the most fundamental one in this work, namely that of methodological differentiation between the natural and human sciences I have differed sharply with Popper. Whereas Popper on a number of occasions has argued that there ought to be no essential difference of method between the natural and human sciences, in Part 3 of this work I shall be arguing that there ought overall (that is, despite some points of convergence of method such as I have outlined in this chapter) to be a radical differentiation between the methods of the natural and of the human sciences.

3.3 A Conclusion Regarding Methodological Study

It will be recalled that in this first part of the book I am seeking to develop a dialectical strategy or argument in defence of a critical philosophically-based methodology of science, guided by the goal of truth. I have now completed this argumentation and it may be useful therefore to state briefly the final synthesis of the argument of the first three chapters. The thesis phase of the argument in Chapter 1 stated the main positive arguments in favour of a critical philosophically-based methodology of science, while Chapter 2 dealt with the antithesis phase – the challenge to such an approach that emanates from the anti-philosophies of positivism and relativism which regard all philosophy as pointless nonsense. Having 'negated these negations' by showing both positivism and relativism to be hopelessly untenable, we may now return to assert with even greater confidence the original thesis, that the methodology of science should be based on a critical philosophical appraisal of the methods used, guided by the regulative criterion of (pursuit of) truth.

In addition to fortifying the original thesis in the course of the antithesis phase we have also considerably deepened our appreciation of certain aspects and implications of a critical philosophically-based approach to scientific methodology so that at this synthesis stage we are really doing a lot more than merely reiterating the original thesis: we are reasserting it in a much more developed and elaborate form, fully conscious of its many implications. For example, the consideration of epistemological relativism has led to a realization that if human inquiry is to retain any semblance of rationality, truth is irreplaceable as its overriding goal. Whatever may be the difficulties of pursuing truth, therefore, it is absolutely indispensable as the regulative criterion of rational inquiry and may *not* be replaced by any other more pragmatic goal or criterion. Having thus firmly established truth as the goal of science, we have also seen that this generates the implication of a 'realist' conception of scientific theory and that it completely rules out the instrumentalist conception. Finally, we looked briefly at how the work of empirical testing should be carried out in any science which is to remain faithful to the goal of truth.

The dialectical strategy of argument of this first part of the book is now complete and there remain only a few much more specific philosophical prolegomena to be dealt with in Chapter 4.

Notes

1 I say advisedly 'so-called' because the conception neither makes the claim to be more 'realistic' in some pragmatic sense nor does it have any particularly close affinity with scholastic 'realism'. It only means that scientific theories should offer a *true* account of how the world really is. The label 'rationalist' might indeed be a better one for this conception of scientific theories.

2 Cf. the outline of instrumentalism in Chapter 2, pp. 32–35.

3   R. Bhaskar (1975), *A Realist Theory of Science* (Leeds: Leeds Books) introduction and ch. 1.

4   See for example K. Popper (1963), *Conjectures and Refutations* (London: Routledge & Kegan Paul), Chapter 3. There are a number of other places in Popper's work also where he has been forthright in his rejection of instrumentalism and in his defence of the realist conception of scientific theory.

5   It will be recalled that the second and third of my specific criticisms of the instrumentalist position remain to be completed (cf. p. 34).

6   Cf. index entry on instrumentalism for page references.

7   How often does it happen in the course of argument that instead of trying to understand another person's view with all its individual nuance, we simply brand it as 'essentialist', 'scholastic', 'Marxist', or 'nineteenth-century liberal' as if there were then nothing more to say or discuss. Any such argument is *ad hominem* and is on a par with the political vice of saying 'What can you expect, he is only a . . .?'

8   K. Popper, *Conjectures and Refutations*, pp. 103–7, 114–19. Popper actually portrays essentialism as a philosophy of science but, as I shall show, it is a theory of meaning which can generate implications for philosophy of science *et alia*.

9   Professor P. Masterson of Dublin has suggested the name 'normative essentialism' for this concept whereby real definitions might emerge only when science had achieved a body of absolute truths. It may also be compared with the American pragmatist C. S. Peirce's notion of the 'general intended interpretant' as the ultimate goal shared by all rational thinkers, however different their interpretations and classifications of the world today may be.

10   Whence the *ad hominem* argument against the realist which says, 'Ah, but you are really adopting essentialism', is clearly refuted.

11   My treatment of the question of what constitutes a genuine scientific explanation is perforce superficial here since it is an extremely tricky issue. For example, once the realist approach is adopted we might say that explanation is most basically the achievement of insight and that generalization is beside the point; it arises only from a belief that there is an 'order in nature' so that any true insight will be a systematic generalization. For a further treatment of these tricky but important issues, see Chapter 16.

12   Some of the Austrian School of economists have upheld such a view, as we shall see in Chapter 10. The German Historical School would also be an example, as would the British philosopher Peter Winch, see P. Winch (1958), *The Idea of a Social Science and its Relation to Philosophy* (London: Routledge & Kegan Paul).

13   Winch, for example, regards the human sciences as a branch of (linguistic) philosophy; Dilthey and his followers use the term 'hermeneutics' to replace the human science label.

14   That is, one whose consequence set is infinite, such as a scientific theory.

15   I. Lakatos (1970), 'The methodology of scientific research programmes', in I. Lakatos and A. Musgrave (eds), *Criticism and the Growth of Knowledge* (Cambridge: Cambridge University Press), pp. 93–132.

16   D. Hume (1969), *Treatise of Human Nature* (Harmondsworth: Pelican).

17   Such as I have already outlined on p. 24 and pp. 45–47.

18   Cf. Section 3.1 where Popper's defence of a realist concept of scientific theory is discussed.

19   To see the similarity of Lakatos and Kuhn, see I. Lakatos, 'The methodology

of scientific research programmes', pp. 132–8. This sharp contrast between Popper and Lakatos should not seem so surprising when we bear in mind that Lakatos is an avowed epistemological relativist while Popper insists on the quest for truth as the goal of all human inquiry.

4

The Methodological Alternatives

The central aim of this book is to make a contribution to some of the debates on methodology which are currently a feature of the human sciences in general. This is to be achieved both by the presentation of general philosophical arguments and, more concretely, by taking the specific case of economics, widely held to be the most mature of the human sciences, and examining its methodological position. Before embarking upon this examination of economics it will be useful to outline in somewhat greater detail the two leading methodological positions in the debate to which I seek to make a contribution, namely the objectivist-behaviourist approach with its efficient causal mode of explanation and the subjectivist-interpretive approach with its teleological mode of explanation.

In addition, I have also sought to clarify in this chapter the philosophical linkages and presuppositions of the above methodological alternatives. The issues that are raised in any critical appraisal of methodology belong to the fields of epistemology and the philosophy of man, and so even if neither of the methodological alternatives to be considered could be said to imply with logical necessity the particular epistemological positions with which they shall be linked below, yet the ultimate resolutions of the controversy must come about on the plane of philosophy. When once these purely philosophical issues have been settled, the appropriate methodology of the human sciences should then be deduced, from the specific positions in epistemology and the philosophy of man which have been found adequate so that in the end the fate and claims of the methodological alternatives will depend critically on the adequacy of the philosophical positions from which they can, but need not necessarily, be deduced.

I hasten to add that this chapter is intended only as a sketch or preview of the two leading methodological alternatives and their philosophical linkages; a comprehensive philosophical appraisal of their merits is left until Part 3, that is until after the illustrative case study of economic methodology has been completed.

4.1   The Objectivist-Behaviourist Approach: A Sketch

It will be as well to begin this survey of the methodological alternatives by drawing a clear-cut distinction between the notions of subject and object. This distinction will be of crucial importance for the discussion throughout the rest of the work. What I have in mind here is not the simple grammatical contrast of subject and object but rather the ontological or philosophical dichotomy. Taking the notion of object first since it presents the least difficulty, an object for philosophy means in the first place simply a *thing*. Added to this vague formulation is the requirement that an object should be a passive thing, or at the very least that it must be under the sway of efficient causal laws of nature. A subject by contrast is characterized as an *actor* or as an active being. The hallmarks of subjectivity are self-consciousness and freedom, and the notion of subject is intimately bound up with that of spirit. A subject knows what it is doing and that it is always free to do otherwise: hence by contrast with passive objects it transcends all efficient causal determination and is the responsible author and originator of all its actions. Although there could be fascinating discussion of where exactly the borderline between subject and object must be drawn in the realm of living things this should not be allowed to blur the sharpness of the distinction drawn[1]: and the radical character of the subject-object dichotomy on the ontological plane is a crucial presupposition of the overall argument in this work. A more lengthy defence and discussion of the philosophical grounds for drawing such a distinction will be presented in Part 3, Chapter 12.

The position which I have labelled as objectivist or behaviourist has had a long history in the human sciences dating back to the Enlightenment and certainly as far as Auguste Comte. Its central conviction is that the human sciences can progress in their understanding of man only by rigorously following the same methods as the natural sciences. For this purpose man must be treated as only another object in nature subject to efficient causal natural laws: as a sophisticated and complex organism but nothing more. All references to subjectivity, to human consciousness freedom and intentional activity must be banished since such subjective states are strictly unobservable and so can have no place in a rigorous human science. Although the objectivists will admit that there are some apparent problems which arise when the human sciences seek to follow exactly the methods of natural science, they hasten to point out that these annoying complications in human science (such as the self-fulfilling prophecy for example) turn out upon examination to have exact analogues in the natural sciences, for example the Heisenberg effect in physics, and so are not good ground for asserting a significant differentiation of methodology between natural and human science.

Once all reference to human consciousness has thus been extirpated objectivist explanations can only be cast in terms of externally observable patterns of behaviour and their correlation with no reference to choices, intentions, aspirations. It follows that explanation in human science can only take the form of a more or less sophisticated stimulus response model – in short an efficient causal model in which all behaviour is explained as some kind of socially or physically conditioned reflex. Once subjectivity has been comprehensively banished we are left only with patterns of observable behaviour of complex organisms and we proceed to explain these on the natural science model of antecedent cause and resultant effect, as correlations between various observed social or physical events (stimuli) and the regularly observed behaviour of the organism thus evoked (response). This is precisely the position which is taken up by behaviourist psychology, for example, and it is the inescapable consequence of any strict attempt to apply the methods of explanation of the natural sciences to the human sciences.[2]

The objectivist-behaviourist position with its efficient causal mode of explanation and which directs the human sciences to imitate in detail the methods of the natural sciences may be presented in three identifiably different ways. These three versions are not often distinguished and so it will be useful to give a brief sketch of each one here:

1   The instrumentalist version

This version says that while for purposes of rigorous human science we must eliminate all reference to (unobservable) subjective states, there is no question of denying that man is a self-conscious, purposive and freely acting being. The moral and political consequences of adopting a literal reduction of man to object, to a complex organism and no more, are abhorrent to these instrumentalists. It must then be clear that what they are proposing is a behaviourist fiction, that for purposes of human science it is useful even if seriously inaccurate to proceed with a purely objectivist picture of a man as merely a complex organism, since thereby the example of the revered natural sciences can be followed. From the discussions in Chapter 3 it should be clear that in this version, the objectivist-behaviourist approach, is adopting an instrumentalism as one of its basic postulates – whence my label, for it is prepared to defend as useful for scientific purposes a conception of man which it admits to be a serious distortion of the human reality, and thus build the human sciences on a fictional foundation. In the light of the decisive arguments against instrumentalism which were presented in Chapter 3 it will be already evident that I regard this version of objectivism as completely untenable.[3]

2   The reductionist version

If the instrumentalist version of objectivism is thus untenable there can be no escape from the adoption of an explicit and literal reductionist conception of man by the objectivists. In this version there is no attempt to sidestep awkward issues by having recourse to 'as if' fictionalist stratagems. Rather the essentially philosophical thesis that man is (literally) no more than a highly complex organism – another object in nature, is more or less openly espoused. Freedom and self-consciousness (that is, spirituality) are held to be only unfounded illusions inherited from religion and with the progress of the objectivist programme in psychology and human science they will gradually be eliminated. Ultimately these theorists look forward to the day when all of the human sciences will be capable of being deduced from physiology and biology: and physiology and biology deduced from physics and chemistry (cf. Comte's conception of a unified positivist science).[4] This extreme materialist reductionism presents a highly pessimistic unromantic view of man and of the possibility of morality and culture, yet it has enjoyed a surprising degree of popularity in all loosely positivist (or empiricist) thinking ever since Thomas Hobbes developed his political philosophy on the blatantly materialist notion of man as a complex material machine in motion. For whenever a positivist-inclined thinker resolves to distrust all assertions with regard to subjective states, the eventual espousal of some such materialist reduction is inevitable (given the illegitimacy of the instrumentalist version of objectivism).

3   Superficial monism of method

There is a third version of the view that the human sciences should follow strictly the methods of the natural sciences which although superficial and philosophically confused I shall mention here because of its widespread popularity among economists. This viewpoint enjoins the human scientist to follow closely the methods of natural science while in no way wishing to assert that man is an object or that he is to be treated as if he were an object for purposes of human science. Rather, proponents of this view hold that man may indeed be a free and self-conscious subject but do not wish to make any firm philosophical commitment on the question of whether man is a subject or object. In examining the potential implications of this subjectivity they merely enumerate a list of specific difficulties or complexities which will arise in applying natural science methods to man as a subject, for example the problems of controlled experiment, of self-fulfilling prophecy and of prediction in general given human freedom. Each of these specific difficulties is then cut down to size by showing analogous problems in the natural sciences or by appealing to the so-called law of large numbers, and any difference of method is said to be only a matter of degree.

The difficulty or superficiality of this position lies in the fact that it does not achieve an adequate grasp of the full implications of human subjectivity. As we shall see below, if man is a free and self-conscious being there can be no question of giving any efficient-causal account of his actions, rather they are to be explained in a strictly teleological manner in terms of the agents' goals and intentions. Since teleological explanation is radically distinct from the efficient-causal mode of explanation of the natural sciences it follows that if a proper recognition is given to the full implications of subjectivity we must arrive at a radical contrast between the methodologies of natural and human science. In fact, given the direct implication of teleology and hence of a dualism of method inherent in human subjectivity, the only way in which a monism of method can be defended at the same time as holding man to be a subject is by falling back on to the instrumentalist version of objectivism already discussed above and shown to be untenable. (Man is a subject but is to be treated for purposes of human science as if he were an object.) In short the superficial version of methodological monism is seriously unsatisfactory because it must either bring out the full implications of human subjectivity which are teleology and a dualism of method, or else it must collapse into the instrumentalist version of objectivism.

From this preliminary survey of the versions of the objectivist-behaviourist position we may already conclude that given the invalidity of instrumentalism and the conclusions arising in the superficial variant the strongest and most satisfactory version of the objectivist position is that which adopts a frankly materialist reductionist conception of man as merely another complex organism in nature.

As I noted at the beginning of the chapter it is of considerable importance to examine also the epistemological presuppositions of the leading methodological positions since it is on the plane of a critical philosophical appraisal that issues of methodology must eventually be settled. Accordingly, the presuppositions of objectivism will be briefly indicated here, although a full discussion of the conception of man and the epistemological linkages of both the objectivist-behaviourist and subjectivist-interpretive approaches must wait until Part 3.

There is a fairly obvious linkage between the objectivist approach and the broad empiricist and positivist tradition in philosophy and epistemology.[5] This linkage is made manifest in two main ways. First, empiricism broadly speaking is the conviction that all valid knowledge is based directly on sense-experience so that strictly valid cognitive claims can only refer to empirically observable realities. Positivism, a latter-day descendant of empiricism, is the view that the only propositions which have any claim to be valid or even meaningful cognitions (apart from tautologies) are those which can be directly tested by observation, that is those which are directly verifiable empirically. It will be immediately obvious how such an epistemological viewpoint must lead to the banishment of all reference to subjective states and acts such as intentions or acts of free choice from the human sciences since none of these are empirically observable as such.[6] Rather from such an epistemology it follows that man must be treated, for purposes of a rigorous human science at the very least, as if he were an object.

Secondly, all positivist and empiricist thought has been inspired by a great reverence and admiration for the accomplishments of natural science. Indeed in positivism, and in certain versions of relativism such as those of Kuhn and Lakatos, the natural sciences are regarded as the very paradigm of valid cognition. From such views the injunction to the human sciences to follow strictly the methods of natural science readily follows, and just such an implication has been drawn out by a long line of empiricist philosophers. Since a full recognition of human subjectivity points towards a subjectivist-interpretive methodology that is radically distinct from that of the natural sciences[7] this methodological monist injunction of necessity implies that man cannot be regarded as subject at least for purposes of human science. Rather he is to be treated as at most another highly complex organism in nature whose behaviour is to be explained along the lines of the efficient causal generalizations of the natural sciences.

The broadly positivist or empiricist position in epistemology is, therefore, quite sufficient to generate a strict objectivist-behaviourist methodology of the human sciences, together with its necessarily reductionist notion of man. It is not necessarily the case that an objectivist methodology conversely implies a positivist position in epistemology. Nevertheless, it is difficult to see what other kinds of epistemological option might produce such a methodology of human science as their consequence, and we may certainly say that if deprived of the empiricist epistemological backdrop the objectivist position in methodology would lose a great deal of cogency and would look peculiarly narrow and dogmatic in the face of man's awareness of freedom and his capability for moral and aesthetic expression. Suffice it to note that at least in the more systematic exponents of the objectivist-behaviourist position there has always been present a fairly strong positivist conviction.

4.2 The Subjectivist-Interpretive Approach: A Sketch

There has for a very long time been an alternative view of the methodology of the human sciences which in some respects has been even more systematically outlined than the objectivist approach. This is the approach which I have labelled above as subjectivist-interpretive, and it presents a teleological model of explanation for the human sciences which is radically different in kind from the mechanical-causal models of the natural sciences. Because of its links with the continental European systems of philosophy, this approach has been looked at askance by natural scientists and until recent times at any rate by most of the Anglo-Saxon human scientists and commentators on method; and there have also been some fierce internal battles known as *Methodenstreit* among proponents of different versions of the subjectivist approach, which have not helped to dispel the skepticism of empiricist-minded thinkers with regard to what is superficially at least a rather appealing position. But first an example which may help to highlight the differences between these two important methodological alternatives. I have taken a minor illustration from Professor H. L. A. Hart's *Concept of Law* concerning the 'internal' or self-conscious aspect of rules[8] and amplified it considerably to try to throw into relief what is at stake in the controversy of objectivist and subjectivist methods in the human sciences, and which is the key focus of this work.

A Martian observer trained to a high degree of sophisticated falsificationism in the methods of natural science escaped from 'star wars' and began some research on human behaviour patterns. Informed that behaviour by motorists at traffic lights was particularly revealing of the nature and predicament of Earthlings, and that in particular national differences in temperament were observable in a clear-cut manner almost as good as that of a controlled experiment, he proceeded to make comprehensive observations there. Following the objectivist mechanical-causal mode of explanation which, after all, had made the mission to Earth possible, he quickly constructed the inductive generalization or hypothesis that 'red light' when seen generates a grating neural response and causes drivers to stop their cars (or transmits automatic signals to the engine which bring the car to a halt), while 'green light' when seen generates a pleasant neural response causing drivers to carry on (or transmit some different signal causing the car to carry on automatically).

The hypothetical generalization holds up quite well at first – at least until our inter-galactic traveller comes to Italy. Here, what had previously been only a rare and minor falsification of the theory put down to errors of observation, and so on, becomes a major anomaly and in effect a clear falsification of the hypothesis, for our Martian scientist observes a wide and unsystematic range of exceptions where cars in Italy continue to move through crossings, even when red lights are displayed. In vain he begins to search for all manner of auxiliary hypotheses which might help to buttress his theory, such as that Italians have neuro-physiological systems on which the effects of colours are different (but even if that were at all plausible how could he then explain the fact that so many Italians do obey red lights) or he may even fall into crude 'ad hoccery' seeking to explain away the exceptions by time of day, make of car, age and sex of drivers – all to no avail. In desperation he concludes that his theory is the best available even if systematically falsified and defiantly challenges us to produce a better one.

Enter the social scientist of the subjectivist-interpretive school, who points immediately to the inevitable source of the Martian's failures. What the objectivist approach cannot under any circumstances grasp is the subjective character of the human being, that man is a *self-conscious* and *free* being whose behaviour must, therefore, be seen not as causally determined by any external stimulus, but rather as action, as the purposive execution of a project, as activity directed to a goal of which the agent is actually or potentially conscious. Self-conscious action cannot be explained in objectivist terms, it can only be understood by grasping the subjective intention of the agent, and herein lies the key to resolving the Martian's enigma over the traffic lights. The behaviour of human beings on such occasions can only be adequately understood as the purposive decision to follow the rules of the road, itself based on a prior decision that to follow these social conventions will contribute to road safety and hence to the universally shared human goal of survival. Neither rules nor the prior subjective decision to follow them in pursuit of some ulterior goal (which may or may not be shared with others) exercise a causally determining impact on human action; we may always decide to disobey rules in general or on specific occasions, and purely private decisions can always be revised. Consquently, the observation of exceptions to normal behaviour at traffic lights indicates only that there is deviance from the rule, that not all subjects feel inclined to obey them, and that this conscious disrespect for rules is stronger in Italy than elsewhere (for reasons which can again be illuminated by interpretive methods).

Hart summarizes the lesson to be drawn from the example succinctly, pointing to the necessity of grasping the 'internal' or self-conscious aspect of any rule:

[The objectivists'] view will be like the view of one who having observed the working of a traffic signal in a busy street for some time limits himself to saying that when the light turns red there is a high probability that the traffic will stop. He treats the light merely as a natural sign that people will behave in certain ways as clouds are a sign that rain will come. In so doing, he will miss out a whole dimension of the social life of those whom he is watching since for them the red light is not merely a sign that others will stop: they look upon it as a signal for them to stop and so a reason for stopping in conformity to rules.[9]

The central feature of this alternative approach to methodology then is its determination to recognize the subjectivity of man and to bring that subjectivity into the very heart of the explanatory theories of the human sciences. Man is a self-conscious being who *knows* what he is and what he is doing, and in the moment of self-awareness he becomes equally aware of his freedom, of the inexorable burden of responsibility that is *choice*. His overt behaviour, apart from purely physical reflexes, will, therefore, have the character of action strictly so-called, it will be the purposive self-conscious execution of a project chosen by the agent. The task of the specifically human sciences, those which deal precisely with man as a self-conscious subject (rather than as a biological organism, as for example physiology) and which includes psychology and all of the social sciences is to seek an explanation, a genuine understanding of human actions. This is to be achieved not through any kind of mechanical-causal account citing external stimuli (for in the moment of choosing his course of action the agent transcends all antecedent determinations and becomes the fully responsible initiator and agent thereof), but rather through an elucidation of the purpose, the reason for, the subjective meaning of the freely chosen action for the agent involved. The explanatory model of the human sciences in dealing with action is, therefore, *teleological*, being an interpretation of the subjective meaning or intention of action for the agent in question.

Since the distinction of this subjectivist-interpretive position from the objectivist-behaviourist approach to methodology will be central to the whole of the discussion which follows, it may be as well to pause for a moment to emphasize how radical the dichotomy of these two approaches is and why it is so. We may begin by noting immediately that both approaches do share certain points of view despite their differences. Thus they both uphold the conviction that the task of any natural or human science is to explain particular phenomena by means of (insightful)[10] generalizations of which they are a case; and that these hypothetical generalizations should be subjected to careful empirical testing.[11] This, however, is as far as the similarity goes and it leaves a wide and significant area of methodological differentiation.

In the first place, where the objectivist approach treats man purely as another object in nature, at least for purposes of human science, the subjectivist approach treats man as a subject, as a self-conscious and free being who in the moment of choice transcends all antecedent determination of an efficient causal type. We have already seen that on the philosophical plane the notions of subject and object are radically distinct and so it follows that a human science whose understanding of man is developed on the notion of man as a mere object will be completely different from and opposed to a human science which is built up upon the notion of man as subject. This sharp contrast will be felt both on the level of the pure theory of human science and also, even more significantly, in the practical applications of that theory to problems of social and economic policy and of psychological therapy. For clearly if man is regarded as a self-conscious and free being rather than as a mere object this will make a crucial difference to the way in which we seek to influence social affairs and improve the human condition in general. (This contrast on the level of practical application is well illustrated by the completely opposed methods of psychological therapy advocated by the behaviourist and the existentialist schools in modern psychology.)

In addition to the difference over their basic conception of man, the objectivist and subjectivist approaches also differ radically in their basic mode of explanation: the objectivist approach adopts a broadly efficient causal mode of explanation such as is used in the natural sciences, while the subjectivist-interpretive approach uses a strictly teleological mode of explanation. This distinction of efficient causal and teleological modes of explanation goes back as far as Aristotle who clearly differentiated between explanation in terms of efficient cause and explanation in terms of final cause, where by final cause he meant the telos, or goal, of an activity.

The essence of the contrast may be indicated in a preliminary way here pending a much fuller discussion in Part 3. An efficient causal explanation (such as the objectivist approach typifies) will be an attempt to explain any piece of human behaviour in terms of some independently identifiable antecedent (and observable) cause or stimulus which gives rise to the behaviour in question as effect or response in a law-like manner; the inspiration of this approach is clearly the natural science model of explanation, especially the physics model.[12] Teleological explanation by contrast is the attempt to explain human action in terms of the agent's own goals or intentions. Not only does attainment of the goal always come after the execution of the action, as I shall show at some length in Part 3 Chapter 15, the relationship of goal or intention to the action which gives it effect is completely different from the relationship of efficient cause to its effect.

Since the time of Plato and Aristotle a clear-cut distinction has been maintained by philosophers between these two modes of explanation. In recent times, however, Davidson[13] and others arguing from the everyday usages of (causalist) language have held that teleological explanation is not really distinctive but only an unusual type of efficient causal explanation. Not wishing to dwell upon this now, it may be pointed out that the linkage of an agent's intention to his action is an intrinsic logical one of a very different kind from the linkage of efficient cause to its effect; hence whatever may be the usages of notoriously sloppy and ambiguous everyday language[14] nothing but unnecessary confusion can arise from this attempt at conflation of efficient causal and teleological modes of explanation. We may conclude, therefore, that both in the basic conception of man and his activity and in the mode of explanation of human phenomena there is a clear-cut and radical differentiation between the objectivist-behaviourist and subjectivist-interpretive methodologies of the human sciences.

The subjectivist-interpretive approach to human science with its literal teleological mode of explanation has a long and sometimes illustrious heritage in European thought. A brief survey of its chequered heritage will therefore prove quite interesting as well as clarifying and guarding against some serious ambiguities and confusions in interpretation of what precisely I have meant in this work by a subjectivist-interpretive methodology. As far back as Plato there have been demands for explanatory models that go beyond the efficient-causal to give reasons why the world is as it is,[15] and teleology was also a central feature of Aristotle's science, although he used teleological explanation in a most implausible analogical manner to apply to natural objects mainly. The abandonment of Aristotelian science brought the teleological mode of explanation into serious disrepute and throughout the Enlightenment right up to Comte the conviction was widely held that the human sciences should be built upon a strict imitation of the mechanical-causal model of the natural sciences (cf. Hobbes on political theory, Hume's psychology). It was only when the human sciences began to establish themselves seriously as separate disciplines in the early nineteenth century that the claims of the human sciences began to be heard again. By the later nineteenth century there had arisen in Germany an influential school of thought which represented an extreme reaction to the crudeness of the early objectivist approach to human science as expressed, for instance, by Auguste Comte: this was the German Historical School, which held that indeed man was a free self-conscious subject, author of his own actions and projects and creative being *par excellence*. Emphasizing the uniqueness of each human subject, the members of this school held not only that understanding human action meant grasping the intention of the agent, but that this subjectivist meaning would also be radically unique and personal to each individual so that there could be no question of systematic generalization in the human sciences. Furthermore, they held that this subjective meaning could be grasped by the human scientist in an 'empathetic intuition' which would be true *a priori*. They held that the interpretive human disciplines were more like the appreciation of literary texts and were to be based on an *a priori* empathetic intuition of the unique meaning of others' actions: they were to be much closer to hermeneutics and history than to the natural sciences.[16]

The extremity of the German Historical School's position, and especially its appeal to empathy as the *a priori* basis of interpretation of subjective meaning, did immense damage to the claims of the subjectivist approach among many serious scientists and was regarded as the typical terminus of any flirtation with continental European philosophical ideas by Anglo-Saxon thinkers especially. After all, from Descartes to Hegel to Husserl and Sartre, self-consciousness and subjectivity have been central to continental philosophy. In Max Weber's methodological essays we come upon a much more moderate statement of a subjectivist-interpretive methodology which insists that the teleological mode of explanation of action is fully consistent with the construction of a generalizing human science and that interpretive hypotheses are just as subject to the requirement of rigorous empirical testing as those of the natural sciences. Individual actions always have their unique aspect, just as single material objects do, and the whole task of interpretive social science is to abstract from those actions or aspects of the meaning of actions which are unique to the individual and to construct ideal-type generalizations which focus on those goals or intentions which are shared by a wide range of human agents and which render certain courses of purposive action typical over a wide range.

If Weber thus demonstrated the possibility of a systematic human science using the interpretive approach, his follower Alfred Schutz outlined a comprehensive statement of the subjectivist-interpretive methodology together with its philosophical underpinnings, deducing his position from Husserl's phenomenology. In Schutz we find a painstaking account of the nature of human subjectivity, of choice, freedom, and of action as the self-conscious execution of a project. From this account he deduces that to understand human actions is to grasp the full subjective meaning of the action for the agent: and this will require that we elucidate what he calls both the 'in-order-to' and 'because' motives of the action[17]. The 'in-order-to' motive is the project or goal to whose realization the action is directed, while the 'because' motive refers to those past experiences and features of the social situation which have influenced the agent to react to them by the construction of the project revealed in the 'in-order-to' motive as purpose of his actions. The unhappily labelled 'because' motive is not in any way to be understood as a mechanical-causal determinant of human actions (either deterministically or probabilistically). Rather than any kind of a stimulus-response model, what Schutz has in mind is a freely chosen purposive reaction by the human agent to the constraints of his environment[18] and the 'because' motive can only be cited together with, and as a part of, teleological explanation in terms of 'in-order-to' motive.

As well as giving a systematic account of how subjectivity demands that the human sciences should adopt an interpretive methodology which explains human action in terms of the subjectively intended meaning of the agent, Schutz strongly insists that such subjective intentions are inaccessible to the observing social scientist. They are certainly not externally observable (as the objectivist would require), but neither are they given to some mysterious empathy which would give us direct intuitive access to the minds of other persons. Consequently, both Weber and Schutz emphasize that the interpretive hypotheses constructed by human science as to the subjective intentions of agents are just as much conjectures as those of the natural sciences; and so they stand in need of some kind of unambiguous empirical testing. This is to be achieved by deducing the consequences for observable behaviour of particular interpretive hypotheses (for example, profit maximization as a purposive explanation of firms' behaviour in economics generates certain clear predictions as to prices) and by checking these against actually observed behaviour patterns of agents. There is no question of an *a priori* validity of interpretive hypotheses via empathy or introspection in the mature statement of the position by Schutz; and the requirement that interpretive social theories be tested is precisely what Weber meant by the requirement he so unfortunately labelled as 'causal-adequacy'.

From this brief historical survey it will be clear that the interpretive approach to human science and the notion of teleological explanation have been associated with a variety of different methodological positions and issues. I should emphasize at this stage that when I speak of the subjectivist-interpretive approach in this work what I shall mean in all cases is the mature Weber–Schutz version of the position.

As we have just seen, the mature Weber–Schutz version of the position insists against the historical school that an interpretive human science will seek explanatory hypotheses which are both generalizations and empirically testable. This leads to an important type of objection to the radical differentiation of the Weber–Schutz interpretive approach from the objectivist approach upon which I have been insisting in this chapter. This often-encountered objection consists in asserting that since the requirements of explanation by means of generalization and the empirical testability of hypotheses are the only significant requirements for purposes of methodological appraisal, and since both objectivist and subjectivist approaches equally insist on these requirements there is after all no methodologically significant difference between the approaches.[19]

Upon a close inspection this objection implicitly invokes, or could only be made plausible by implicit invocation of, instrumentalism as a premise. What the objection amounts to is an assertion that for purposes of methodological appraisal what matters is that a scientific hypothesis should be universal and above all that it should have a high degree of predictive power (empirical testability). The precise content of hypothesis is a matter of no methodological importance. But if the content of a hypothesis is a matter of no methodological consequence this implies that blatantly unrealistic fictional hypotheses (of the Friedman variety) as well as realistic hypotheses will be on an equal methodological footing provided they predict with similar accuracy. Consequently, the above-mentioned objection of necessity invokes an instrumentalist conception of scientific theory as a premise.

I have already outlined in Chapter 3 why I regard any form of instrumentalism as completely untenable. Against instrumentalism I have proposed that if science is to be guided by the regulative ideal of truth it must seek hypotheses which offer a genuine understanding of or insight into the phenomena under study; it must seek to give a true and accurate account of how the world really is and functions. If this is the goal of genuine scientific explanation then blatantly fictional hypotheses are absolutely ruled out and an appraisal of the content of scientific hypotheses becomes a matter of considerable methodological importance. Applying these conditions to the question of the contrast of subjectivist and objectivist approaches to the human sciences, I have sought to show that the two approaches involve radically distinct conceptions of man and consequently that a human science built around the conception of man as subject differs radically both in the content of its explanatory theories and in their practical implications from a human science built upon the conception of man as object. Since the realist notion of scientific theory insists that any such radical contrast in the content of scientific hypotheses is of the utmost methodological significance, the differentiation which I have sought to draw between the subjectivist and objectivist approaches turns out to be in every sense a fundamental one, and the objection which seeks to minimize the methodological significance of this contrast of content is, I would suggest, seriously mistaken.[20]

Since any methodological position can ultimately be defended only on the plane of a critical epistemology and ontology, I turn now to give an indication of what the philosophical presuppositions and linkages of the subjectivist-interpretive position are. In the first place, in sharp contrast to the pessimistic reductionist view of man, which I have shown to be necessarily linked with the objectivist position,[21] we find in the interpretive position an optimistic and quasi-romantic conception of man as a self-conscious, choosing, purposive agent responsible author of his own actions. This broadly humanist conception of man is forcefully stated by all of the protagonists of the interpretive approach as their central conviction. The humanism that is thus central to the interpretive approach has contributed greatly to its overall attractiveness as a methodological position, in particular with the vanishing of the shibboleths of extreme 'scientism' in recent times, and it is a leading factor in my own (fairly transparent) philosophical preference for the position.

While both the subjectivist and objectivist approaches necessarily bring with them certain definitive positions in the philosophy of man, the same cannot be said of their epistemological presuppositions. We have already seen that although the objectivist position is most plausible when deduced from a positivist-empiricist type of epistemology it does not necessarily imply such an epistemology. In the case of the subjectivist-interpretive methodology we find that it has in fact been deduced (together with a humanist philosophy of man) from two philosophical systems which are *prima facie* strikingly opposed in modern thought: namely from post-Wittgenstein linguistic analysis in Anglo-Saxon thought and from phenomenology in the continental European tradition.[22] Linguistic analysis from study of everyday uses of language has come to an insistence on the irreducibility of action, will, and other concepts referring to conscious states to the objectivist model of efficient cause and effect (or stimulus-response) in any form and on the consequent differentiation of man as actor, as subject, from objects or organisms. Winch and others have gone on to deduce from this broad humanism a clear-cut interpretive methodology for the human sciences.[23] In phenomenology the insistence on subjectivity, on the irreducibility of man to an object and on self-consciousness and freedom is even more forthright and it was from Husserl's pure phenomenology that Alfred Schutz deduced his systematic statement of an interpretive methodology for the human sciences.

Since I have as yet said very little about phenomenology, and since I shall be making a number of references to it in the course of Part 2, I shall now give a brief account of the main features of phenomenology and of its linkages with the subjectivist-interpretive methodology of human science. This is very much of a preliminary sketch, however, because a much fuller treatment of the topic will be found in Chapter 12.

Within phenomenology we may distinguish two rather different although not opposing approaches: the pure phenomenology of Husserl and the later existentialist phenomenology of Sartre, Schutz and others. Husserl was led to develop his pure phenomenology from a reflection on the inadequacies both of the positivist and relativist anti-philosophies, on the one hand, and of the speculative excesses of continental European rationalist thought in the nineteenth century (for example, Hegel and Marx) on the other. In particular, having shown that the positivist view that the natural sciences are the paradigm of valid cognition is dogmatically uncritical and that the relativist position only leads to nihilistic absurdities (for the reasons such as I have already outlined in Chapter 2, pp. 27–30), Husserl insists that it is the inescapable task of philosophy to provide a critical-rational foundation of absolute certainty (which will, therefore, not itself be in need of any further critical examination) for all human cognition, and in particular for the methods of the sciences.

In this search by a critical reason for a foundation of absolute certainty for all human cognition there is an unmistakable echo of Descartes, and indeed Husserl followed Descartes closely in arguing that the only field where such certainty could be attained was that of self-consciousness, of consciousness made present and fully transparent to itself in reflection. From this turn to self-consciousness Descartes produces his famous *cogito* ('*cogito ergo sum*', 'I think, therefore I am, I exist'). When I reflect I cannot possibly deny that I am thinking (reflecting), nor can I possibly deny that I actually exist, at least as a thinking being. To deny either would involve an untenable performative contradiction.

Descartes had not taken the exploitation of the field of self-consciousness very much further than the *cogito*. Husserl in his pure phenomenology seeks to extract a great deal more from the field of self-consciousness. Where Descartes had emphasized the *cogito* Husserl now examines also the *cogitatum*, the object-for-consciousness. He points out that in a reflection by consciousness on itself we can not only know with certainty that we exist and are thinking, we can also elucidate with absolute certainty what we are thinking about. However, what can be given with certainty is not the real essence of some external material object or event about which we are thinking, but only the object or event as it is construed by our consciousness. In short what we can elucidate with certainty is only *phenomenon*, the object as it appears to consciousness, rather than as it is in itself. It is for this reason that Husserl's approach to philosophy is known as phenomenology, and in particular that Husserl spoke of the 'bracketing of existence' – the suspension of any attempt to make assertions about actually existing objects-in-themselves as a crucial step of his phenomenological method for philosophy.

Existentialist phenomenology grew up from a concern precisely over the 'bracketing of existence' in Husserl's pure phenomenology. All of the existentialists are fully in accord with Husserl's rejection of positivist and relativist absurdities and with his critical rational quest for a foundation of certainty upon which human cognition can be built. Moreover, they agree with Husserl's Cartesian-inspired turn to the field of self-consciousness in order to find such certainties. Within this field they seek to find if there are any propositions at all which can be asserted with certainty and yet which do pertain to actual existence – if there are any propositions which can be asserted with certainty without the need to bracket existence. Descartes' *cogito* already provides an instance of one proposition pertaining to existence which can be asserted with absolute certainty. The existentialists then go on to argue that in reflection upon any conscious state (such as joy, fear, lethargy) or activity (such as thinking, laughing, choosing) we can not only elucidate with certainty what is involved in the state or activity (of joy, fear, thinking, laughing, etc.) following Husserl's phenomenological method; equally we cannot possibly deny the existence of such conscious states (at some time) hence their actual existence is also given with absolute certainty. For in order to be able to elucidate the essence of various conscious states or activities in reflection, I must at some stage have actually experienced them, whence they must have existed (at some time or other). Thus existentialist phenomenology finds in the area of the elucidation of conscious states and activities a rich field where the phenomenological method can be applied without any need to bracket existence; and the fruits of this application will be an elucidation of the real essence of conscious states of activities as they are in themselves (rather than merely as they appear to consciousness).[24]

A full outline and discussion of both pure and existentialist phenomenology must wait until Chapter 12 and hence rather than taking the discussion of phenomenology any further here I shall indicate how it leads towards a subjectivist-interpretive methodology for the human sciences. In the first place in virtue of its definitive refutation of positivism and of relativism phenomenology undermines a crucial pillar which supports the objectivist-behaviourist approach to the human sciences, namely the presumption that the natural sciences are the paradigm of valid human cognition and that the human sciences should therefore follow closely the methods of natural science. Secondly, and much more decisively both pure and existentialist phenomenology make human subjectivity, man's self-consciousness, the very starting point of all human cognition and the most fundamental certainty of all. Hence there can be no question of man being merely another object in nature; rather human subjectivity should be the very first principle of the human sciences. As we shall see below in Chapter 14, Alfred Schutz has built up a comprehensive outline of the subjectivist-interpretive methodology drawing directly on existentialist phenomenology. From the conception of man as free self-conscious subject and from a careful phenomenological analysis of the essence of actions, choices, and various types of inter-subjective experiences and interactions, Schutz deduces the imperative of explaining human action in terms of the goals of the self-conscious agent and to contrast this teleological mode of explanation with the efficient causal mode of explanation of the natural sciences.

Thirdly, we may note another less widely recognized linkage between existentialist phenomenology and a subjectivist approach to the human sciences. We have seen that the real essence or form of various conscious states or activities can be given with absolute certainty in a reflection by consciousness on itself. This leads to the possibility that existentialist phenomenology may be able to make some direct contributions of *a priori* validity to some human sciences. If the real essence of say the emotion of joy or the act of deliberate choice can be revealed in a phenomenological reflection this will constitute a valuable foundation of (non-tautological) certainty upon which for example the specific psychological theory of joy or the economic theory of deliberate choice may be built. As examples of this I may mention Sartre's work on the psychology of the imagination[25] (and of emotions) and also my own discussion of the economic theory of deliberate choice in Chapter 5, where I suggest that the optimization principle can be deduced to be true *a priori* for every case of deliberate choice (as economists have in effect presumed) from phenomenological examination of the act of deliberate choice.

To forestall misunderstanding, it will be as well to emphasize here the limitations of this potential *a priori* contribution from existentialist phenomenology to the human sciences. The subjectivist-interpretive human sciences typically search for generalized interpretations of human actions. Now what can be known with certainty in phenomenological reflection regarding the conscious states and activities of large numbers of people other than oneself is only the purely *formal* or universal aspect of such conscious states or activities. That aspect alone is common to all human agents, while the detailed contents of other people's conscious states and activities differ widely. Hence, apart from the formal aspect which is common to all agents, all that I can ever hope to know with certainty in a phenomenological reflection is the contents of my own conscious states and activities. As soon as we begin to fill out the widely diverse contents of the conscious states of other persons (as a generalizing human science must if it is to get beyond a mere formalism), the *direct* contribution of existentialist phenomenology to the human sciences is at an end. There is, therefore, no question of existentialist phenomenology being capable of providing a whole range of *a priori* empathetic intuitions regarding the details of other people's conscious states as the historical and hermeneutical schools suggested in the last century. The direct and *a priori* valid contribution from existentialist phenomenology to the human sciences is a good deal more limited being confined as I have shown to the purely formal level of elucidating the real essence of various conscious states or activities in general.

It will be obvious from the tenor of my outline of the two leading methodological positions, objectivist-behaviourist and subjectivist-interpretive, in this chapter where my own preference lies, and even what are the philosophical arguments which I regard as decisive for that preference. For in seeking to make a contribution to the controversy between the objectivist and subjectivist approaches I seek specifically to resolve that debate in favour of the subjectivist approach and to show that the conclusive philosophical grounds for such a resolution can be found in existentialist phenomenology. As I have repeatedly emphasized, it is only on the plane of a critical philosophical discussion that these methodological issues can ultimately be settled and so in Part 3 I shall present in detail the philosophical arguments for my proposed resolution of the methodological debate in favour of the subjectivist position. Before moving to present these arguments, I have paused to consider, in an extended methodological case study, mainstream economics as an illustrative example of a mature human science as it is actually practised. The outline of the two main methodological alternatives in this chapter will serve as a useful prologue to that case study as well as being a sort of cocktail to be sampled before the main philosophical banquet of Part 3.

Notes

1 Just as the distinction between baldness and non-baldness is not blurred by the difficulty of saying how many hairs constitute the maximum for baldness in borderline cases.
2 The intermediate case that biology seems to constitute as a seemingly teleological natural science will be considered below and shown to be thoroughly efficient-causal and not teleological. Thus there is no escape from the conclusion that to follow the methods of natural science in human science implies objectivism (cf. Chapter 15 and pp. 236–39).
3 A fuller discussion must await, Part 3, Chapter 13.
4 A. Comte (1877), *Cours de Philosophie Positive* (Paris: Ballière, 1877).
5 See A. Rosenberg (1981), *Sociobiology and the Preemption of Social Science* (Oxford: Basil Blackwell), for example. In chs 1 and 2, he outlines clearly the linkage between a reductionist version of objectivism and empiricist philosophical premises.
6 Thus we may observe behaviour which an agent tells us is free or directed to some goal. But neither the freedom of choice itself nor the agent's intention is given directly to observation.
7 This point has already been referred to briefly on p. 55. A fuller discussion of why methodological monism must imply an objectivist approach (that is, the untenability of the superficial variant of monism mentioned on p. 55) will be presented in Part 3.
8 H. L. A. Hart (1970), *The Concept of Law* (Oxford: Clarendon Press). The

example is generalized from Hart's discussion of obeying rules at traffic lights and contrasting external (that is, behaviourist) and internal (interpretive) understanding of this phenomenon.

9 H. L. A. Hart, *The Concept of Law*, p. 87. It may be added that while Hart uses the example to illustrate the rule following aspect of much human action and the necessity of paying attention to the 'internal' aspect of rules, I have sought to draw from the example a wider lesson concerning the self-conscious character of the human agent; the freely chosen purposive character of his action and the consequent necessity of explaining action by grasping the agent's subjective meaning or purpose.

10 Clearly, the instrumentalist version of objectivism would dispense with the adjective 'insightful'.

11 Only the mature Weber–Schutz version of the subjectivist approach clearly insists on the need for testing interpretive hypotheses (cf. discussion on pp. 62–63).

12 The case of biology as a supposedly teleological natural science may be mentioned in this connection. However, as I shall show in Part 3, Chapter 15, biology is teleological only in virtue of a loose use of language. It is not strictly teleological at all; it is efficient-causal in its mode of explanation.

13 D. Davidson (1968), 'Actions, causes, reasons', in A. White (ed.), *The Philosophy of Action* (Oxford: Oxford University Press).

14 Upon reflection, could anything be more stupid than to take 'everyday uses of language', or common sense, as the basis for philosophy or for knowledge in any field. The great task for human cognition is precisely to overcome the illusions of common sense in all fields (cf. Plato's conception of the task of human inquiry: the pursuit of *episteme* and the dissipation of *doxa*).

15 Cf. Plato (1982), 'The Phaedo', in *The Last Days of Socrates* (Harmondsworth: Penguin), pp. 153–7.

16 In all of his works, W. Dilthey reiterates this theme in criticism of the positivist project of the human sciences in Comte, and so on. For a much fuller discussion of the Historical School's methodology, see cf. Chapter 14, pp. 211–14.

17 The methodology of Weber and Schutz together with references are discussed in much greater detail in Part 3. However, A. Schutz (1972), *The Phenomenology of the Social World* (London: Heinemann), *passim*, but especially chs I, II, and V may be mentioned. See also M. Weber (1947), *Economy and Society*, Talcott Parsons (trans.), (London: Macmillan).

18 This may be compared with K. Popper (1957), *The Poverty of Historicism* (London: Routledge & Kegan Paul), where he discusses action in accordance with the 'logic of the situation' (pp. 140–1, 149).

19 Such objections have been raised in the course of numerous seminars and discussions, notably by Professor M. Blaug and Professor P. Salmon.

20 Mistaken because it involves an instrumentalism.

21 Necessarily, if the instrumentalist and superficial variants of objectivism are rejected.

22 M. Roche (1973), *Phenomenology, Language and Social Science* (London: Routledge & Kegan Paul), chs 1, 2. Here is shown the striking convergence on humanism by these otherwise quite opposed schools.

23 P. Winch (1958), *The Idea of a Social Science and its Relation to Philosophy* (London: Routledge & Kegan Paul).

24 The point being, of course, that the essence of a conscious state as it appears to consciousness in reflection is the same as the essence of that state as it is in itself.

25 J.-P. Sartre (1972), *The Psychology of the Imagination* (London: Methuen).

PART 2

Economic Science:
A Methodological Case Study

Introduction to Part 2

The purely philosophical discussion of methodological issues often seems rather barren and abstract, as if it were dealing at times only with illusory dichotomies and non-issues. Some of the discussion presented here may have already given such an impression to the reader. Accordingly, in this second part of the book I have sought to bring the abstract philosophical argument to life and to show its relevance to the practice of the human sciences by considering in detail the methodology of a leading human science, both as practised and as preached by its leading exponents.

Part 2 may therefore be looked upon as an illustrative case study in which the abstract issues of the debate between the objectivist-behaviourist and subjectivist-interpretive approaches are examined in a more concrete manner as they manifest themselves in the theories of a well-established human science. For purposes of this case study I have chosen to examine in detail mainstream economic science for two reasons. First, economics is arguably the most mature and well-established of the human sciences. It has transcended the aura of vagueness and self-doubt which characterizes many of the less mature human sciences. Secondly, my own background and competence fits me to speak with much greater authority of economics than of other human sciences.

In taking economics for this case study I should hasten to add that what I have examined is the broad mainstream body of economic theory upon which there is a wide degree of consensus among economists and which will be found expounded in detail in any good intermediate level textbooks of microeconomic and macroeconomic theory. Thus when speaking of mainstream economics I do not mean to refer to some of the extremely narrow, so-called neo-classical versions of economics, which are sometimes set up as whipping-boys by critics of economics. These so-called neo-classical versions, which would be better labelled as neo-conservative, focus exclusively on the perfectly competitive model of the firm, and at the macro level have hardly got beyond the stage of the purest and simplest version of the Walrasian general equilibrium model in which all markets are cleared automatically through the offices of the all-seeing auctioneer. Adherence to such pure, perfectly competitive versions of neo-classical economics is, it should be emphasized, very much the exception among mainstream economic theorists. For the bulk of economists, mainstream theory today embraces besides perfect competition and market exchange a whole range of theories of the firm under conditions of imperfect competition and oligopoly, a wide set of non-market exchanges and a careful analysis of the 'anatomy' of various types of market failure and disequilibrium behaviour. A cursory glance at any of the leading textbooks will verify this range of interests of modern mainstream theory: and as we shall discover in the following chapters the unifying principle of mainstream economic theory is not the model of perfect competition but rather the 'optimization' principle.

I shall now summarize the main points which are to be made in the course of this methodological case study of mainstream economics. The early chapters consider at some length the fields of microeconomic and macroeconomic theory, reaching the conclusion that mainstream economic theory is an outstanding exemplification of a Weber–Schutz type of subjectivist-interpretive methodology together with its teleological mode of explanation. This unmistakably interpretive character of economic theory I show to arise from the pervasiveness and centrality of the 'optimization' or 'maximization' principle to all economic explanations.[1] Since the optimization principle has been the subject of some controversy in regard to rationality postulates in recent years I have paused in Chapter 7 to examine what precisely are the assumptions regarding the rationality of human agents that are involved in the optimization principle.

Having clarified the interpretive character of economic theory, I then turn to examine what economists themselves have had to say about their methodology. A survey of the remarks of leading spokesmen on methodology in both the last and present centuries reveals, astonishingly, that virtually none of the great economists have recognized the interpretive character of the methodology they have been practising. There is no mention whatever of either Max Weber or Alfred Schutz. Nor has there been any recognition that economic theory exemplifies a subjectivist approach together with its teleological mode of explanation which is radically distinct from objectivism and the efficient-causal modes of explanation of the natural sciences.[2]

In whatever little they have had to say explicitly about their methodology economists have urged a monism of method, that is that economics should follow as closely as possible the (efficient-causal) methods of explanation of the natural sciences and that there is no inherent radical differentiation between the methods of the natural and the human sciences. In terms of the classification of the various versions of the objectivist approach which was given in the last chapter economists have adopted the 'superficial methodological monism' variant[3] – the view that does not deny that man is a free and self-conscious being but holds that this does not generate any significant differences of method between the natural and the human sciences.

Arising from these considerations I conclude Part 2 by suggesting that there is a two-fold methodological gap between economist's precepts and practice on matters of methodology. There is in the first place a widely recognized gap between economists' precepts as regard the need to test their theories carefully and rigorously and their practice which has been extremely lax in this regard. This gap has been outlined well by Mark Blaug in his work *The Methodology of Economics*[4] where he shows that while economists have been following such leading exponents of natural science methodology as Lakatos and Popper in preaching the logic of falsification and of severe testing of theories, in practice they have been fighting shy of serious empirical testing.

In addition to his gap of precept and practice in regard to testing I have discovered what from a philosophical point of view is an even more serious incompatability between precept and practice. For while economists have been preaching a monism of method (and in some cases an outright instrumentalist version of objectivism), the body of main-stream theory has become the homeground and shining exemplification of a Weber–Schutz type of subjectivist methodology with a teleological mode of explanation which as we saw in the last chapter is *philoso-phically* radically distinct from any form of objectivism and in particular from the efficient-causal modes of explanation of the natural sciences.

Notes

1 Explanation of action by the 'optimization' principle is clearly interpretive. It explains action in terms of the goals which the agent seeks to maximize.
2 There has been one notable exception – the Austrian School (Mises, Robbins, and Hayek, for example). As we shall see below, these thinkers have rightly recognized the interpretive character of economics, but have fallen into other equally serious methodological errors, as has the bulk of the mainstream spokesmen. They have not advocated the interpretive methodology in the mature Weber–Schutz version which I have defended.
3 In some cases economists and other commentators have adopted the 'instrumentalist' version of objectivism as outlined in the previous chapter (cf. M. Friedman, E. Nagel).
4 M. Blaug (1980), *The Methodology of Economics* (Cambridge: Cambridge University Press), especially ch. 15.

5

The Economic Theory of
Deliberate Choice

A clear definition of economic science is provided in the seminal essay by Lord Robbins. Economics he defines as a 'study of human behaviour insofar as it is a relationship between ends and scarce means which have alternative uses'.[1] Economics, therefore, is concerned above all with the way in which mankind allocates and distributes its scarce resources; it is the science of human choice in the face of scarcity.

It will be appropriate to commence our case study of economic science with a careful examination of the economists' theory of deliberate choice. We shall find that this theory is of central importance to economics not only in virtue of the above definition but also in so far as its central principle – the optimization principle – is an all-pervasive element in the explanatory hypotheses of mainstream economics.

5.1   The Theory Outlined

The economic theory of choice is one of *constrained* choice, of choice in the face of scarcity, and it is worth pausing briefly to note the significance of this qualification. If the resources requisite to the realization of human goals and aspirations were not scarce, i.e. if they were available to all as free goods, there would no longer be a 'problem of choice'. To illustrate this, consider time, which for each man is the scarce resource *par excellence*. If one could live for ever without fear of death from any source, then, with the promise of an infinite tomorrow, there is literally nothing which a human agent could not eventually do, and there is no problem of time preference. Consequently, the 'problem of choice' would lose most of its significance since alternative courses of action forgone now can always be chosen, and sampled at some time in the infinite future. Put another way, the agonizing burden of choice of which the existentialist philosophers have spoken arises essentially from the fact of scarcity. When resources in general, and time above all, are scarce, then when an agent chooses certain courses of action he is forgoing for ever the possibility of certain alternatives. Therein lies the existential drama. The responsibility of human choice and the fact of scarcity are, as we shall see, central features of the economic theory of choice.

I shall now give a brief outline of the economic theory of choice for the case of an *instantaneous* choice. I have taken this simplified case which abstracts from the difficulties of preference through time and of uncertainty as to the future because my purpose here is not to expound any part of economic theory in detail but only to focus on those aspects of economic theory which are methodologically of the greatest significance. In the field of choice theory, the case of instantaneous choice (i.e. choice pertaining to the immediate present ignoring passage of time) will illustrate the methodologically significant aspects with ample clarity and without loss of generality.

The most basic postulate of the economic theory of choice is that there is a stable and well-defined utility function which indicates the strength of a typical human agent's preferences.

$$U = U (X_1, X_2 \ldots, X_n)$$

where U is an indicator of the agent's level of *subjective* satisfaction or well-being and $X_1, \ldots, X_n$ are all and only those goods, services and activities which contribute to the agent's satisfaction and which are scarce. It is to be remarked that there is no suggestion here that $(X_1, \ldots X_n)$ are only material goods and services – any good service or activity which for the agent is scarce and a source of well-being (*in his view*) must be included among the arguments $(X_1 \ldots X_n)$. Moreover, despite the potentially misleading term 'utility', the modern utility function does not carry with it any hedonistic suggestion nor any suggestion that the levels of well-being (the levels of U) could actually be measured or compared as to intensity among different individual agents.[2]

Having specified a utility function, economic theory introduces four axioms which will guarantee a well-defined and stable utility function for the typical agent. These are sometimes called axioms of 'consumer rationality' but as I shall be suggesting in a later chapter the whole question of rationality postulates and their precise meaning in economics has been a source of much controversy and confusion (cf. Chapter 7). These four axioms are:

1   *Consistency.* This stipulates that if a vector of goods and services $\bar{X}_1$ $(= X_{11}, \ldots, X_{n1})$ is preferred to a vector of goods and services $\bar{X}_2$ $(= X_{12}, \ldots, X_{n2})$, (i.e. if $\bar{X}_1$ gives a higher value of U than does $\bar{X}_2$), and if the vector $\bar{X}_2$ is preferred to the vector $\bar{X}_3$, then the vector $\bar{X}_1$ is preferred to the vector $\bar{X}_3$. This is a simple statement of consistency of preferences and from a mathematical standpoint it stipulates that the utility function is single-valued.

2   *Continuity.* This is an essentially mathematical axiom stipulating that the utility function is continuous and differentiable. In economic terms it means only that the quantities of the various goods and services $(X_1, \ldots, X_n)$ are infinitely divisible, either literally or at

least approximately (so that the axiom would be an idealized case type of abstraction).

3   *Dominance*. This stipulates that if vectors of goods and services $\bar{X}_1 = (X_{11} \ldots X_{n1})$ and $\bar{X}_2 = (X_{12}, \ldots, X_{n2})$ are such that

$X_{i1} > X_{i2}$ for at least some goods and services i, $1 \leq i \leq n$,

and if we also have

$X_{i1} \geq X_{i2}$ for all i, $1 \leq i \leq n$

then the vector $\bar{X}_1$ is preferred to the vector $\bar{X}_2$ i.e. it is associated with a higher level of U. Mathematically, this axiom states that all of the partial derivatives of the utility function (the so-called marginal utilities of goods and services) are positive, i.e. that

$$\frac{\delta U}{\delta X_i} > 0 \text{ for all i, } 1 \leq i \leq n$$

In simpler terms, what this axiom amounts to is a stipulation that what we include as arguments of the utility function are goods or, in the case of such 'bads' as pollution, the level of exemption for such bads: the arguments of the utility function are all and only those entities which yield well-being or satisfaction to the agent and are scarce.[3]

4   *Convexity*. Again this is largely a mathematical stipulation and it states that if the utility function is maximized subject to a linear constraint (by means of differential calculus) the resulting zero partial derivative solution will give a maximum rather than a minimum of satisfaction level (U). This axiom is usually defended as being realistic by the argument that both lexico-graphic preferences and 'corner solutions' are very rarely observed in reality. The latter defence of the convexity axiom turns out to be most revealing from a methodological standpoint as we shall discover below (Section 5.2). In everyday language what the convexity axiom amounts to is an abstraction for purposes of the economic theory of choice from the case of the extreme addict (such as the heavy drug addict) whose preferences are entirely dominated by one single good which is the sole index of his well-being and an assumption on the basis of empirical observations that typical human agents almost always choose a combined mix of all of the goods and services which yield them satisfaction and which are attainable within the constraints they face.

These four axioms stipulate the properties of the utility function that is used by economists. It should be clear that they are not at all restrictive since what they postulate is no more than that human agents have a well-ordered and consistent set of preferences that is stable through time. They constitute a minimum set of assumptions for the development of a theory of deliberate choice in the face of scarcity such as the economist seeks.

It is worth noting in passing that the utility function implicitly assumes the stability of preferences through time. This assumption, known as the constancy of tastes, is not introduced as an axiom because it is evident that human agents' preferences do evolve through time. However, it is fully defensible to introduce as a simplifying assumption the notion of constant tastes over limited time periods on the ground that while preferences evolve we do not, in the case of typical agents, observe empirical preferences which fluctuate wildly all of the time. Thus economists, while recognizing the indispensability of the constant tastes assumption to their basic theory of choice, have at the same time been aware of the hypothetical, empirically falsifiable and hence non-axiomatic character of that assumption.[4]

Scarcity of means in relation to ends is of the essence of any existentially significant choice as we have already seen, and economics is the science of such constrained choices. We turn now to specify the constraint function of a typical human agent for the simplified case of an instantaneous choice. The most basic constraint on an individual's scope of choice is the set of initial endowments of goods, services and activities which he owns at the beginning of the decision period. In a society where free exchange is possible the agent can greatly improve his level of satisfaction by exchanging some of his initial endowments (of labour, for example) for other goods and services (for example, cars and concerts) which he may not possess.[5]

Any good, service or activity which is exchanged will have an explicit or an implicit rate of exchange and in a monetized economy these exchange rates can all be expressed as prices in terms of money. In effect in a monetized economy money is itself a good which can contribute to an agent's level of satisfaction in virtue of its role as a universably acceptable medium of exchange and as a store of value; and since the price of money in terms of money is unity, money becomes the obvious good to use as a *numéraire* in terms of which all of the exchange ratios between various goods and services can be readily expressed. If we then assume that the typical individual is a price-taker, that is to say that he can have no influence over the prices prevailing in the economy, we may write the generalized constraint function for a typical individual in the following way:

$$\sum_{i=1}^{n} P_i \left(\bar{X}_i - X_i \right) = 0 \text{ ,}$$

where $\bar{X}_i$ = initial endowment of good i, X_i = level of consumption of good i p_i = price of good i in terms of money. Each of these are flow variables defined (as in the case of the variables of the utility function) for the decision period of the instantaneous choice under consideration.[6] Both $\bar{X}_i$ and p_i are constants for the typical agent, and money is included as a good in both the utility function and the constraint with a price of unity.[7]

Having defined the utility function

$$U = U(X_1, \ldots, X_n)$$

and the constraint

$$\sum_{i=1}^{n} P_i (X_i - X_i) = 0$$

we come to the final step of the economic theory of constrained choice: the postulate of utility maximization. This postulate amounts to a minimal requirement in cases of deliberate choice, and indeed the notion of utility maximization is pervasive in economics if not also almost second nature to the economist. This simple postulate we shall also discover to be of the utmost methodological significance.

Given the utility function and the constraint $\sum p_i \bar{X}_i$ which is linear because the p_i's are constant we can derive the formal mathematical solution for a constrained maximum of utility by means of the Lagrange technique. With linear constraint and the axiom of convexity of the utility function the turning points solution of the Lagrange functions will yield a maximum rather than a minimum of utility subject to constraint, and so we have:

Define a Lagrange function $\phi(X_1, \ldots, X_n)$ as

$$\phi (X_1, \ldots, X_n) = U(X_1, \ldots, X_n) + \lambda \sum_{i=1}^{n} p_i(\bar{X}_i - X_i).$$

The turning points of this Lagrange function will give the solution in $(X_1 \ldots X_n)$ which will give a maximum of U subject to the constraint, that is,

$$\text{Set} \quad \frac{\delta\phi}{\delta X_1} = \frac{\delta\phi}{\delta X_2} = \ldots = \frac{\delta\phi}{\delta X_n} = \frac{\delta\phi}{\delta\lambda} = 0$$

$$\rightarrow \frac{\delta U}{\delta X_1} - \lambda p_1 = \frac{\delta U}{\delta X_2} - \lambda p_2 = \ldots \frac{\delta U}{\delta X_n} - \lambda p_n = \sum pi(\bar{X}_i - X_i) = 0$$

putting all partial derivatives equal to zero.
Hence,

$$\frac{\dfrac{\delta U}{\delta X_1}}{p_1} = \lambda = \frac{\dfrac{\delta U}{\delta X_2}}{p_2} = \ldots = \frac{\dfrac{\delta U}{\delta X_n}}{p_n}$$

Thus the formal mathematical result for a maximization of utility subject to constraint in the case of instantaneous choices is that there should be equi-proportionality in marginal utilities and prices for all goods and services. This result is a generalization of the more familiar economic textbook solution for constrained utility maximization as the tangency between indifference curve and budget constraint line (for a two-good case).

There is one point which has been implicit in all of the above discussion and which perhaps deserves emphasis. In the case of instantaneous choices the whole question of the accuracy of an agent's information about prices, goods, and the ability of the latter to satisfy his wants is only of minor significance, for in an instantaneous choice with a very short time horizon an agent will usually have virtually perfect information regarding most relevant aspects of the choice. It is none the less true that given the explicitly subjective character of the fundamental utility notion in the theory that what has been outlined is in effect a theory of *expected utility* maximization by an agent in the light of information available to the agent. What is maximised is what the agent believes to be best for him or her since agents can rarely know with perfect certainty what is best for them.

I shall be discussing this aspect of the economic theory of choice later on[8] and showing that fundamentally the same theory of constrained maximization applies in a world of uncertainty, of imperfect information. I shall not discuss here any further complexities of the theory such as choice over many periods because my purpose here, as noted already, is not to expound the theory of choice in detail but to focus on those aspects of the theory which are of greatest methodological significance. These are already present in a clear-cut manner in the simple theory of instantaneous choice just outlined, as I shall show in the next section.

5.2 A Methodological Characterization of the Theory: Subjectivist, Teleological and A Priori

Turning then to a methodological appraisal of the economic theory of choice, the first and most striking feature of it is its unmistakably subjectivist-interpretive character. For the utility theory deals with man as a self-conscious being freely choosing his courses of action in the world, thus embodying a conception of man as subject. The utility function specifies in a purely formal manner the various goods, services and activities which contribute to an agent's well-being and so it may be regarded as a goal function or an 'objective' function as it is sometimes called by economists. Human action is then explained by utility theory as the attempt by agents to realize these goals subject to the limitations of their situation.

A more clear-cut case of the subjectivist-interpretive approach to explanation (such as was outlined in the last chapter) could hardly be imagined. Moreover, since utility theory explains human action in terms of the agent's own goals it is also *strictly teleological* in character. Since in the course of the following chapters I shall be showing how fundamental the theory of choice as utility maximization is to all branches of economic theory, this unmistakably subjectivist-interpretive character of the theory will be of far-reaching significance to the overall methodological appraisal of mainstream economics.

The interpretive character of mainstream economic theory will be discussed at greater length in later chapters and what I wish to focus upon in this chapter is the formal generality of the utility theory and its methodological implications. The utility function as we have seen remains entirely neutral regarding the question of what a typical agent's goal might be. The rest of economic theory can therefore be regarded as a process of unfolding of the content of the formal utility function by means of specific conjectures as to the actual goals of typical agents in various kinds of situations. Thus demand theory makes such conjectures as that wide ranges of agents will regard food, housing, etc., as well as luxury yachts as goods and with the aid of the principle of utility maximizing will deduce predictions regarding the shape of the demand curve (relating price to quantity demanded) for those goods. Similarly, the theory of the firm is based on such conjectures as that economic profit (*qua* pure surplus) is an overriding goal of business enterprises, and specific predictions regarding the behaviour of typical firms then can be deduced from the principle of profit maximization.

The whole of mainstream economic theory can thus be seen as an unfolding of the content of the purely formal utility theory of choice. This impression is only heightened if we consider the extremely wide scope which has been revealed for the principle of utility maximization in modern times. In the past twenty years economic theories of such areas as portfolio choice, of brushing one's teeth, of sex, politics and even of crime and discrimination have been built around the principle of utility maximization in choice. Moreover, it must be insisted that this wide-ranging modern utility theory is not subject to the hoary old charge that economic theory somehow portrays man as a narrowly selfish, calculating and unromantic being for there is no reason why the well-being of other agents should not be an actual variable in a utility function.

Thus, when one buys an extravagant present for one's lover, or when one is prepared to sacrifice important job opportunities or inheritances in order to remain close to the person one loves, at least where such choices are based upon a careful reflection, they are utility maximizing and would be rightly defended as optimal for our romantic agent given the constraints he faces. Even in the case of a genuine and illustrious statesman[9] who has sacrificed much in order to work for the well-being of his people, this is surely because he derives an immense satisfaction from seeing significant advances in the level of well-being of his people (their utility levels are an important set of variables in his utility function), and he may even be delighted at the prospect of monuments to him in the future. It is a sad and often wilful misunderstanding of economic theory which seeks to portray it as heartless and incapable of dealing with actions which spring from emotional or altruistic motivations.[10]

What I have been trying to suggest from this sampling of the scope of the utility theory and the sorts of choice and resultant courses of action[11] that it can encompass is that for any case of human choice preceded by reflection and deliberation about the alternatives available, the principle of utility maximization provides the key to its explanation. This is the case whether the activities be market or non-market, the goals noble or basely materialistic, the motivation emotional or ruthlessly calculating: indeed even the most austere monk, in so far as he deliberately chooses his penitential way of life, must be regarded as maximizing his expected spiritual well-being in an after life!

There are of course certain spheres of action to which the economic theory of utility maximizing choice is not applicable. Where an action is simply a physiological response to some physical stimulus or direct physical coercion (for example, being pushed over a cliff by someone else), there is no question of the agent having in any way chosen it and so any theory of choice would be inapplicable. More important, there are many cases where an action has an identifiable purpose and where the agent could have elected otherwise but which cannot even be said to be attempts at optimization. Where a freely chosen action is not preceded by at least some reflection but is rather a purely impulsive reaction or utterly spontaneous act, it should be obvious that any notion of maximization would be inapplicable. The central feature of utility theory is, after all, the notion of an agent weighing up the merits of various courses of action in the light of preferences and constraints, and where no such deliberation at all precedes an action, the principle of utility maximization is again obviously inapplicable.

It is often alleged that the imperfection of agent's information regarding the eventual consequences of their choices seriously undermines the scope of the utility maximization principle. It is true that the future is always shrouded in uncertainty and hence that agents' information regarding the consequences of their choices is imperfect. The theory of utility does not, however, assume perfect knowledge. Stated in its most strictly general form for a world of uncertainty it is a theory of expected utility maximization, that is to say that in cases of deliberate human choice human agents will seek to maximize their (expected) utility levels on the basis of the information available to them. It is to be remarked that this qualification, though obvious, is not simply a slick verbal amendment. Some of the most interesting work in macroeconomic theory is concerned with disequilibrium situations arising from imperfection of information and how agents will purposely adjust to them.[12] Thus for example when because of imperfect information agents fail to realize the goals they sought to maximize, modern disequilibrium theory examines how agents will seek to learn from their mistakes and acquire better information in order to achieve a utility maximizing equilibrium more successfully in the future. As we shall see in somewhat greater detail in the next chapter, disequilibrium theory just as much as equilibrium theory is built upon the notion of attempted expected utility maximization in the light of the (imperfect) information available to the agent, and so the undoubted imperfection of agent's information is not, after all, a limitation of the scope of the economic theory of choice.

Drawing together all of these considerations as to the scope of the utility maximization principle we are inevitably led to the suggestion that the utility theory is true *a priori* for any case of deliberate choice. That is to say that we can lay down as a non-trivial *a priori* truth that in any case where a human agent is faced with a constrained choice among competing ends and where that choice is preceded by at least some reflection and deliberation, the agent will always seek to maximize (expected) utility in the light of the information available.

This *a priori* character of the utility maximization principle arises from the formal generality of the utility function in its modern version; from the fact that the generalized utility function is completely neutral regarding what are the actual goals of agents and specifies only that any entity or activity which is regarded by an agent as a source of well-being should be included as an argument of the function. In view of this I propose from here onwards to refer to the *a priori* principle of utility maximization by the shorter and more suggestive label, the optimization principle.

Since the utility theory has not always been presented in the above manner as a formally generalized theory it will be useful to review briefly its history over the past one hundred years. This is a valuable exercise because many of the objections to utility theory which are voiced right up to the present day are more applicable to the nineteenth-century version rather than to modern utility theory.

The origin and inspiration of the economic theory of choice was Bentham's utilitarian ethical theory. Bentham had viewed human well-being as dependent entirely upon the avoidance of pain and the pursuit of pleasure, and these were conceived in a narrowly materialistic manner as sensual pleasure and pain only. He envisaged that the satisfaction or 'utility' of sensual pleasure and pain could be measured (in 'utils') and he proposed a 'felicific calculus' of pleasure and pain as the basis of ethical theory and practice. Any action or policy was to be appraised by examining mathematically the amounts of pleasure and pain to which it would give rise for various agents; and was to be approved if it contributed to the greater utility of the greatest number.[13]

Bentham's utilitarianism provided the inspiration for the utility theory that was first introduced into economics during the 'marginalist revolution' of the last century. Although Jevons, Menger and Gossen, its early exponents, were wary of the extremely materialist aspect of Bentham's presentation, their conception of utility was still a narrowly hedonistic one and they envisaged the possibility of cardinal measurement also like Bentham. Even an economist with such breadth of vision as Alfred Marshall clung to a largely hedonistic conception of utility which could be measured in cardinal units. This persistent narrowness of nineteeth-century utility theory conceived as a felicific calculus of pleasure and pain as well as being due to its Benthamite origins was also bound up with the notion of 'economic man' which caused so much difficulty and methodological misunderstanding in nineteenth-century economics.[14] According to this conception, man was indeed a being capable of much more than the pursuit of sensual pleasures; but for purposes of economic theory it was regarded as a useful abstraction to deal with only those human actions and choices which were motivated by the pursuit of sensual pleasure and 'material wealth'.

At the beginning of this century Vilifredo Pareto began to break away from the narrow hedonistic conception of utility to insist that a much wider range of activities could be encompassed by the economic theory of choice. Cultural and purely spiritual activities could be included as arguments in the utility function. Pareto also demonstrated that the central theorems of choice theory could be derived on the basis of ordinal utility considerations, that is without the need to assume that utility is cardinally measurable in utils. Athough Pareto did not go so far as to assume the *a priori* truth of the utility theory, it is clear that his conception is much closer to the modern formally generalized theory than to the hedonistic version of the early marginalists. Indeed in order to avoid the hedonistic overtones with which the term 'utility' had come to be associated Pareto suggested that it should be replaced by the much more generalized and neutral term 'ophelimity', meaning gain or well-being.[15] With these significant steps away from the cardinally measurable hedonistic utility function Pareto laid the foundations for the wide-ranging extensions of utility theory such as were discussed earlier in this chapter, and which led inevitably towards the formal generalization of the utility function (the maintenance of a strict neutrality regarding what are the actual goals of agents) and to the resulting conclusion that the formalized optimization principle is true of every case of deliberate choice.[16]

Economics is generally considered to be an empirical science, subject to testing of its theories against observations of actual human behaviour, and I shall argue in later chapters that this view is basically quite correct. Since I have suggested that the optimization principle is true *a priori* and since such *a priori* theories would generally be out of place in an empirical science it would be appropriate to give some indication of the methodological underpinning of such a strong claim. The quest for such an underpinning of the optimization principle will raise questions as to the epistemological status of certain knowledge claims and so will of necessity be philosophical in character.

In Chapter 4 we have already seen that existentialist phenomenology can in principle make a direct *a priori* contribution to any of the human sciences. This would be achieved by means of an intuition of the essence of some typical conscious state or act (such as the essence of fear or of the act of imagining), and would constitute a valuable even if purely formal starting point for a human science (for example, of psychology in the cases of fear and imagination). I have already emphasized that this potential contribution from phenomenology remains a purely formal one since there is no claim to be able to intuit in detail the contents of other people's conscious states by empathy; what can be given to phenomenological intuition is only the form of a conscious state or act that is common to all of its particular instances.

Since the optimization principle is put forward as being true *a priori* only when the utility theory has reached its most generalized and purely formal statement, it would be possible in principle to ground the optimization principle in an existentialist phenomenology of deliberate choice. Such a phenomenological analysis would aim to reveal the essence of any act of deliberate choice as utility maximization or more precisely as optimization (where utility is given its purely formal meaning). It would involve a long digression to present such a phenomenology of deliberate choice in this work. However, I shall indicate briefly here the line which such an analysis would take.

As a method, phenomenology relies on an appeal by the author to the reader to consider certain of his own conscious states or acts and to seek to intuit their essence or form by abstracting the element of identity among the differences of detail in each instance of the conscious state in question.[17] A phenomenology of deliberate choice would thus involve a survey of a wide range of typical cases of deliberate choice together with an attempt to achieve an insight into the element which is common to all of the instances. The outlines of just such a survey are already present in the discussion at pages 83–85 which led up to the suggestion that the optimization principle is true *a priori*.The cases of everyday market choices – the typical choices of statesmen, politicians and of ultra-romantics – were all considered before reaching the insight that, in all cases of choice preceded by reflection, human agents always choose that course of action which they believe to be best for them.

A second line of phenomenological approach to the optimization principle might be provided by the Platonic conception of human action and ethics. Plato held that no man willingly does that which he believes to be bad for himself. When taken in conjunction with man's social dependence on other human beings for his well-being (so that the well-being of other agents is a key variable in an agent's formal utility function), this axiom generates the famous Socratic – Platonic theory of rationalist ethics – that virtue is knowledge. If only we knew what was good for us we would automatically act accordingly: man's moral imperfections are at root problems only of ignorance.

Since the axiom that no man willingly does that which he believes to be bad for himself may be roughly translated into the proposition that any man will, at least upon reflection, always take that course of action which he believes to be best for himslf, that is that in cases of deliberate choice every human agent will optimize, it may also be suggested that the assertion of the *a priori* truth of the optimization principle in its formal version is by no means a novelty, but rather has a long and illustrious philosophical heritage as an axiom of the rationalist approach to ethics stretching back to Plato.

I shall not attempt to take this sketch of the philosophical foundations of the *a priori* truth of the optimization principle any further here. Enough has been said to show (a) that it is possible to give a rigorous philosophical foundation to the claim that the optimization principle of economic theory is true *a priori* by deducing it from a phenomenology of deliberate choice and (b) some brief indication of the lines which such a philosophical derivation of the principle might follow has also just been given.

Economists themselves have for the most part fought very shy of giving any recognition at all to the two significant methodological features of the economic theory of choice which I have been discussing here. This we shall see is probably due to a strong residual positivist prejudice among leading mainstream theorists. In the first place, there can be no doubt whatever that in its modern formalized version, the theory of utility and the optimization principle are unmistakably subjectivist – interpretive in character and employ a teleological mode of explanation. Despite the centrality of the theory of choice and of the optimization principle in modern economic theory, there has been virtually no recognition at all of its subjectivist character and teleological mode of explanation on the part of economists. This, however, is part of a more general failure by economists to recognize the subjectivist-interpretive character of the whole body of mainstream theory, and it will be discussed at greater length in Chapters 8 to 11.

In the second place, there is equally no doubt that economists have treated the optimization principle in its modern purely formal version as true *a priori*. We have already seen how wide the scope of the principle is since economists have applied it successfully to every kind of deliberate choice. Particularly revealing is the typical defence of the convexity axiom of the theory of choice. Economists have typically defended this axiom by saying that we very rarely observe 'corner solutions' in an agent's choice among those goods and services in which he is interested.[18] What is fascinating about this defence of the axiom is that it already presumes the optimization principle; for it is only on the presumption that human agents always seek to maximize their utility within the constraints that convexity will imply no corner solution;[19] and that observation of a corner solution will imply non-convexity. Therefore, in their typical defence of the convexity axiom, economists have in effect been treating the optimization principle as true *a priori*; that is to say, they have been presuming the truth of the optimization principle before, and as a presupposition of, engaging in any empirical tests of the utility theory of choice.

Despite the fact that economists have clearly been treating the optimization principle as true *a priori* of any deliberate choice, there has again been virtually no recognition of this methodologically most significant feature of utility theory. It may be suggested that both this failure and the failure to grasp the subjectivist character of utility theory are due to a strong residual sympathy with positivist philosophical ideas among mainstream economists. Since economics as an independent discipline may fairly be said to have been dominated by Anglo-Saxon thinkers and ideas, this positivist leaning is not at all surprising. In the last chapter we saw how a broadly positivist position in philosophy will lead towards adoption of an objectivist – behaviourist position in methodology of human science and to a profound distrust of any reference to empirically unobservable conscious states or acts, whence positivism is decidedly suspicious of, if not wholeheartedly opposed to, a subjectivist – interpretive approach to the human sciences. This may help to explain why positivist-leaning mainstream economists have failed, or at least been very reluctant to recognize, the subjectivist character of the utility theory of choice.

The unifying strand of all versions of positivist thought is the dogma that the only meaningful propositions are either tautologies or empirically testable propositions; put another way, a rooted opposition to all meta-physics. Consequently, positivist-leaning economists have expressly feared that if they were to accord to the optimization principle the status of an *a priori* truth they would thereby make it into a trivial tautology, into a proposition which merely defines how certain economic terms are to be used. Since economists would be very unwilling to trivialize such a fundamental element of the corpus of mainstream theory in this manner, they have fought shy of a proper recognition of the *a priori* methodological character of the optimization principle even though in practice they have undoubtedly treated it as being true *a priori* of all cases of deliberate choice.

This methodological appraisal of the mainstream economic theory of choice has been long and exhaustive because, as we shall see below, the optimization principle has been central to all explanatory theory in the mainstream of economics. What I have sought to establish in this chapter is that the theory of choice as the maximization of purely formal utility function involves an explanation of human action in terms of the subjective goals of freely choosing human agents and is therefore a clear-cut case of the subjectivist – interpretive approach to the human sciences with its teleological mode of explanation. I argued, furthermore, that in its modern most generalized version where the utility function is understood as a purely formal goal function without any prejudice as to the actual objectives of agents, the utility maximization – or, more felicitously, the optimization principle – may be asserted to be a true *a priori* of any case of deliberate choice. Finally, I sought to show how the optimization principle conceived as an *a priori* truth can be given a full rigorous and non-trivial foundation by being deduced from an existentialist phenomenology of deliberate choice.

Notes

1 L. Robbins (1936), *An Essay on the Nature and Significance of Economic Science* (London: Macmillan), p.16.

2 Some further discussion of the modern utility function by contrast with earlier hedonistic versions will be found in the next section of this chapter.

3 There is, of course, the possibility of reaching a saturation point with a good/service where it goes from having a positive to a negative partial derivative at some level; and of reaching a 'bliss' point when saturation level is reached for all of $(X_1 \ldots X_n)$. These possibilities are ignored here because, as will become clear when we have analysed the mathematical condition of maximized utility, the saturation points can only be reached by a maximizing agent as a 'bliss point' (that is, simultaneous saturation in all scarce goods) and the likelihood of any human agent ever reaching a bliss point is so remote that we may ignore this possibility altogether and stipulate positive partial derivatives for $U(X_1 \ldots X_n)$.

4 The significance of this treatment will be discussed in more detail in Part 3, Chapter 14.

5 Note that in the case of goods and services which he cannot exchange an individual is stuck with his initial endowment. Such goods remain constant and so may be ignored in a theory of choice since the agent is powerless to change their level. They are not, strictly speaking, variables of the utility function.

6 Note that this decision period could be 'this week', 'this month' or 'this year' depending on the agent. The 'this' underlines the instantaneous character of choices considered here for simplicity.

7 That is, money is being used as a convenient *numéraire*. The notion of a

numéraire good is that since in a market economy all goods and services can be exchanged there is an advantage in expressing the exchange ratios with some selected single good in the system. This good is called a *numéraire* and in a monetized economy where all exchange ratios are already expressed in the market in terms of money, and where money is itself a good, then money is the obvious choice as *numéraire*. The exchange ratio of any *numéraire* must obviously be unity.

I should, of course, add that when I say that money is itself a good, what I mean strictly is that the 'real purchasing power' of money is a good (an asset) for the agent. Hence when we include a money good in a utility function we should strictly speaking be including what monetary theorists call 'real cash balances'. For the case of an instantaneous choice, however, prices cannot change during the period of choice and for such cases nominal money holdings and real cash balances will be effectively the same thing.

8   Cf. Chapter 7, pp. 113–18 for a full discussion of the utility maximization theory of choice in a world where agents' information is imperfect.

9   By genuine statesman, I mean one who has abjured all pursuit of narrow personal gain in material terms to work for the greater good of his people.

10 This point is discussed again in later chapters in connection with rationality postulates (cf. Chapters 7 and 15).

11 To have genuinely chosen a course of action is to have already begun to take some steps towards its realization (cf. the existentialist notion of commitment and the discussion of it in Part 3, Chapter 16).

12 The most obvious examples are the discussions of unemployment as market failure in such theories as those of Clower and Leijonhufvud. For fuller discussion and references, see Chapter 6, p. 110.

13 Bentham's 'greatest good of the greatest number'; for Bentham, good was synonymous with (increasing) utility.

14 Cf. F. Machlup (1978), 'The universal bogey', in F. Machlup, *Methodology of Economics and Other Human Sciences* (New York: Academic Press), for a discussion of the 'economic man' abstraction.

15 From the Greek word *ophelos*.

16 We have already seen the optimization principle is unmistakably subjectivist-interpretive in character. However, it is worth remarking that the earlier hedonistic versions of utility theory could conceivably be construed as a kind of 'drive' theory of stimulus-response variety, and hence as efficient-causal in character. However, notice that (a) such an efficient-causal construal would be impossible for the modern generalized utility function which certainly involves more than a 'drive' theory of human action, it is inherently subjectivist being built on the notion of man as a freely choosing subject, and (b) even the narrow hedonistic version of U theory can be construed as a stimulus-response model of behaviour only with extreme implausibility. Thus the subjectivist-interpretive character of modern utility theory remains firmly established.

17 This is the process known in phenomenology as the 'eidetic reduction'. For a full discussion of phenomenology, see Chapter 12, pp. 175–79.

18 A corner solution is one in which consumption of some good or service is zero. We therefore specify that there should be no corner solutions in those goods which enter an agent's utility function, that is, those goods in which he is interested, since even with convexity there will always be zero consumption levels for those goods which do not enter an agent's utility function.

19 There is, of course, the unlikely possibility of convexity and optimization giving a corner solution with a very oddly shaped constraint. Most constraints are linear (in utility theory), however, and with linear constraints optimization and a corner solution necessarily imply non-convexity.

6

Teleological Explanation in Microeconomics and Macroeconomics

In the last chapter I suggested that the purely formal optimization principle is treated by economists as being true *a priori* of any case of deliberate choice and that this can be seen from the manner in which the optimization principle underlies all branches of mainstream economic theory as a principle of explanation. Having once established the formal optimization principle the rest of economics can be regarded as a gradual unfolding of the content of the formal function by means of specific conjectures as to what the actual goals of typical agents are in various types of situations.

In this chapter I shall be seeking to substantiate in detail this way of looking upon economic theory as a whole. I shall seek to show how we can regard wide areas of both microeconomic and macroeconomic theory as consisting of: (a) a conjecture as to the goals of typical agents (b) the development of a theory on the basis of the conjecture by invocation of the optimization principle (having specified the relevant constraints) and (c) the derivation of testable predictions about the observable behaviour of agents from the theory. This sort of schema is fairly easily seen to be pervasive in mainstream microeconomic theory, but I shall be suggesting that at least much of the advanced modern work in macroeconomics also follows a similar pattern. From a methodological point of view, what is most significant about such a schema of explanation is its unmistakable subjectivist – interpretive character: it seeks to explain human actions in terms of the attempts of human agents to realize their goals to the maximum degree consistent with their constraints. If, therefore, we can show that the vast bulk of mainstream micro and macroeconomic theory in addition to the utility theory of choice is subjectivist – interpretive in character involving a teleological mode of explanation, we shall have arrived at the conclusion that mainstream economic theory is, in virtue of the pervasive role therein of the optimization principle, a clear-cut exemplification of the Weber-Schutz interpretive approach to the methodology of the human sciences.

6.1   *The Subjectivist Character of Microeconomics*

We may begin our examination of mainstream economic theory by considering the simple case of consumer demand. Taking first the derivation of the demand curve for a good or service let us consider the choice of a typical consumer between two goods only. This simple case will serve adequately to illustrate the methodological principle which is at stake.

Let the two goods among which the consumer chooses be food and real cash balances,[1] where real cash balances is the purchasing power of money income and may here be taken as a composite proxy for all other goods and services in which the agent is interested. The theory of demand begins from the (often implicit) conjecture that both food and real cash balances are actual variables in the utility function; that the acquisition of food and of purchasing power are actual goals of agents. If we assume that the individual agents are price-takers and that the choice is an instantaneous one we may then represent these conjectures with an indifference map which indicates agents' preferences as between food and real cash balances, and a constraint which is linear (price-taker assumption) and which indicates the consumption levels of the two goods which the agent can afford given his money income (Fig. 6.1).

The indifference curve analysis is very well discussed in any intermediate level textbook in economics and so I shall not try to expound it here. It will be sufficient to note that since each indifference curve indicates various combinations of goods X and Y among which the agent is indifferent and since higher indifference curves (further to the north-east) represent higher levels of satisfaction or well-being,[2] then the indifference map of Fig. 6.1 adequately represents the conjecture that both food and real cash balances are regarded as utility-yielding by the agent. The relevant constraint on an individual's choice among food and other goods and services will typically be the level of his money income since this defines how much he can afford to spend in any given period.[3] Since we have assumed a price-taking agent this will give rise to a linear constraint line such as B_0 or B_1 in Fig. 6.1. The position of the constraint line will depend on the agent's current income while its slope will depend on the relative price of food. (Real cash balances are the same as nominal money for an instantaneous choice and so have a price of unity.) The equation of this constant line is

$$g = X . P_x + Y$$

where g = agent's money income

$$X = \text{food}, \, p_x = price \, of \, food$$
$$Y = \text{(remaining) real cash balances,}$$

which simply states that agents will use up all of their money income during the decision period on various goods and services.

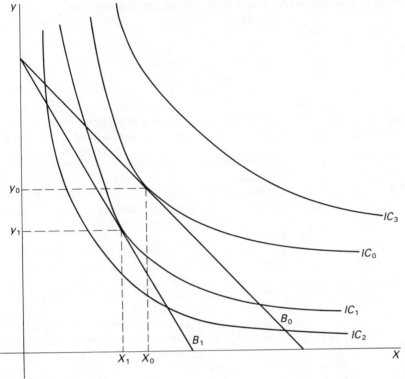

IC = indifference curve
B = budget constraint line

6.1 *Indifference Curve Analysis of a Consumer's Demand for Food*

Having thus defined the typical agent's actual utility function for this simplified two-good case and having defined the constraint function, the economist proceeds to develop a theory of consumer demand using the optimization principle and to derive various predictions about behaviour from that theory. The optimization principle tells us that faced with the conjectured utility function and constraint B_0 an agent will choose to consume a quantity X_0 of food. This is the utility maximizing combination of food and all other goods and services given the constraint B_0; the point of tangency (X_0, Y_0) represents the highest possible indifference curve IC_0 that could be reached when faced with a constraint line B_0.

This is the position of consumer equilibrium and we may proceed from this to examine by the method known as comparative statics the implications for the equilibrium quantity demanded of food (X_0) of changes in the price of food, p_x, and in the agent's money income. To give a simple example, consider the effect of a definite rise in the price of food. This will give rise to a new and steeper constraint line B_1 (in Fig. 6.1) and so to a new level of equilibrium consumption of food X_1. In almost all cases $X_1 < X_o$, as illustrated in the diagram, although it is just conceivable (but not very likely) that we could have $X_1 > X_o$ – the theoretical possibility known as the 'Giffen good'.

Given that the Giffen good is a most unlikely possibility, and indeed it can *only* arise in the case of goods with a strongly negative income elasticity of demand, we can derive an important prediction from the above theoretical analysis based upon the optimization principle: for all but Giffen goods the effect of a rise in price of X will lead to a fall in quantity demanded of X, *ceteris paribus*.[4] In the case of food,[5] which we conjectured to be a good for all typical agents, this leads to the specific prediction of a negatively sloped demand curve for each individual agent, that is to say that when the price of food rises *ceteris paribus* the quantity demand will fall. From this the prediction of a negatively sloped market demand curve (relating price to total demand for food *ceteris paribus*)[6] can also be readily deduced.

From a methodological point of view the points of greatest importance to emerge from this brief study of demand theory are:

(1)   that in virtue of being based upon the optimization principle the theory of demand is a clear-cut instance of a subjectivist – interpretive approach to explanation; it seeks to explain agents' demand for goods and services in terms of the actual goals of agents – goals which they pursue to the maximum degree consistent with the constraints they face. (Such an interpretive explanation in terms of optimization by freely choosing agents may be contrasted with a stimulus-response theory of demand of objectivist-behaviourist variety, for example.)

(2)   that we have also seen how the theory of demand rests upon a refutable conjecture as to the actual goals of agents.[7] This is to be contrasted with the *a priori* truth of the purely formal optimization principle of the previous chapter. Moreover, the theory of demand built around the optimization principle serves as a first illustration of the assertion that the whole of economic theory may be regarded as a gradual unfolding of the purely formal utility theory of choice by means of various conjectures as to the goals of typical agents.

As our next exemplification of the subjectivist-interpretive character of microeconomic theory I turn to the theories of the firm and of market structure. Again we find that all of the leading theories of the firm are based upon some conjecture as to the goals which firms seek to pursue and to maximize subject to constraint, and so may be regarded as further instances of the unfolding of the content of the formal *a priori* optimization principle of the previous chapter, in this case for the typical firm.

The leading hypothesis in the theory of the firm has undoubtedly been that of profit maximization: that the goal which a typical firm sets itself is to realize the maximum level of (economic) profits consistent with the demand and cost conditions which it faces. It is of some importance to notice that 'economic' profit which is the maximand of the firm is not the same as accounting profit: economic profit is defined as the surplus of revenue over cost which remains when all opportunity costs have been counted. These opportunity costs will include, in addition to the direct outlays on factor inputs and raw materials, the time and efforts of managers and/or owners and the rate of return available on alternative uses of the funds invested in the enterprise. Since the economic profit so defined is a pure surplus or economic rent then provided the decision-takers of the firm (owners or managers) can be confident that they will be able to secure some share of the surplus for themselves, maximization by the decision-takers will imply a profit-maximizing strategy for the firm.[8]

Let us begin by illustrating how the profit maximization conjecture provides the basis for a theory of the firm under conditions of perfect competition. In the market structure known as perfect competition there are large numbers of buyers and sellers, a homogeneous product and freedom of entry into and exit from the industry by firms. Under such conditions each individual firm is a price-taker: it cannot exercise any influence over the price it receives for its product, and in the long run if there are economic profits being made by firms in the industry some new firms will be attracted into the industry thus expanding supply and competing away the economic profits.

Since my main purpose here is methodological appraisal rather than systematic exposition I shall confine my illustration of the details of the theory of the firm to the case of perfect competition in the short run where profit maximization is the conjectured goal of firms. The constraints which a typical perfectly competitive firm faces arise from the conditions of demand and cost of production illustrated in Fig. 6.2.

The short run is by definition any period within which not all a firm's factor inputs are variable, and so with some fixed inputs increases in supply of output will be subject to the law of diminishing returns. This is reflected in the U-shaped short-run marginal cost curve, SMC — after a certain point diminishing marginal returns to variable factors and thus rising marginal costs set in. The shape of the short run average cost curve SAC will then be as shown in Fig. 6.2 with SMC cutting SAC at its (SAC) minimum point.[9] The demand curve facing the firm is a horizontal straight line since under perfect competition the firm is a price taker. We have p = p and MR (marginal revenue) = p, where p is the fixed market price.

With the aid of the hypothesis of profit maximization we can now develop a theory of the firm's output and pricing decisions in the short run (assuming perfect competition). Since costs are defined as opportunity costs the level of economic profit is

Total Revenue − Total Cost, ($TR - TC$)

and if profit is to be maximized we can show by elementary differential calculus that

$$\begin{cases} MR - MC = 0 \quad \text{i.e. } MR = MC \\ \\ \dfrac{dMR}{dq} - \dfrac{dMC}{dq} < 0 \text{ i.e. } \dfrac{dMR}{dq} < \dfrac{dMC}{dq} \end{cases} \begin{array}{l} \text{for long-run and} \\ \text{short-run decisions} \end{array}$$

and

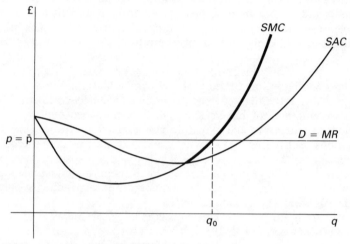

SMC = short-run marginal cost curve
SAC = short-run average cost

Fig. 6.2 *Short-run Equilibrium of a Perfectly Competitive Firm*

where q = output, MR = marginal revenue, MC = marginal cost, and by definition $MR = \dfrac{dTR}{dq}$ and $MC = \dfrac{dTC}{dq}$.

Under conditions of perfect competition price is constant and so

$$TR = \bar{p}.q \text{ and } MR = \bar{p}.$$

Therefore the condition of profit maximization for the firm in perfect competition in the short run is in terms of Fig. 6.2

that $SMC = \bar{p} \ (= MR)$

and that $\dfrac{dMR}{dq} - \dfrac{dSMC}{dq} < 0.$ i.e. $0 - \dfrac{dSMC}{dq} < 0.$

i.e. that $\dfrac{dSMC}{dq} > 0.$

The profit maximizing firm will thus produce where price is equal to SMC and where SMC is rising. This will be at an output level of q_0 (see Fig. 6.2).

Having determined the level of a firm's output when market price is $\bar{p}$ we may go on to examine what would be the level of output at different levels of market price (which is always fixed for the perfectly competitive firm). It can easily be seen that at prices above or below $\bar{p}$ in the diagram the profit-maximizing output can simply be read off from the intersection of different horizontal price lines (demand curves) with the rising part of the SMC curve. The only caveat to be entered is that we must have $\bar{p} \geq SAC$, for if $\bar{p} < SAC$ then $TR = \bar{p}.q < SAC.q = TCo$, i.e. $TR < TC$, then the total value of a firm's sales would not even be sufficient to cover total costs and the firm would close down $(q = 0)$. Since the firm's supply curve is by definition a curve relating the level of market price to the output which will be produced by the firm at that price, the firm's short run supply curve will be its SMC curve over the range where $SMC \geq SAC$ (that is the part of the SMC curve shaded heavily in Fig. 6.2).

The short-run industry or market supply curve can be derived by means of a summation of individual firms' supply curves and in virtue of the pervasiveness of the law of diminishing returns the market supply curve will also be upward sloping in the short run. This prediction of the theory may be checked by examining the short-run effect of increases or decreases in demand on prices in the short run. Similarly, the effect of sales taxes, such as VAT, will be to push up the cost curves of firms and so should lead to an upward shift of the supply curves and *ceteris paribus* to some increase in the prices of goods taxed in the short run.[10]

It is not, however, these testable qualitative predictions of the profit maximization hypothesis under perfect competition which are my main interest here. What I wish to emphasize is the methodological character of the theory. There are two main features. First, the theory of the profit maximizing firm under perfect competition is once again an unmistakable instance of the subjectivist-interpretive approach to the human sciences, being a teleological explanation of the firm's actions in terms of the goals which it seeks to maximize. Secondly, this theory is also an instance of the formal *a priori* optimization principle discussed in the last chapter and derives its interpretive character precisely from that fact. It embodies a specific testable conjecture as to the goals of a typical firm under perfect competition (that profit is the overriding aim) and explains the firm's supply curve in terms of the attempt to maximize realization of that goal.

The above discussion has illustrated how the profit maximization hypothesis can provide the basis for an elaborate theory of the firm that will yield testable predictions; and it has shown how such a theory will be unmistakably subjectivist-interpretive in character. The profit maximization hypothesis also provides in a similar way the basis for the theory of perfect competition in the long run, for the theory of the firm under the market structure known as imperfect competition[11] and also under conditions of pure monopoly. In each of these cases the profit maximization hypothesis renders the theory subjectivist-interpretive in character and teleological in its mode of explanation (in virtue of being further specific instances of the optimization principle).

The modern economic system, to repeat a platitude, is characterized by a significantly large sector where the market structure is neither perfectly nor imperfectly competitive, nor purely monopolistic; where, that is, the assumptions of these comparatively simple theories of the firm are completely violated. This is the sector of the large-scale industrial corporation, typically found in manufacturing industry rather than in services, and the market structure here is that of oligopoly – of competition among a small number of very large firms. The essence of an oligopolistic market is that unlike perfect and imperfect competition where an individual firm's actions have no impact on the market as a whole, in oligopoly firms cannot but explicitly recognize the interdependence of their various actions. Consequently, the notion of atomic optimization by an individual firm taken in isolation breaks down and there is always an element of the gaming situation present in oligopoly in so far as a firm must take into account the likely reactions of its rivals when planning its own courses of purposive action.

Since my purpose again is methodological appraisal rather than exposition I shall give here only a brief review of some of the leading theories of oligopoly. There are first of all a number of theories which retain the hypothesis of profit maximization as their basic conjecture as to the goals of firms, but which modify it in order to recognize the element of interdependence of firms' actions under oligopoly. Under this heading, two theories may be mentioned.

One is the *game theory* approach outlined by Von Neumann and Morgenstern.[12] This is based upon an explicit recognition of the 'game' character of the market situation in oligopoly, where so much depends upon the correct prediction by a firm of the reaction pattern of other firms. In game theory the hypothesis of atomic profit maximization by an individual firm is replaced by the hypothesis of a maximin strategy: that each firm will seek to maximize its own gains (profits) while minimizing those of its opponent. All of the proposed solutions of game theory models are built around the maximin hypothesis, and this is again very clearly an instance of the optimization principle and, hence, an interpretive explanation of the actions of firms in terms of the goals which they seek to maximize.[13]

Another theory is the *kartel* or *joint profit maximization model*. Facing the futility of price wars and maximin type of competition (which can easily be shown to be mutually frustrating in most market situations) the kartel model proposes that firms, having recognized their interdependence and the futility of cut-throat price competition, will adopt the purposive strategy of maximizing the joint profits of the whole group of firms in the market; the group of firms will act, in other words, as if they were a pure profit-maximizing monopoly, and will refrain from price competition in order to achieve the result which will maximize total profit for the group as a whole. Once again this theory is based on a conjecture as to the goals which firms will seek to realize under oligopoly conditions and is therefore subjectivist-interpretive in character (and another instance of the optimization principle).

A large number of theorists of oligopoly in recent times, among them Galbraith and Baumol, have suggested that a large-scale corporation, rather than being controlled by a single owner or by its shareholders, is controlled in effect by its managerial technostructure, that is by the team of highly specialized top management who make all of the critical decisions affecting a firm's future. Given the degree of technical competence required for decision-making in many technologically advanced modern corporations, for the shareholders or any other group to try to interfere with managerial decisions is only to court commercial disaster through ignorance. If the managerial technostructure becomes the effective controller of the large oligopoly corporation,[14] then the goals to which the operation of the firm is directed will presumably be the technostructure's goals and therefore when framing conjectures as to the goals of typical firms in oligopoly (or indeed in pure monopoly) careful attention must be paid to the pertinent variables which we might expect to find in the utility functions of top managers.

Since high economic profits mean, *inter alia*, that the top management can afford to pay themselves higher salaries or take more perks there can be little doubt that profit is one goal if not the overriding goal of the technostructure. In any case the commercial viability and survival of the enterprise depends upon attainment of an adequate level of profits. Consequently, the hypothesis of profit maximization is still a plausible one for the managerially controlled corporation. It has been suggested, however, that in many cases top management may also have other goals such as the attainment of a maximum degree of symbolic social prestige or political influence and that these are best achieved by strategies other than outright profit maximization. It has also been suggested that in other cases because of persistent criticism of the evils of capitalism or possibly because of a certain magnanimity on the part of managers, the large corporation may also pursue goals of a philanthropic or publicly-minded nature, in all cases subject to the constraint of making sufficient profit for commercial survival and independence.

I shall now give some brief illustrations of non-profit maximizing hypotheses under conditions of oligopoly, beginning with *Baumol's sales maximization* hypothesis. This was an early venture in the field and it suggested that since the prestige of managers and even their political influence was a function of the size of the corporation they controlled rather than of the level of its profits, managers would pursue the goal of a maximal rate of expansion of the firm subject to a profitability constraint (that is, making adequate profits for commercial survival). A closely similar hypothesis, argued along an analogy with the theory of bureaucratic expansion (Parkinson's Law) may also be found in Galbraith's *New Industrial State*.[15] Notice that this hypothesis explains the behaviour of firms in terms of the goals they seek to maximize and so is an instance of the optimization principle.

Underlying the sales maximization hypothesis and all of the other specific non-profit maximizing hypotheses which have been put forward is an approach to the theory of the large corporation known as the *managerial* theory of the firm. This approach states as a general principle that since large corporations are controlled by their top management rather than by their owners, it is to the utility functions which we might expect typical managers to have that we must look when framing conjectures as to the goals which such firms will pursue. Under the broad heading of managerial theories a wide range of conjectures as to the actual goals of firms have been suggested, and their implications for the theory of the firm and their testable predictions have been worked out. Thus, for example, as well as sales maximization the pursuit of good labour relations, social justice, loyal service to the community and even the pursuit of technical excellence, artistic merit or fashion have all been cited among the goals which a technostructure of top managers might decide to pursue, and maximize subject to a minimum profit level constraint. What is important here is not the detail of these hypotheses but the fact that they are all built upon the optimization principle – the explanation of a firm's actions in terms of the goals which its decision-taking executives seek to maximize.

There has, however, been one hypothesis regarding the actions of a large managerially controlled corporation which has purported to be opposed to the optimization principle: this is the *satisficing* hypothesis. What this asserts in effect is that the modern large corporation will usually have a number of goals other than profit maximization, that it will face complex cost and demand data as well as considerable uncertainty regarding future demands and costs, and hence that rather than going for an outright maximum of profit, sales or any other goal, the firm will prefer to 'satisfice', that is to say, it will gear its activities to reaching a 'satisfactory' rather than an optimal level of these goals. This theory has enjoyed some popularity in recent years, but from a methodological point of view it is to be remarked that:

(1)   This theory of the firm is still subjectivist-interpretive in character in so far as it explains a firm's actions in terms of the goals which the management pursues. Hence the label of 'behaviourist' which is sometimes attached to such models (for example, by H. Simon) is seriously misleading.[16]

(2)   Upon a closer examination it seems to me that the satisficing model still embodies the optimization principle. To say that firms will not seek an outright maximum of profit or of any other goal but rather some satisfactory combination of a number of managerial goals is only to say that managers are maximizing a complex goal function and seeking an *optimal*mix or combination of these goals. If it be replied that the point is that managers will only seek a 'satisficing' rather than an optimal *combination* of goals because of uncertainties and the complexity of the decision, then provided we recognize that the collection of information relevant to a complex decision requires managerial time and effort and is therefore a relevant cost associated

with the decision, the supposedly satisficing decision will turn out to be an *optimal* one once the costs of information collection are taken into account.

From the point of view of this work, whose aim is to develop a methodological appraisal of mainstream economics, the most important point to emerge from this survey of theories of the firm is the pervasiveness of explanation based on the optimization principle. From the profit maximization hypothesis as used in perfect and imperfect competition right through to the joint profit maximization, sales maximization and even, I have argued, to the satisficing hypothesis in conditions of oligopoly, we have found that the theory of the firm is in all cases built around a conjecture or hypothesis as to the goals of the firm's decision-takers, and explains the actions of the firm as the attempt to achieve a maximum realization of those goals subject to the constraints that are operative. Consequently, all of the leading theories of the firm in mainstream economics are unmistakably subjectivist-interpretive in character and involve a strictly teleological mode of explanation; they are, moreover, instances of the optimization principle.

If my arguments concerning the interpretive character of all leading theories of the firm and in particular of the satisficing model are correct then there is only one well-known theory of the firm which has been excepted from the above. This is the Hall–Hitch type of theory according to which firms pricing decisions are not based on any kind of purposive optimization at all but simply on the application of a fixed and customary mark-up percentage over costs. This theory parades itself as highly realistic and has a decided appeal to unanalytical minds. However, upon closer methodological examination it turns out not to be a theory at all but merely an unimaginative re-description of data on firm's pricing decisions. There are two main reasons why the mark-up theory of pricing must be rejected by any serious analytical economist:

(1) The aim of scientific theory is to *explain*, to achieve some kind of insight into why things are as they are.[17] The mark-up theory of pricing, far from providing us with any kind of explanation, merely re-describes and codifies data on the actual pricing decisions of firms and can hardly therefore be called a 'theory' of the firm or of its pricing. To state the mark-up thesis is merely to define the explanandum of a theory of the firm.

(2) The really crucial question, therefore, is to examine the origins of the mark-up used by firms. Why they should habitually apply some mark-up over costs? The most revealing aspect of the mark-up is the manner in which it varies widely both among different industries and through time in a given industry. Given these variations the obvious conjecture or hypothesis that suggests itself is that the currently employed mark-up is the result of a maximization decision at some stage in the past. That is to say, that on some past occasion the firm collected relevant information and decided in the light of its goals, such as profit maximization, what mark-up percentage it should

employ as a general rule-of-thumb in order to realize those goals to the maximum extent consistent with the constraints. A rule-of-thumb approach is adopted precisely because of the complexity of an optimizing decision and the need to save scarce decision time; and when significant changes occur in the demand and cost conditions relevant to the firm's decision, the rule-of-thumb will be promptly revised in the light of the firm's goals and the new data. Consequently, if the mark-up thesis is developed into a genuine explanatory theory (by examining the origins of the mark-up) it will inevitably come to be based on some conjecture as to the firm's goals in setting the mark-up and thus upon the optimization principle.

It follows from these considerations that if the mark-up thesis were developed into a genuinely analytical explanatory theory it too would be based on the optimization principle, and so we may conclude that the whole spectrum of mainstream theory of the firm clearly embodies the optimization principle as the basis of its explanation. By this stage, then, we have established that the main branches of mainstream microeconomic theory, – the theories of demand, of the firm and market structure – are all clearly subjectivist-interpretive in character in virtue of being based upon the optimization principle. We may also mention before concluding that in such areas as the theory of public goods, free riders and spillover effects, the analysis is based firmly on the notion of a utility maximizing individual agent or consumer. Similarly, in the economic theories of sex and politics, analyses based on conjectures as to the specific goals of typical agents and the attempt by agents to achieve a maximal realization of these goals have proved to be extremely fruitful and illuminating (for example the behaviour of politicians analysed as maximization of their private goal function subject to various constraints).

Our methodological appraisal of mainstream microeconomic theory in the previous pages thus allows as to arrive at a most clear-cut conclusion, a conclusion which I have been repeatedly emphasizing and which may be summarized in two key points:

(1) Mainstream microeconomic theory is the attempt to explain the actions of various typical agents by means of conjectures as to the specific goals they pursue and the attempt by agents to realize those goals to the maximum degree consistent with the constraints which they face. It therefore adopts an unmistakably subjectivist-interpretive methodology with a strict teleological mode of explanation.

(2) More specifically, it is clear that the interpretive character of microeconomic theory arises from the pervasive centrality of the optimization principle to its explanations. This bears out a point made in the last chapter, namely that the whole of economic theory could be regarded as a gradual unfolding of the content of the formal *a priori* optimization principle of deliberate choice by means of specific conjectures as to the goals which various typical agents actually pursue.

6.2 The Methodological Character of Macroeconomics

The last section has shown that the whole of mainstream micro-economic theory is the preserve of a clear-cut subjectivist-interpretive methodology of Weber–Schutz type. The same cannot be said of macroeconomic theory, at least not upon a *prima facie* examination, although I shall argue that in more recent advanced work on macroeconomics an interpretive methodology has definitely been employed.

Macroeconomic theory, in contrast with microeconomics, seeks to deal with the economy taken as an interdependent whole, with economic events in the large rather than focussing upon the activities of any one type of agent taken in isolation. A quick glance at any of the textbook expositions of macroeconomics will reveal a set of theories and relationships which *prima facie* are in sharp contrast to those of microeconomics. Such relationships as the aggregate consumption function, the aggregate investment function, the Phillips curve, the neo-quantity theory of money or the Harrod–Domar growth theory will be found, each of these being put forward as a stable causal relationship among aggregate variables (such as gross national product, overall price level, total money supply) and with little or no reference to the optimization activities of individual agents which are the stock-in-trade of microeconomics. Since this aggregate macroeconomic theory is well outlined in any of the introductory textbooks I shall content myself with giving three examples of it here: the consumption function, the Phillips curve and the neo-quantity theory of money.

The consumption function was first introduced into economics by Keynes and proposed that there is a stable and systematic relationship between aggregate real consumption in a community and aggregate real income. According as aggregate real income rises so also will aggregate real consumption but the latter not by as much as the former so that if

$$\text{where } C = \text{aggregate real consumption}$$
$$\text{and } Y = \text{aggregate real income}$$
$$\text{then } 0 < C'\,(Y) < 1.$$

This yields the familiar graphical presentation given in Fig. 6.3.

In the figure, C is real consumption expenditure and is measured on the vertical axis, Y is real income and is measured on the horizontal axis. It should be immediately added that other variables such as the rate of interest and the expected rate of inflation are also held to have significant influence on aggregate consumption, but in the short run Keynes suggested that real income would have a preponderant influence in giving rise to changes in aggregate consumption.[18]

As a second example of aggregate macroeconomic theorizing we may take the Phillips curve hypothesis. This curve, which grew originally out of some statistical work, proposes that there is a negative relationship between aggregate unemployment and either the rate of overall wage inflation or the rate of price inflation. (Wage inflation and price inflation are very closely linked since wages are a large element in costs of production.) A typical Phillips curve is shown in Fig. 6.4.

The Phillips curve shows a negative relationship between aggregate unemployment and overall price inflation and suggests specifically that if the rate of unemployment falls below a certain minimum level there will be progressively higher inflation rates. At what level of unemployment inflation will set in remains controversial but it will be obvious that this hypothesis has had a considerable influence on economic policy-makers in treasuries, etc., who speak about the policy trade-off between curbing inflation and eliminating unemployment.

A third example of aggregative macroeconomic theorizing is provided by the neo-quantity theory of money of the Chicago School. The basic view of these theorists is that if we take the classical quantity theory of money as expressed by the equation of exchange

$$MV = pY$$

where M = aggregate money supply, V = income–velocity of circulation

Y = aggregate real income, p = overall price level,

and if we hypothesize that V is a highly stable variable,[19] insensitive to interest rate changes, and so on, then the equation of exchange becomes a simple and powerful theory of the determination of aggregate money income. The level of money supply M will be the single overriding factor governing aggregate money income pY according to the simple equation $MV = pY$.

These three examples will give a clear idea of the kind of aggregative macroeconomic theory which is found in textbooks and which is highly popular with civil servants and central bankers. It has, however, become a central feature of mainstream economics only since 1945. For this reason it has been subjected to comparatively little methodological appraisal, and such appraisal as there has been has tended to extol its immense practical usefulness and its operational character.

In the light of the distinctions made in Chapter 4 between the objectivist and subjectivist approaches to the human sciences we may now proceed to a more detailed methodological appraisal of this aggregative macroeconomic theory. The most obvious point to suggest itself is that with these aggregative macroeconomic relations we are far removed from the sphere of optimization by individual agents. Rather we are presented with sets of supposedly stable relationships among highly aggregated variables and over which no individual can have any influence by means of his isolated actions. These relationships may be understood after the manner of what Emile Durkheim called 'social facts',[20] that is to say as brute facts pertaining to society as a whole which the individual cannot but accept because he is powerless, at least as an individual, to change them. Rather than being conceived, therefore, as the result of the purposive activity of individual agents these aggregative macroeconomic

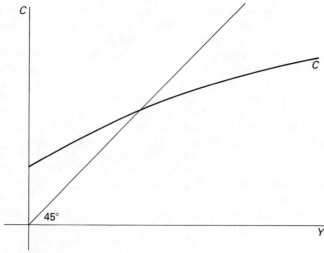

Y = aggregate real income
C = aggregate real consumption function (short run)

Fig. 6.3 *A Keynesian Aggregate Consumption Curve*

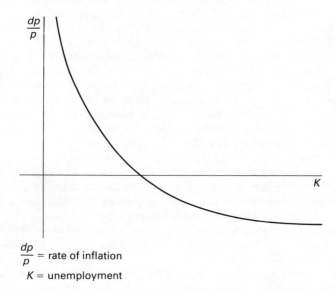

$\dfrac{dp}{p}$ = rate of inflation

K = unemployment

Fig. 6.4 *A Simple Phillips Curve*

relationships are regarded as stipulating stable efficient-causal linkages among various economic aggregates:[21] as enunciating macroeconomic 'laws', analogous to the (efficient) causal laws of the natural sciences, between for example aggregate money supply and aggregate money income or aggregate real income and aggregate real consumption.[22]

If, therefore, aggregative macroeconomic theory adopts an efficient causal mode of explanation this is directly incompatible with the methodology of microeconomic theory. For we have already seen that the whole of micro theory is built upon the optimization principle and involves a strictly teleological mode of explanation – an explanation of action in terms of the goals of the agents involved. We have seen in Chapter 4 that the efficient causal and the (strictly) teleological are radically distinct modes of explanation and so it follows that there is a definite incompatibility of method between the aggregative macro theory of the textbooks and microeconomic theory.

This methodological incompatibility between aggregative macro and micro theory would by itself be sufficient ground for concern since it must inevitably give rise to some tensions and contradictions in the ways in which micro and macroeconomists understand certain sets of phenomena. There are, however, even more direct incompatibilities in the substance of micro and macro theory. Thus, for example, if there were a relation of compatibility between microeconomic and macroeconomic theory it should be possible to derive macro-theoretic relationships (such as those given in the above examples) by means of a generalization from micro-theoretic relations. It is firmly established, however, that because of the 'problems of aggregation' no such derivation of macro theory from a micro theory foundation is possible[23] or at least the set of assumptions which would have to be made in order to achieve such a rigorous derivation of macro from micro theory are so restrictive as to be hopelessly unrealistic.[24]

In addition to this, there are some even more blatant incompatibilities of substance between micro and macro theory in cases where directly contradictory assumptions are embodied in their various theories. The most notorious instance of this is in regard to factor input ratios in production. The centrepiece of the micro theory of production is the principle of factor substitution – the notion that there is always a variety of different techniques, that is of combinations of factor inputs which can be used to produce any given level of output in a technically efficient manner. If such factor substitution were not possible then the famous law of diminishing returns would have no meaning since it refers only to cases where one factor input in production is held constant while some others are varied, that is, it refers only to (certain cases of) production with variable factor ratios.

In the field of macroeconomic theory we find a number of cases where the principle of factor substitution is replaced by the opposite and blatantly incompatible assumption[25] of rigid or fixed factor ratios in production. The rigid factor ratio assumption is seen most clearly in the input-output models of the economy where every industry is assumed to operate with fixed factor proportions. It can also be seen in some versions of the aggregate investment function and in economic growth theory where the assumption of fixed capital:output ratio is freely made.

It will be clear, therefore, that there is a very definite incompatibility between aggregative macro theory and micro theory, and that this is not merely a matter of adopting different modes of explanation but pertains also to the very substance of macro and micro theories. The hiatus between textbook macro and micro theory has for long been a source of profound malaise to students of economic theory and of a kind of schizophrenia among its teachers. Consequently, it is not surprising to find that in recent years a number of leading economists have turned their attention once again to the quest for a rigorous microeconomic foundation of macro theory which would close off the hiatus of incompatibility.

Quite apart from a feeling of schizophrenia in this matter there are also compelling philosophical reasons why this hiatus of macro and micro theory should be closed off; indeed, from the philosophical standpoint the incompatibility of the two branches of theory amounts to a serious intellectual scandal. Any science, I have argued in Chapter 3, should be guided by the ideal of searching for truth. Since micro and macroeconomics both deal with the same set of phenomena (that is, with economic phenomena) and since their only difference is one of perspective (partial equilibrium versus looking at the economy as a whole) it follows that the theories of micro and macro levels should be mutually compatible. It is possible that an appearance of incompatibility can arise because of wide differences in the terminology and analytical apparatus used by the two branches of economic theory. This, however, may only be due to a problem known to philosophers of science as that of theoretical terms and the different focus of abstraction which they embody. Where the foci of abstraction of the theoretical terms of two branches of a science differ, giving rise to an impression of incompatibility, what is required is that a mutual translation of the different theoretical terms should be carried out and when achieved the theories will be comparable in their terminology and should be then seen to be compatible.

Unless one is to fall back on a crude instrumentalist conception[26] of scientific theory which would hold that what matters is only the predictive power of a theory while its content is of no consequence, it follows that if we have two incompatible theories between which no mutual translation of theoretical terms is possible at least one of the theories must be false and must, therefore, be jettisoned. (Two contradictory theories cannot both be true of the same set of phenomena, and since we seek true theories in science at least one of two incompatible theories must be discarded.) What we have discovered in the case of micro and macroeconomics are two theories referring to the same set of phenomena, albeit from a different perspective and which appear to be seriously incompatible. Since the problem of aggregation prevents or fouls up any attempt at a mutual translation of the terms and functional relations of micro theory into macro theory the incompatibility remains, and so from a methodological standpoint it is imperative for the economist either to solve the problem of mutual translation (overcome the aggregation problem) or else to grasp the nettle of jettisoning either aggregative macro theory or micro theory based upon the optimization principle.

In the past fifteen years economists have become acutely aware of the intellectual scandal that this hiatus between macro and micro theory constitutes. It is interesting to remark in particular from the point of view of methodology, that in seeking to close off the hiatus economists have shown a distinct preference for or belief in the analytical superiority of microeconomic theory. In the first place, this preference can be seen in work directed to deriving macroeconomic aggregative relations as rigorous generalization from well-established mainstream microeconomic theory: if the problem of mutual translatability, that is, in this case the problem of aggregation is to be solved, this is to be achieved by deriving macro theory from established micro theory and not vice versa. In the second place the preference for micro theory can be even more clearly seen in those cases where faced with completely incompatible macro and micro theories of which at least one must be jettisoned, economists invariably drop the aggregative macro theory.[27]

There are a number of reasons why economists should prefer to turn to microeconomic theory when faced with the scandal of incompatibility. The aggregative macro theory of the textbooks and treasuries has proved to be quite barren as regards further development and elaboration, and in any case has to a very large extent been empirically falsified. Few, if any, of the aggregative relations postulated (the consumption function is the possible exception) have turned out to be at all plausible or corroborated, and in some cases macro hypotheses have been irredeemably falsified. The simple Phillips curve hypothesis and the Harrod–Domar theory of growth are examples of the latter. Other macroeconomic aggregative relations have been falsified in their simplistic textbook versions but more elaborate statistical work on them has rendered them more acceptable by means of introducing a greater degree of disaggregation. Such disaggregation inevitably turns macro theory back towards microeconomic foundations.

Equally disappointing has been the record of aggregative macro theory as a basis for economic policy making. Although, in the period of virtually continuous economic boom from 1945 to 1965, aggregative Keynesian economics was hailed as providing the great policy antidote to the trade cycle, the record of simple aggregative Keynesian economics as well as of the more recently fashionable crude monetarist economics (based on the neo-quantity theory of money) as bases for sound economic policy has been nothing short of abysmal. Upon reflection, however, these serious failures of aggregative macroeconomics, whether Keynesian or monetarist, are not really surprising. The aggregative macroeconomic relationships which they propose are simplistic and crude in the extreme; while, as we saw, the attempt to improve and sophisticate them inevitably leads to disaggregation by sector, industry, etc, and so points back towards the need for a microeconomic foundation.

By contrast with these tribulations of crude aggregative macro theory, mainstream micro theory based upon the optimization principle has shown a remarkable resilience and scope for development as witnessed, for example, in the various theories of the firm and in the whole theory of public goods and spillover effects that have emerged in recent years. Furthermore, in relation to matters of economic policy advice micro theory has offered a much more modest contribution than macro theory (for example, in relation to taxation, the optimal supply of public goods, cost-benefit analysis of projects, and so on); but arguably that modest contribution has met with considerably more success in practice than more pretentious macroeconomic policies.

There has, therefore, been a definite turn by leading macroeconomists in the past fifteen years to eliminate the scandalous hiatus which had developed between aggregative macro theory and micro theory and this has taken the form of a concerted effort to base macroeconomic theories on a rigorous foundation in well-established mainstream microeconomic theories based upon the optimization principle. Perhaps the strongest expression of this turning is the great renewal of interest in the 'general equilibrium' approach to macroeconomics. This approach antedates the aggregative Keynesian approach by some forty years. It abjures all attempts at aggregation and builds up a theory of the economy as a whole as a complex matrix of individual optimization activities. In this approach every distinct optimizing agent can be separately recognized and so the problem of aggregation is entirely eliminated. Indeed because of the insuperable difficulties which have arisen in the attempts to deduce macroeconomic relationships of the aggregative type such as the consumption function, Phillips curve or neo-quantity theory of money from microtheoretical foundations, much of the most advanced work in macroeconomics today is carried out entirely within the disaggregated framework of general equilibrium theory.

The general equilibrium approach, pioneered at the end of the last century by Leon Walras,[28] may best be described as a strictly *micro*economic approach to macroeconomic theorizing. The economy as a whole is conceived as a complex set of interrelationships between purposive optimizing individual agents, and macrolevel phenomena are to be explained as either the intended or the unintended side-consequences of myriad purposive individual actions. Each agent in the economy is in principle separately represented and so the problem of aggregation is simply eliminated in this approach. Macroeconomic theory becomes micro theory writ large and the unity of substance as between micro and macro theory is fully restored. Furthermore, since general equilibrium theory is built up directly from the purposive optimizing activities of individual agents and their complex interactions with each other, the methodological unity of economic theory is fully restored. With the abandonment by modern advanced macroeconomics of the crude aggregative brand of theorizing the last vestige of efficient causal explanation disappears and the whole of modern mainstream economic theory becomes the preserve of a strict teleological mode of explanation.

When Walras first developed the general equilibrium model he was addressing himself to the question of whether or not, in a decentralized market system, there could be a simultaneous equilibrium solution for all agents, that is a solution in which all agents would be successfully optimizing subject to their constraints. Since his purpose therefore was only to demonstrate the existence of a possible general equilibrium solution, Walras abstracted from all of the problems of disequilibrium adjustment processes and stability of equilibrium by means of the famous postulate of the all-seeing auctioneer. This auctioneer would be in touch with every agent in the economy and would call out prices, listen for the bids of agents and allow no exchanges (deals) to take place until all agents' bids could be simultaneously satisfied. The auctioneer fiction has thus the effect of guaranteeing a smooth and unproblematic process of adjustment by prices to disequilibrium situations. It was, however, an explicitly provisional fiction introduced by Walras for his own theoretical purposes precisely to abstract from disequilibrium adjustments and to focus exclusively on the question of whether or not a simultaneous general equilibrium solution is possible in a market economy.

By contrast, a good deal of the more recent advanced work on macro-economics within the general equilibrium framework may be viewed as the study of general equilibrium (and general disequilibrium) without the auctioneer fiction, or in other words without the assumption of a smoothly operating process of adjustment to general disequilibrium in the economy by means of price changes. In fact a great deal of attention has been paid to the processes of adjustment of an economy in situations of general or macrolevel disequilibrium. As examples of this work I may mention Hahn's article[29] on the new general equilibrium approach to macro theorizing in economics, where he argues in fact that by far the most important insights of Keynes' work are entirely missed and obliterated in the conventional textbook presentations of Keynes' theory in the crude aggregative format of IS and LM curves; and that these insights can only be adequately grasped through an analysis of the typical disequilibrium adjustment processes of a modern economy within the framework of a disaggregated general equilibrium theory. Other examples may be found in the works of Clower, Leijonhufvud and Malinvaud (to cite a few well-known names), all of whom have sought to restate various aspects of Keynes' macroeconomics within a general equilibrium framework.[30]

From the point of view of this book the most significant aspect of these modern developments in macro theory is that they restore the methodological unity of mainstream economic science. It allows us to reach a very definitive conclusion at the end of our long case study. For we have found in the case of economics, arguably the most mature of the human sciences, that the whole corpus of mainstream theory, both microeconomic and the best of modern macroeconomic, is the unmistakable preserve of the subjectivist-interpretive methodology with its strict teleological mode of explanation. This conclusion arises above all from the centrality of the optimization principle to all explanations in mainstream economics. We have also seen in this chapter how a good deal of economic theory may be viewed as a gradual unfolding of the content of the purely formal *a priori* optimization principle (as discussed in Chapter 5) by means of specific conjectures to the actual goals of typical agents in various kinds of situations.

Notes

1   We have already seen in Section 5.1, that by restricting our attention to the instantaneous and price-take-simplification we do not undermine the generality of the methodological appraisal of utility theory (as interpretive) that was built from this simple case. The same is true of demand (and labour supply) theory since they are as we shall see only specific instances of the utility theory of choice (where the variables of the U function are specified).

2   The formal axiom of consistency ensures that the indifference curves do cross while the axiom of convexity gives them their distinctive shape.

3   For more complex cases, and in particular for multi-period choices, the relevant constraint would be the agent's total wealth. Here, however, we are dealing with an instantaneous choice and so current income in the period is the appropriate constraint.

4   That is, if all else remains the same: if income and tastes remain unchanged so that we are dealing with a pure price effect.

5   Food taken as a general category rather than specific types of food is very unlikely to be Giffen.

6   The *ceteris paribus* clause must now include income distribution.

7   As noted before, what we do know for certain is that in cases of deliberate choice an agent will seek to optimize. What cannot be known with certainty are the actual goals of agents and so these must remain a matter of conjecture.

8   Utility maximization will imply profit maximization at least if the conjecture that the decision-takers like to earn more money (at zero cost in terms of effort, and so on) is true. The real difficulty with the profit-maximizing hypothesis is not that the firm's controllers do not desire more money: it is rather that the controllers sometimes have other goals as well (such as of a philanthropic nature).

9   This follows from the mathematical property arrived at by differentiating total variable cost: $SMC = SAC + q \frac{dSAC}{dq}$

10   *Ceteris paribus and* provided the good is not Giffen.

11   Imperfect competition is the same as perfect competition except for the homogeneity of product assumption. In imperfect competition there is product differentiation and hence negatively sloped demand curves for firms.

12   J. von Neumann and O. Morgenstern (1947), *Theory of Games and Economic Behaviour* (Princeton, NJ: Princeton University Press). See also any good intermediate microeconomics textbook for an outline of the principal theories.

13   Notice in passing that any other explanation than an interpretive one in terms of the purposive strategies of the players would be preposterous in the case of a 'game' strictly so-called. The game is almost as effective as the traffic light example given in Chapter 4 for illustrating the inadequacy of an objectivist-behaviourist approach to human science.

14 The theory of the technostructure is applicable only to oligopoly and to monopoly. The small firms in perfect and imperfect competition are still very largely owner controlled.
15 J. K. Galbraith (1967), *The New Industrial State* (London: Hamish Hamilton).
16 Cf. the discussion of Chapter 4 where the radical contrast of subjectivist-interpretive and objectivist-behaviourist approaches to human science was drawn.
17 Cf. my discussion of the 'realist' conception of scientific theory in Chapter 3.
18 Also, we may note that, strictly speaking, it is aggregate permanent income rather than aggregate current income which is the appropriate income variable to include a consumption function.
19 The Chicago School claims that the hypothesis of a stable V is well borne out in empirical tests.
20 E. Durkheim (1962), *The Rules of Sociological Method*, 8th edn (Glencoe, Ill.: Free Press).
21 R. Boudon (1981), *La Logique de Social* (Paris: Hachette) argues that Durkheim's methodology is not efficient-causal but focuses instead upon the unintended macro-level consequences of large numbers of purposive individual actions. This, however, is an unusual reading of Durkheim.
22 Keynes spoke of the consumption function as a 'fundamental psychological law'.
23 There are many sources on this problem, but see, for example: H. Green (1977), 'Aggregation problems of macroeconomics', in G. Harcourt (ed.), *The Micro Foundations of Macro-Economics* (London: Macmillan).
24 Not only are the aggregative relations not derivable from micro theory, it is even questionable whether or not 'real' economic aggregates such as real GDP, or the 'overall price level' have any significant economic meaning because of the aggregation problem. Thus, although we can measure something which we label real GDP, it is doubtful whether or not it can be used as an aggregate analogue for the microeconomic notion of real output: this is simply because real GDP will be an aggregate measure of 'output', strictly speaking, only if *all* relative prices remain constant. This is simply never a remotely realistic assumption to make.
25 It would be possible to render them compatible by assuming, for example, homogeneous production functions, *and* fixed relative factor prices. The latter assumption is hopelessly unrealistic whatever may be said about the former.
26 I have decisively rejected instrumentalism in Chapter 2.
27 Cf. the turn to general equilibrium approach to a variety of macro-theory problems to be discussed below.
28 L. Walras (1977), *Elements of Pure Economics*, W. Jaffe (trans), (New York: Augustus Kelley).
29 F. Hahn (1977), 'Keynesian economics and equilibrium theory', in G. Harcourt (ed.), *The Micro Foundations of Macroeconomics* (London: Macmillan). The Harcourt edited collection of essays is a valuable compendium from an IEA Conference (1976) on the micro foundation of macro theory.
30 For example, R. Clower (1965), 'The Keynesian counter-revolution, a theoretical appraisal', in F. Hahn (ed.), *Theory of Interest Rates* (London: Macmillan) or A. Leijonhufud (1968), *On Keynesian Economics and the Economics of Keynes* (Oxford: Oxford University Press).

7

Rationality Postulates in Economic Theory

This chapter constitutes something of a digression from the main themes of the book, but I have deemed it important to include it in view of some widely-voiced but not always well-directed criticisms of mainstream economic theory which have been expressed in recent years. These criticisms focus upon the vexed question of the rationality postulates that are involved, implicitly or explicitly, in economic theory.

In this chapter I shall seek first to define precisely in what sense mainstream economic theory necessarily involves postulates as to the rationality of agents. Having clarified the various meanings of the term 'rationality' I shall then go on to attempt a pre-emptive strike against some of the leading criticisms of those rationality postulates finding that in most cases these criticisms are misconceived, as a result of confusion over the various meanings of the ambiguous term 'rationality'.

The discussion of rationality postulates in economic theory has also a wider significance since the whole topic of rationality and its meanings has always been closely bound up with the subjectivist-interpretive methodology of the human sciences.

7.1 Epistemic Rationality and Practical Rationality

The first task then must be to define the various meanings of rationality. In a work which does much at least to clarify the issues at stake, Benn and Mortimore suggest that there is a fundamental distinction to be drawn between epistemic rationality and practical rationality.[1] Very roughly this distinction corresponds to that of the rationality of belief and the rationality of action.

Epistemic rationality as defined by Benn and Mortimore may be predicated only of a belief or an opinion, not of an action. Deriving from the Greek word *episteme*, meaning absolutely certain or proven knowledge, a belief can be said to be epistemically rational when it is *known* with absolute certainty, when the agent has conclusive rational grounds for holding the belief. As thus stated, epistemic rationality is a highly stringent criterion for selection of rational belief and various less demanding definitions of what is required for a belief to be rational have been suggested. Thus, for example, Gibson,[2] echoing a long line of positivist thinkers, has suggested that a belief is rational if it is founded upon an induction from past experience. Since, however, any belief founded upon an induction must commit the logical fallacy of induction (of arguing from the particular to the general case) it must ultimately fail if arraigned before the court of Reason and so while there may be good grounds for defending such inductively-based beliefs as *reasonable* they cannot merit the title of being (epistemically) *rational*. Since any other suggested definition of epistemic rationality (other than that given in the first instance above) must fail in the same way when subjected to a thoroughly rational examination, the notion of epistemic rationality may be predicated only of those beliefs which are known with absolute certainty.

If, therefore, we speak of an epistemically rational agent we can only mean one who has reached a state of perfect knowledge – an agent all of whose beliefs are held with absolute certainty. From what has been said about mainstream economic theory in the last two chapters, it should be clear already that economics does not involve an assumption that all agents have perfect knowledge or perfect information, hence that economics does not adopt a universal postulate of epistemic rationality.[3]

'Practical rationality' may in some cases be predicated of beliefs, as for example in the highly specialized sense in which certain propositions of Kant's philosophy are held to be practically but not necessarily epistemically rational (for example, those propositions to which the mind must assent *if* science or morality is to be possible). However, this highly specialized usage of the term is not of much relevance to the human sciences; of much greater relevance is the matter in which an *action* may be said to be practically rational.

Again following Benn and Mortimore, an action may be said to be practically rational when the following three conditions are fulfilled: (a) the action must be purposive, that is, directed to realization of the agent's goals; (b) the agent's goals must be mutually consistent; (c) most important of all, the action must be geared to achieve a maximum realization of the goal(s) to which it is directed subject to the constraints of the agent's situation and in the light of the (best) information available to the agent.

Once the meaning of practically rational action is spelled out in this manner it will be obvious that practical rationality is the exact logical equivalent of the purely formal optimization principle of the economic theory of choice which was discussed in Chapter 5. We saw there that economics restricts its attention to cases of deliberate choice and that having assumed a well-defined and consistent set of premises, the economic theory of choice proposes that in any case of choice preceded by reflection (deliberation) the agent will maximize his utility (subject to the constraints) in the light of the information available to him. The optimization principle so defined is held to be true *a priori* of any deliberate choice and since (as we saw) the optimization principle is central to the whole corpus of explanatory theory in mainstream economics one may say that economics adopts a postulate of *practical rationality* of action that is of fundamental importance to the whole science.[4] We have also seen in Chapter 5 that if the sphere of economic theory is confined to the field of actions proceeding from deliberate choice,[5] the optimization principle and hence the practical rationality postulate which is its logical equivalent, can be shown to be true *a priori* by means of phenomenological elucidation of the essence of deliberate choice. Thus we arrive at the important conclusion that while economics does not involve a postulate of epistemic rationality it does adopt a well-founded *a priori* postulate of practical rationality (of action).

7.2 Rationality Assumptions in Economics: Some Standard Criticisms Rebutted

Having clarified the relevant meanings of the term 'rationality' let us turn to examine some of the criticisms which have been levelled at the rationality postulates of economic science. Possibly the most widely-voiced but vaguely-formulated objection is that which holds that in a world where uncertainty is an inescapable feature of human existence, the rationality postulates of economics are untenable because they are hopelessly unrealistic.

If what this criticism is trying to suggest is that economics involves an untenable postulate of *epistemic* rationality of agents, then it is seriously misconceived. For while it is indeed true that if economics were to assume perfect information on the part of all human agents it would be a hopelessly unrealistic and therefore untenable assumption,[6] we have just seen that economics does *not* adopt a universal postulate of epistemic rationality, and so any criticism which suggests that it does is simply misconceived.[7]

A much more significant question which can be raised is that concerning the implications of uncertainty for the practical rationality postulate, that is, for the optimization principle. We shall find that the optimization principle is still fully tenable under conditions of uncertainty, and a number of telling points may be made in this regard. To begin with, there is nothing in the formal statement of the optimization principle to suggest that it is inapplicable in choices where the agent is uncertain about the future. We already saw in Chapter 5 how in such cases of uncertainty the optimization principle is modified to read 'the maximization of *expected* utility subject to constraint in the light of the (best) information available to the agent'.

In the above restatement of the optimization principle for cases of uncertainty the really significant qualification is the phrase 'in the light of the (best) available information'. Here it is acknowledged that agents rarely have perfect information and that choices are based on expectations rather than certainties. What is crucial, however, is that this qualification rather than in any way undermining the formal optimization principle turns out upon examination to be yet another instance of it. For in the case of a choice preceded by reflection and deliberation and where the agent faces uncertainty a vital part of his deliberation process will involve the collection of more information, and the agent will continue to collect such information relevant to his choice until such time as the expected further gain in utility from further information is just equal to the cost of collecting it (the main cost of collection being lesiure time lost in searching for information). In other words, in a deliberate choice in conditions of uncertainty, (a) the level of an agent's information will itself be the result of an optimizing (utility-maximizing) decision; (b) the subsequently chosen course of action will then be a maximization of expected utility on the basis of that 'optimal' information. Thus in conditions of uncertainty, not only is the optimization principle still valid, but the search for the 'best available information' will itself be an optimization which is a component part of the agent's act of choice. It is interesting to remark that it is this simple notion of 'optimal collection of relevant information' which underlies theories of rational expectations, even if it is usually well hidden behind a thicket of obscurantist econometrics. For arguably that much misunderstood theory amounts in the end to nothing more than the application of the practical rationality postulate, that is, the optimization principle, to the process of expectation formation by human agents in a world of uncertainty.

It is also arguable that in any case the protagonists of uncertainty have grossly overstated their case and that imperfection of information is by no means as serious and widespread as they seem to suggest. As Tisdell points out,[8] the only information which is relevant and affects an optimization decision is that which is in (or pertains to) the neighbourhood of the constraint function and the preference patterns of the agent (also in the neighbourhood of the constraint). Thus although any individual agent is steeped in considerable ignorance in relation to the goal of perfect all-embracing knowledge, the typical agent will usually be highly knowledgeable in those matters which are relevant to his deliberate choice. That this is the case may be seen both from the fact that when faced with imperfection of information a deliberately choosing agent will engage in a process of 'optimal search' to collect further relevant information and thus to form 'rational' expectations; and from the even more important fact of 'learning by doing', i.e. of acquiring information relevant to one's deliberate choices by means of a trial and error process. Both of these will result in acquisition by the agent of a high level of information in matters relevant to his deliberate choices.

The above points concerning optimal search and the adequacy of relevant information may perhaps be best illustrated by a number of examples. Thus what is happening at present in outer Mongolia or in Sumatra is indeed quite uncertain for a typical European, but is on the other hand of no consequence whatever for the bulk of decisions made by European firms and consumers. If it is of consequence to some of those firms (for example, rubber producers) or consumers (holidays in far-away places), they will make it their business to acquire fairly precise information about happenings in those places; they will engage in an 'optimal search'[9] for relevant information. Similarly, the performance figures, and so on, for a Ferrari 308 GTB are of little or no consequence to an agent for as long as such a car is way out of the range of the potential purchasing power of the consumer. Presumably, however, if he were to become capable of buying such a delightful adult toy he would find out something about those details and about the performance details of such competing goodies as Maserati Merak, De Tomaso Pantera or TVR. Lastly, it should be emphasized that the process of learning by doing, that is, by trial and error, plays a crucial role in the acquisition of information relevant to an agent's choices and this process often allows a rapid approach to a fairly high quality of relevant information. For example, by a process of trial and error among the restaurants in a new city, I can fairly quickly arrive at a set of restaurants which are utterly reliable in terms of satisfaction of my tastes. The process of search by trying out alternatives thus results in fairly rapid learning after which the choice of restaurant for dinner will effectively have fallen into the category of choice among a set of certain alternatives.

The arguments above suggest that there is no inherent conflict between the postulate of practical rationality (the optimization principle) and the presence of uncertainty as an inescapable feature of human existence. There is, however, one important consideration to be borne in mind. If uncertainty were so extensive and serious that agents possessed only the most scant and utterly unreliable information even in matters that were relevant to their choices, then any attempt at optimization or at purposive activity of any kind would be pointless because it would be doomed in almost all cases to complete failure. It is, strictly speaking, impossible to pursue or to attempt to pursue a goal unless one has a fairly clear idea of some paths or strategies whereby it may be reached; purposive or optimizing action in the absence of adequate relevant information is, therefore, nonsensical and impossible.

This suggests a qualification to the view that there is no conflict between the optimization principle and uncertainty. Although the optimization principle is still applicable in a world of imperfect information, it will be so only if agents are fairly well informed in matters relevant to their choices, that is, only if agents possess a level of relevant information sufficient to make purposive optimizing activity possible. But I would argue that uncertainty is rarely of a sufficient scale thus to conflict with and destroy the optimization principle – as may be seen from the following two considerations:

(1) The simple fact that human agents *do* engage in purposive and optimizing activities (and with a high degree of success).[10]
(2) The fact that agents are generally very well informed in matters pertaining to their choices and where they are not, that they can and do acquire the relevant information by a process of search and learning from experience that may occur quite rapidly (cf. the discussion and examples given above).

We therefore reach an important conclusion. While there is no inherent conflict between the postulate of practical rationality and the presence of uncertainty, the optimization principle (= practical rationality postulate) requires a further postulate that the quality of agents' information in matters pertaining to their choices is sufficient to make optimizing activity possible and meaningful. I have also noted that such a further postulate is fully defensible and tenable.

Let us now turn to a second and quite different line of criticism which has been proposed against the rationality postulates of mainstream economics. This second type of objection has been urged by S. Latsis and by H. Simon[11] but I shall argue that it also has been seriously confused. Discontent has been expressed by both writers against what they call the 'single-exit' solution of the theory of the firm and Latsis cites in particular the perfect competition and monopoly theories which allow only one possible pattern of action by firms, in the case of perfect competition to 'produce the profit-maximizing output or go bankrupt'. Simon speaks of economists' use of a substantive rationality postulate which he identified as, first, the tendency of economics to produce only one single optimal solution in various models and, second, to assume that this optimum is always successfully achieved. Since equilibrium in economics or in any human science means a situation in which agents' plans or aspirations are fulfilled, this latter part of Simon's criticism is strictly speaking an objection to economists' predilection for equilibrium theories and comparative static analyses rather than an objection to the practical rationality postulate. I may note in passing that there is much to be said for this second criticism by Simon: economists have devoted far too little time to examining the activities and adjustment processes of human agents in situations of disequilibrium – where their plans fail to be fulfilled. However, since equilibrium analyses focus on situations in which agents optimize successfully and since we have seen that information in matters relevant to choices is generally adequate enough to make such optimization possible, equilibrium analyses retain their validity and importance within economic theory. All we can say is that there has been over-emphasis on such analyses at the expense of analysis of disequilibrium situations.

Turning now to the first part of Simon's criticism, which he shares with Latsis, we find that both authors are opposed to single exit solutions in the theory of the firm and they see this somehow as a criticism of the rationality postulates of economics. If this objection were directed at some supposed epistemic rationality postulate of mainstream economics then it would be entirely misconceived, since economics does not involve such a postulate as we have already seen. Consequently, we must understand it as directed against the practical rationality postulate – the optimization principle. There seems to be some vaguely formulated suggestion in both Latsis and Simon that the 'single-exit' solutions produced by economic theories based upon the optimization principle are somehow inconsistent with the assumption of freedom of choice that is also central to economic theory and indeed a presupposition of the optimization principle (Chapter 5, pp. 77–82); that the single-exit solutions imply some kind of a straitjacket which negates freedom of choice.

It seems to me, however, that as an objection to the practical rationality postulate the Latis–Simon criticism is sadly confused and that it amounts in effect to a rather different and well-known objection to economic theories of the firm. For the derivation of a single exit solution in various theories is not in any way inconsistent with freedom of choice. Given the goals of an agent, the constraints he faces and, in the case of uncertain choices, the information at his disposal and his expectations, *there is only one overall optimum solution* to his deliberate choice. Therefore, in the various theories of the firm, having specified the conjectured goals of the typical enterprises the constraints it faces and the information available to it, there will only be a single formally defined optimal solution and to say this in no way suggests that firms are not free decision-takers.

It will be obvious, however, that if firms have different goals then the production and pricing strategies which they adopt in pursuit of those goals will also be different, in which case the optimal solutions for such firms will not be even formally similar. Consequently, it may be suggested that the Latsis–Simon objection to single-exit solutions is, strictly speaking, an objection to the widespread assumption by economists that all firms pursue the same goal, that goal usually being taken to be outright maximization of profits.

If this is what the Latsis–Simon objection amounts to, then it is hardly a revolutionary, or even a very new, criticism of theories of the firm. In the past twenty years, mainstream economics has begun to recognize that in managerially controlled corporations, especially under oligopoly conditions, the pursuit of profit may very often be only one among a number of goals pursued by firms; and various theories of the firm have been built around conjectures as to the typical goals of firms other than the pure profit maximization hypothesis (Chapter 6, pp. 99–101)[12]. If, therefore, the Latsis–Simon objection amounts to a criticism of mainstream theory for specifying the goals of firms much too narrowly, then it is one of which mainstream economics has already taken cognizance and has moved some way towards remedying by constructing new theories of the firm, upon conjectures as to the typical goals of firms other than profit maximization.

A third leading type of objection to the rationality postulates of economics is the 'economic man' objection. According to this view, which is particularly prevalent among non-economists, economics is held to portray man as a narrowly self-interested and coldly calculating being in virtue of the centrality to all economic explanations of the practical rationality postulate. This criticism draws nourishment from the unfortunate and misleading remarks of a range of nineteenth-century economists who held that economic science involved as a basic abstraction a notion of 'economic man'. Economic man they portrayed as a being who was narrowly self-interested and devoted solely to the pursuit of material wealth. The trouble is that economics does not involve such a narrowly defined focus of abstraction today and probably never did.

We have already seen that the focus of abstraction which defines the
specialized field of economic science is a good deal wider than the
nineteenth-century economic man conception. Economic theory focuses
upon cases of deliberate choice, – or choice preceded by some reflection
on the part of the agents – and holds the optimization principle or
practical rationality postulate to be true *a priori* of any such choice. There
is nothing in the purely formal optimization principle which suggests that
it is confined only to cases where agents pursue material goals, nor is
there even a suggestion that the typical optimizing agent is a narrowly
self-interested or a coldhearted being. As emphasized in Chapter 5, the
optimization principle which lies at the base of the whole of economic
theory is a purely formal and generalized principle, and its status as an *a
priori* truth stems precisely from its formal character.[13] Consequently,
the optimization principle retains a strictly neutral or non-committal
attitude as to what the goals of agents, i.e. the variables of their utility
function may be. These may include, as well as the pursuit of personal
wealth, the well-being of other persons, the pursuit of purely spiritual
goals and various objectives for which the agent's motivation is
emotionally super-charged. The only requirement for economic theory to
be applicable is that the actions under study should proceed from a
deliberate choice and thus come under the aegis of the optimization
principle, i.e. the practical rationality postulate.

It follows, therefore, that such actions as those of an ascetic monk, of
a great statesman who cares profoundly for the well-being of his people
and of a man who deliberately buys an extravagant present for his lover
are all practically rational, and hence that there is no implication in the
practical rationality postulate of modern economics of a nineteenth-
century economic man, that is, of confining economics to dealing with
ruthlessly self-interested and purely materialist behaviour. This last line
of criticism of the (practical) rationality postulate of economics thus turns
out also to be seriously misconceived. It is possible, however, that this
particular criticism is an instance of a wider and more dangerous literary
(and sometimes philosophical) misconception: the view that there is
somehow an implacable and unbridgeable antithesis between reason and
emotion. This, I have argued elsewhere (Chapter 15, pp. 228–29), is a
bogus dichotomy since in a great variety of cases it is eminently rational
(practically) to choose (on reflection) to follow the siren-calls of various
emotional motivations.

7.3   The Precise Meaning of the Rationality Postulates of Economics

From the clarification of meaning of rationality postulates in economics
and from a consideration of some of the leading criticisms which have
been directed at them, there are three main points to emerge at the end
of this chapter.

First, economics adopts a postulate of practical rationality which is the logical equivalent of the optimization principle. Since the focus of abstraction which delimits the field of economics is upon human actions that proceed from a deliberate choice,[14] and since a phenomenological examination of the formal optimization principle will show it to be true *a priori* of any such choice economics is fully warranted in adopting practical rationality as a fundamental *a priori* postulate.

Secondly, economics does not involve a postulate of full epistemic rationality – of omniscient agents. However, if optimizing activity, and hence the practical rationality postulate, are to have any meaning or be possible at all, we require a postulate of 'the adequacy of agents' information in matters pertaining to their choices'. If agents have information adequate enough to render optimization meaningful, i.e. are sufficiently well informed in relevant matters to give optimization a reasonable chance of being successful, then the wide field of equilibrium and comparative static analysis are fully defensible as idealized case abstractions. In establishing the postulate of 'adequacy of information' I relied both on the simple fact that optimizing activity is engaged in and meaningful in the world and upon an examination of how when faced with imperfect information in matters pertinent to their choices agents can quickly acquire the relevant information by 'optimal search' and/or by a process of learning through trial and error.

Thirdly, in the light of the above clarification of the rationality postulates necessarily involved in mainstream economics, various leading criticisms were considered. I found that in almost all cases these objections were seriously misconceived, the misconception arising in many cases from ambiguities in the term rationality. I sought to show in particular that there is no inherent conflict or incompatability between the *practical* rationality postulate – the optimization principle, of economic theory – and the presence of uncertainty in human existence.

Notes

1   S. Benn and G. Mortimore (eds) (1976), *Rationality in Social Science* (London: Routledge & Kegan Paul), cf. introductory essay for the discussion of the epistemic versus practical rationality distinction.

2   Q. Gibson (1976), 'Arguing from rationality' in S. Benn and G. Mortimore (eds), *Rationality in Social Science*.

3   Further discussion of what economics assumes in regard to the quality of agents' information will be found below in this chapter.

4   The interpretive approach to any human science has often been alleged to involve a practical rationality postulate. This is not the case, however, since only economics adopts such a postulate. Other interpretive human sciences do not. What we can say is that an interpretive methodology (elucidating the goals of an agent's actions) is much easier to apply to practically rational actions than to other types of action. This is why both Weber and Schutz speak of a 'preferences for [practically] rational ideal types' in any interpretive human science (cf. Part 3, Chapter 15 for a fuller discussion of these points).

5   Economics, precisely in virtue of the centrality of the optimization principle, confines its attention to cases of deliberate choice. It is this focus of

abstraction alone which underlies the much-maligned 'economic man' abstraction, rather than some narrower abstraction such as nineteenth-century theorists used to propose (for example, focusing exclusively on the motive of accumulating material wealth).

6 Only an instrumentalist will be prepared to defend blatantly unrealistic assumptions (cf. my rejection of instrumentalism in Chapter 2, and the alternative realist conception of scientific theory outlined in Chapter 3).

7 We shall see presently that in certain specific instances economists do make 'perfect knowledge' assumptions, and we shall assess their tenability in such restricted cases. However, it is clear that economics does not involve a general assumption of perfect knowledge.

8 Tisdell, 'Rationality in economics', in S. Benn and G. Mortimore (eds), *Rationality in Social Science*.

9 By 'optimal search' I mean a process of information collection in accordance with the optimization principle as described above (p. 116). The notion is sometimes also labelled as the theory of (practically) rational expectations.

10 This way of establishing the 'inadequacy of information' will be recognized as a Kantian style 'transcendental' argument from the (undeniable) fact of (largely successful) optimization activity to the conditions for its possibility. This line or argument finds an echo in a recent work by G. O'Driscoll and M. Rizzo (1985), *The Economics of Time and Ignorance* (Oxford: Basil Blackwell). See for example ch. 5, especially p. 76 where they argue that excessive uncertainty would rule out any purposive action.

11 S. Latsis (ed.) (1976), *Method and Appraisal in Economics* (London: Cambridge University Press). See articles by Latsis and Simon in this collection.

12 There is one possible way of interpreting the Latsis – Simon objection which should be noted. It might be held that in conditions of uncertainty the expectations of firms will vary widely and hence that the optimal solutions of firms will differ widely. This is true but irrelevant, since what differs is the detailed content of each firm's optimizations decision, *not* its formal character. For example, all firms may still be attempting to maximise expected profits. Moreover, it would be a mistake, as we saw, to overstate the degree of variance in the content of optimal solutions in firms, since they usually have a high quality of relevant information and usually also fairly closely convergent expectations.

13 Cf. Chapter 5, pp. 83–85. See in particular the examples of actions which can be brought under the optimization principle.

14 We saw that it is deliberate choice rather than pursuit of material wealth or the like which defines the field of economic studies. This follows directly from the economists' basic pervasive approach to analysis of choice. The focus of abstraction of economics is on actions proceeding from a *deliberate* choice.

8

Methodological Precepts and Practice in Economics

8.1 The Methodological Gap

Chapters 5 to 7 have shown at length that the whole corpus of mainstream economic theory adopts an unmistakable Weber – Schutz subjectivist – interpretive methodology with a teleological mode of explanation, a methodology which we have seen in Chapter 4 to be radically distinct from the methodology of natural science with its efficient-causal mode of explanation. We should now be able to conclude our case-study of the methods of mainstream economics were it not for the fact that when economists themselves have commented on their methodology they have put forward a view of it which is quite different from the subjectivist – interpretive view which I have been outlining.

To be precise almost all mainstream economists have endorsed the view that there is no essential difference between the methods of natural and of human sciences and they have conceived of the mode of explanation of economics in particular as efficient-causal. Since mainstream economic theory embodies a subjectivist-interpretive approach and a teleological mode of explanation which is radically distinct from the mode of explanation of natural science, it follows that there is a serious conflict between economists' *precepts* in matters of methodology and their *practice*.

It is because of the presence of this 'methodological gap' on the question of differentiation between the natural and human sciences that I shall now turn aside from the main themes of this work to a digression which will examine more closely the conflict of precept and practice on methodological questions in a long line of mainstream economists. This is I believe an important exercise because my assertion in the preceding chapters that economics is an outstanding exemplification of the Weber – Schutz interpretive methodology could be challenged by appealing to what a range of mainstream economists have actually pronounced on the issue. In this and the following chapters (8–11) I shall seek to counter any such objection by showing that while a majority[1] of mainstream economists have indeed preached a methodological monism, in practice these same economists have been using a subjectivist–

interpretive methodology which is radically distinct from the methods of explanation of natural science. My central argument, therefore, will be that on this methodological issue economists' own precepts are a seriously misleading guide to the character of their practice.

That there should be such a serious misunderstanding of the nature and philosophical status of their own methodology by economists is not entirely surprising, for economists have in the main been largely untroubled by methodological issues and controversies and their remarks on methodology have been extremely cursory. Very often, as we shall see, these remarks appear only as a brief preface or appendix to major treatises of economics. Enthusiasts of Thomas Kuhn's conception of normal science might view this lack of attention to methodology as a mark of maturity (of having passed the pre-paradigmatic stage) of economic science, in particular by comparison with certain other human sciences which are riven by methodological controversy.[2] However, it seems to me that the neglect of serious methodological study by economists has allowed a totally inaccurate understanding of their actual practice to have persisted for over a century; and it has also contributed to a certain superficiality or even to outright crudeness in matters of philosophy which we shall be able to detect in the following survey of economists' methodological precepts and their sharply contrasting practice.

8.2 The Typical Methodological Precept of Economists: Objectivism

I shall now outline the main features of the methodological position which has been adopted by mainstream economists, a position which has hardly changed at all since John Stuart Mill first clearly enunciated it in the middle of the last century. I should add that what I have presented below is a distillation of a typical viewpoint which brings together a variety of points made by different economists into a single systematic statement of their common position. Since economists' own discussions of methodological questions are usually brief and sketchy the typical position will rarely be found expressed in quite so forthright a manner as I have outlined it below. It is, however, a statement of the position with which the vast majority of mainstream economists would be fully in agreement.

The typical position which has been espoused by mainstream economists is that which I have identified in Chapter 4 as a 'superficial methodological monism'. Economists have shrunk from making any firm commitment on the purely philosophical question of whether man is subject or object. Although tending towards the admission of subjectivity by generally holding that man is a free and self-conscious being, economists have argued that subjectivity does not give rise to any significant or essential differences between the natural and human sciences.[3] Economics should follow as closely as possible the methods of the successful natural sciences and in particular its efficient-causal mode of explanation. The problems arising from human subjectivity are only minor annoyances; they do not constitute a radical difference of method between natural and human sciences.

A range of possible difficulties arising from human self-consciousness and freedom have been recognized by economists, only to be dismissed as not giving rise to any serious differentiation between the methodology of natural and human sciences. We shall now review the most important of those difficulties and how economists have dealt with them.

Human freedom means that each agent is the responsible author of his own courses of action and so the possibility arises that all human actions (and reactions) may be quite unique. If this were so it would be impossible to develop any systematic generalizations in human science and we could do little more than interpret and comment on each individual human action taken singly.[4] Economists have sought to quash this possibility by appealing to the so-called 'law of large numbers'. Individual actions may be unique and capricious, but it is argued that in the aggregate these individual eccentricities will offset each other so that some systematic generalizations about the actions of large numbers of people considered as a group will be possible. Since economics is not particularly interested in the details of specific individual actions (as, for example, psychology must be) but operates at a fairly high level of generality, it can therefore ignore the problem of uniqueness of human actions that arises from a recognition of human freedom.

It is worth remarking that this often-repeated argument is seriously fallacious as stated. There is no a priori law of large numbers; or at the very least if it is meant to be some kind of a generalization about statistics, it involves a serious misconception to apply it to the question of human freedom and its consequences. For it is quite possible to conceive of a universal eccentricity of human choice, an eccentricity so rich and multi-dimensional that there would be no question of individual idiosyncrasies cancelling each other out in the aggregate or at group level.[5] There is, therefore, no a priori law of large numbers to which economists can appeal in order to guarantee the possibility of systematic generalization in the presence of human freedom.

In order to overcome this difficulty economists have introduced as a provisional and indeed falsifiable assumption the axiom of constancy and convergence of tastes and preferences. To the extent that preferences converge, generalizations about the actions of those with convergent preference will be possible. This axiom, while acceptable, remains provisional and refutable and it cannot be underwritten by appeal to some a priori law of large numbers.[6]

A second difficulty for the human sciences arising from human subjectivity and which economists have recognized is the difficulty of achieving controlled experiments. The idea of constraining men to participate in strictly controlled laboratory experiments would be widely regarded as a serious infringement of their moral right to freedom of action. However, economists have correctly pointed out that since some of the natural sciences equally cannot carry out controlled experiments, this is not a significant difference between the natural and human sciences. Furthermore, controlled statistical inquiry can be used instead of controlled experiment when seeking to carry out careful empirical tests of theories. The most obvious example of a natural science which must substitute controlled observation of events, for controlled laboratory-type experiments, is astronomy.[7]

A third possible difficulty arising from human subjectivity concerns the self-consciousness of agents and the effect which this may have on attempts to make careful empirical tests. In some cases once human agents know that a certain theory (together with the predictions about their actions which it implies) has been propounded in their regard, they may proceed to take the theory into account and to act in such a way as to fulfil or refute the theory. This is the famous problem of the self-fulfilling, or self-destructive prophecy, the former being well illustrated, for example, by the way in which business expectations tend (via the multiplier-accelerator interaction) to be self-fulfilling in both the boom and the depression phases of the trade cycle.

Whenever economists have recognized this problem and the ambiguity which it introduces into empirical testing they have quashed it by pointing to an analogous problem which has been recognized in the philosophy of natural science; the Heisenberg effect. When making a strictly controlled experiment in small particle physics the possibility arises that the physical presence of the scientist in the laboratory may affect the behaviour of the particles and so the result of the experiment. This will introduce an ambiguity in the results of the experiment (are they genuine tests of the theory or merely the result of the physicist having been present) – an ambiguity which is closely analogous to that of the self-fulfilling prophecy in the human sciences. For example, did the exchange rate fall because of underlying balance of trade difficulties or was it just because a number of economists predicted a fall and gave rise to a loss of confidence in the currency? In the latter case the observed fall is purely the result of economists' remarks. Consequently, economists conclude that the difficulty for empirical testing posed by the self-fulfilling prophecy does not, after all, give rise to any significant difference between natural and human science since natural sciences face a closely analogous[8] problem.

The final important difficulty arising from human subjectivity and recognized by economists is the problem of value neutrality in human science. It is widely and correctly held in the philosophy of science that any science, in seeking a genuine understanding of the world, must first divest itself of all prejudices, and in particular of moral evaluations. Whether or not one approves morally of some of the uses of nuclear technology, the study of nuclear physics can and must be carried out independently of such views. Indeed, such an unprejudiced understanding is a prerequisite for arriving at a rational, well-founded moral conviction in regard to most phenomena. It has been suggested, however, that when dealing with the human sciences the moral evaluations of agents are so central a feature of such sciences that it will be impossible to maintain a strict value neutrality. Economists have argued, however, that while it may be difficult to preserve strict value neutrality it is not impossible and indeed must be attempted, so that once again there is no essential difference between the natural and human sciences on this score either. Any more than being a nuclear physicist commits a person to being an advocate of nuclear weaponry, the study of a free enterprise economy does not make one an advocate of *laissez-faire*.

Having gone through a list of considerations such as the above concerning the points of difference between natural and human sciences that arise from human subjectivity, mainstream economists have typically concluded that even if man is a subject this does not generate any essential difference of method between natural and human science. It should be emphasized that provided we make the modification of replacing the law of large numbers with the provisional axiom of convergent preferences, each of the above arguments is substantially correct. Thus, as far as they have gone in the examination of the problem, economists have been correct in reaching a methodological monist conclusion.

The trouble is that economists have not gone far enough: they have very largely ignored[9] what is by far the most important implication of subjectivity for the human sciences. In Chapter 4 I showed how a full recognition of man's character as a free and self-conscious being leads towards a subjectivist-interpretive methodology of human science with a teleological mode of explanation that is radically distinct from the efficient causal mode of explanation of the natural sciences. Far from giving any recognition to this most important implication of subjectivity a number of leading economists have argued explicitly that economics should adopt the efficient-causal mode of explanation of the natural sciences. The typical methodological position espoused by mainstream economists will therefore be immediately recognizable as the third version of the objectivist position which I have identified in Chapter 4, namely, superficial methodological monism: the view that whether or not man is a subject does not matter since even if he is a subject, this does not generate any significant difference of method between the natural and human sciences.

What makes matters so confusing and paradoxical is that despite this espousal of a clearly objectivist position in methodology, economists have in practice been developing theories of a very different methodological character. In the course of Chapters 5 and 6 we have discovered that mainstream economic theory has been the outstanding exemplification of a Weber – Schutz type of subjectivist-interpretive methodology, and this was so in virtue of the central role played by the optimization principle in all economic theory. In Chapter 4 I have shown why the subjectivist-interpretive approach to human science with its strict teleological mode of explanation of action (in terms of the agent's own goals) is radically distinct from the methods of the natural sciences which adopt an efficient-causal mode of explanation. Consequently, when we confront these considerations from Chapters 4 to 6 with the typical methodological precept of economists we encounter a serious inconsistency. For while adopting in practice a subjectivist – interpretive methodology with a clearly teleological mode of explanation, economists have been preaching a precept of superficial methodological monism and specifically within this, an efficient-causal mode of explanation. It is this conflict between methodological precepts and practice which I shall call a *methodological gap*.

That there should be such a serious inconsistency between economists' precepts and their practice in matters of methodology is not surprising when we bear in mind how very little time economists have devoted to consideration of methodological questions. Methodology has typically been treated by economists as a soft and rather boring preliminary to be shunted quickly aside in the introductory chapters of leading texts, and I have already suggested that economists' grasp of the philosophical issues at stake in any serious methodological critique[10] is hopelessly superficial. Indeed the presence and persistence of the methodological gap just described is clear testimony to such superficiality.

Notes

1 The only exception has been the so-called Austrian School which has recognized the subjectivist character of economics and argued for a 'dualism' of method. This school is discussed in Chapter 10.

2 T. S. Kuhn (1970), *The Structure of Scientific Revolutions* (Chicago: Chicago University Press), ch. 2.

3 It is partly because of this view that economists can fight shy of making a commitment on the philosphical issue of subjectivity versus objectivity.

4 This latter will be recognized as the position adopted by the German Historical School in the last century. The human sciences are reduced to either history or hermeneutics.

5 Furthermore, if eccentricity were widespread but tending to be offset in the aggregate, it might be seriously misleading to make generalizations at aggregate level. Thus 7 is the average of 4, 6, 8, and 10, also of -10250, -57, $+3210$ and $+7125$.

6 Cf. the discussion of this point in Chapter 5, p. 80.

7 As we shall see in Chapter 9, the related study of tides – known as tidology – has often been cited by economists as the sort of natural science with which economics should be compared. (Tidology cannot make experiments.)

8 Analogous, because clearly the problems are not identical. The Heisenberg effect does not assume self-conscious atoms. As regards empirical testing, however, the effect of both problems is to introduce the same ambiguity.

9 The only exception has been the Austrian School who have recognized the implication of the subjectivist-interpretive approach and hence have advocated 'methodological dualism'. This exceptional school is discussed in Chapter 10.

10 I recall here the central argument of Chapter 1: that any critical methodology raises issues of and can only be based upon pure philosophy.

9

What Economists Have Said
and
What They Have Done

In this chapter I shall seek to document in more detail the methodological gap between the precept of a unity of method in the sciences, and of an efficient causal mode of explanation for human science and the practice of mainstream economics, which adopts a clear-cut teleological mode of explanation and is therefore radically distinct from the methods of natural science. I shall do this by examining the methodological precepts of a number of leading exponents of mainstream economics from the nineteenth century up to the present day and I shall show that, in their theorizing, the practice of these self-same economists has been directly at variance with their precepts.

Since this discussion of the methodological gap is strictly speaking a digression from the main theme of the work I shall not try to offer an exhaustive survey of what economists have preached on matters of methodology. Instead I shall deal with the precepts and practice of a sample of leading economists from John Stuart Mill up to the present. Specifically, I shall be looking at J. S. Mill, Marshall, J. N. Keynes, Friedman, Samuelson and Lipsey as instances of leading theorists who have made significant comments on methodology. There have, of course, been other commentators on economic methodology such as Senior, Hutchison and Koopmans, but the views of the six economists I have selected are fully representative of the typical mainstream economics position.[1] At the end of the chapter I shall refer briefly to the remarks of a number of leading modern philosophers of natural science on the question of methodological differentiation since these comments have helped to reinforce the economists' precepts of a monism of method.

9.1   John Stuart Mill on the Question of Methodological Differentiation

We may open our survey with John Stuart Mill, the first great exponent of specifically methodological considerations in economics. It is of some interest to remark that the position expounded by Mill has continued virtually unchanged to constitute the mainstay of economists' methodological precepts right up to the present day, despite the fact that economic theory has come such a long way since Mill.[2]

In his philosophical work, *A System of Logic*, Mill devoted a specific section to the 'Logic of the Moral Sciences' by which he meant the human sciences. He adopts a clear-cut methodological monism urging economists, psychologists and other human scientists to follow as closely as possible the methods of the successful natural sciences: He says: 'The methods of investigation applicable to moral and social science must have already been described if I have succeeded in enumerating and characterizing those of science in general.'[3]

Furthermore, Mill quite explicitly advocates an efficient-causal mode of explanation for the human sciences and he speaks of the endeavour to achieve causal laws, that is, generalizations about 'uniformities of succession in human affairs that would be analogous to the causal laws of physics'.

At the same time Mill is fully aware of the freedom of action of the individual human agent. He denies, however, that this generates any significant difference between the methods of natural and human science and holds that such differences as do arise from human freedom are minor ones of degree rather than major ones. Specifically, he argues that the effects of individual caprice arising from free choice will, to a large extent, cancel out if we cast our generalizations at a sufficiently aggregative level; in other words the law of large numbers somehow submerges the effect of freedom.

He also argues that when we speak of freedom of action what we are really saying, at least for the purposes of science, is that the factors which govern human action are extremely diverse and complex, so much so that it would be difficult to take account of all of them in any particular case. Thus the generalizations of a human science will typically be much less precise than those of say physics. In order to illustrate this point and to show that it gives rise only to a difference of degree between natural and human science Mill says that when we compare a human science with a natural science we should consider 'tidology', the study of tidal rise and fall, as an example of the latter. The general laws of the tides follow from those of the moon's gravitational pull but the exact prediction of the tide level on a particular day and at a particular time is very difficult indeed because of the effect of a range of local factors, such as estuary width and wind speed and direction.

Human freedom, therefore, gives rise to no significant difference of method between natural and human science for Mill; it points only to a certain complexity of the subject matter and to a difference in the degree of precision of causal laws (by comparison with physics but not with tidology), and this difference is further reduced by taking a sufficiently aggregative approach. As Mill himself puts it:

> The agencies which determine human character are so numerous and diversified . . . that in the aggregate they are never in two cases exactly similar . . . [However[an approximate generalization is in social enquiries for most practical purposes equivalent to an exact one; that which is only probable when asserted of individual human beings indiscriminately selected being certain when affirmed of the character and collective conduct of masses.[4]

It will be clear that the above discussion of freedom presented by Mill is carried out entirely within the presumption of an efficient-causal mode of explanation for the human sciences: it is concerned with the degree of accuracy which can be achieved by formulations of causal laws in human science. There is certainly no trace whatever of a recognition that human subjectivity generates the requirement of a subjectivist – interpretive methodology with a teleological mode of explanation, and hence of a radical differentiation between the methods of natural and human science. Since from Mill's various writings, and especially from his political philosophy it is clear that he would not want to deny or to denigrate man's freedom of action, it follows that the position he adopts may best be classified as a 'superficial methodological monism'. This is just the position which I suggested in the last chapter and is typical of a long line of mainstream economists' methodological precepts: the view that man may or may not be a free and self-conscious being but that in any case this subjectivity does not generate any significant difference of method and specifically that the human sciences should follow the efficient causal mode of explanation of the natural sciences.

While I have labelled Mill as a 'superficial monist' above, it may perhaps be remarked in passing that there are some hints of a more forthright, objectivist position, that is to say of the instrumentalist and even the reductionist version of objectivism in Mill.[5] Thus, for example, his treatment of the implications of freedom for the human sciences points towards the conclusion that man is after all only a highly complex organism so that there are at most difficulties in achieving the same degree of precision in the causal laws of the human sciences. Furthermore, Mill seems to approve of Auguste Comte's project for the creation of a unified body of science. Comte adopted the blatantly reductionist version of the objectivist approach to the human sciences whereby man is held to be *only* a complex organism and hence the laws of the human sciences may ultimately be reduced to laws of physiology and biology, and these in turn to laws of physics and chemistry (of brain processes, for example).[6]

However, these are only flirtations or suggestions in Mill. He actually rejected Comte's reductionist programme as a practical possibility in the current state of the human sciences and harboured doubts about whether or not it could ever be achieved. Moreover, although he speaks of the complexity of causal laws pertaining to human action he never explicitly says that for purposes of science man is to be treated simply as another object in nature. Additionally, since the theme of human freedom predominates in certain other fields of Mill's thought it seems to me that his position on human science is most accurately characterized as superficial methodological monism rather than as either of the more explicit versions of objectivism, namely the instrumentalist and reductionist versions.

Having outlined Mill's methodological precepts let us now examine briefly his practice. Mill was one of the last of the great classical economists, an eclectic synthesizer of the doctrines of a range of classical economists who had preceded him rather than an original theorist. In classical economics the optimization principle, although present, did not have the same central role as in all economics since the marginalists, and there are indeed certain parts of classical theory which look decidedly efficient-causal in character. The Malthusian theory of population and the 'Iron Law of Wages' might afford examples of explanations which could at least be construed in efficient-causal terms.

There is not, therefore, the same outright conflict between a precept of methodological monism and a subjectivist – interpretive practice in Mill as we shall find in later post-marginalist economists. At the same time since there are large areas of classical theory which are built quite clearly around the notion of purposive maximizing activity by self-conscious agents the methodological gap is none the less present in Mill. Examples of classical economic theories that adopt an interpretive approach with a strictly teleological mode of explanation are the theory of the competitive firm, Ricardo's theory of differential rent and Smith's theory of wage differentials (as due to equalization of net advantages).[7] Thus we find that while Mill urges economists to follow exactly the methods of natural science and in particular to adopt an efficient-causal mode of explanation, at the same time over large areas of his own theorizing he adopts a subjectivist – interpretive approach with a teleological mode of explanation which is radically distinct from the (efficient-causal) methods of the natural sciences.

The conflict between Mill's precept of a superficial methodological monism and certain other areas of his theorizing is perhaps most clearly illustrated by his political philosophy rather than by his economics. In what is his greatest and most original masterpiece, the 'Essay on Liberty',[8] Mill developed a radical-liberal political theory which accorded pride of place to human freedom and indeed regarded the right to freedom of individual action as the supreme moral and political value. It is difficult to square such a political philosophy, in which freedom is the predominating theme, with a methodology of human science which holds that freedom is only a minor annoyance or complexity giving rise to no essential difference of method between natural and human science.

Thus in summary we may conclude that taking the works of John Stuart Mill as a whole there is an undoubted conflict between the precept of a superficial methodological monism urging the human sciences to follow closely the efficient causal modes of explanation of the natural sciences and trivializing the implications for methodology of human freedom, and various parts of his own practice. Large areas of his economic theorizing involve a subjectivist-interpretive approach with a teleological mode of explanation that is radically distinct from the methods of natural science, while in his political philosophy man is nothing if not free: freedom is the supreme value.

We shall find that a very similar methodological gap to that which I have identified between Mill's precepts in the *Logic* and his practice in *Principles of Political Economy* and the 'On Liberty' recurs in a succession of leading mainstream economists.

9.2   Alfred Marshall

Between the time of John Stuart Mill and of Alfred Marshall economic theory underwent an important transformation known as the 'marginalist' revolution or break-through. In addition to bringing the optimization principle into the centre of the stage of economic theory, marginalism also brought with it the first use of mathematics on a wide scale in economic theorizing. Because of the precision and clarity which this conferred on the new marginalist economics it was hailed, by Jevons, Marshall and many others as an important step forward which would bring economics closer to the methods of the more precise and successful natural sciences. Thus in the first instance the marginalist breakthrough only served to strengthen economists' methodological monist convictions despite the fact that it also based all branches of economic theory on the optimization principle.

Alfred Marshall was the first great exponent of a comprehensive system of the new marginalist economic theory[9] and he is the next leading economist whose precepts and practice in matters of methodology we shall be examining here. Unlike Mill, who wrote whole works in the philosophy of science, Marshall's comments on methodology are very brief being confined to an early chapter and an appendix of his *Principles of Economics*.[10] Like Mill, whom on questions of methodology at least he seems to have followed very closely, Marshall holds that the human sciences and economics in particular should follow as closely as possible the methods of natural science, and in particular they should adopt an efficient causal mode of explanation. As he says: 'All the devices for the discovery of the relations between cause and effect which are described in treatises on scientific method have to be used in their turn by the economist.'[11]

Like Mill, Marshall does not want to deny the existence of human freedom. However, he argues explicitly that it does not generate any special methodological difficulties for the human sciences. Echoing Mill, Marshall argues that the effect of human freedom is to introduce a wide variety of potential factors or causes governing human action so that to arrive at precise and reliable causal generalizations in regard to human action is a good deal more complex or difficult than in such natural sciences as physics. This remains a difference only of degree of precision and complexity, however, and if we consider a natural science such as tidology, whose predictions and generalizations about specific tidal rise and fall in a given place are equally imprecise, even the difference of degree will evaporate.[12]

It is clear that Marshall's whole discussion of human freedom and its implications is carried out entirely within the presumption of an efficient-causal mode of explanation for the human sciences. Throughout his discussion of methodology both in the main text and in the appendix of the *Principles* he repeatedly insists that economics must adopt an efficient-causal mode of explanation like that of the natural sciences, and he conceives of efficient-causal explanation in a definitely deterministic manner. Thus for example he says: '[Economics] like every other science undertakes to study the effects which will be produced by certain causes not absolutely but subject to the condition that other things are equal and that causes are able to work out their effects undisturbed.'[13] And again: 'Let us then consider the nature of economic laws and their limitations. Every cause has a tendency to produce some definite effect if nothing occurs to hinder it.'[14]

Thus the presumption of an efficient causal mode of explanation in the human sciences is explicit and pervasive in Marshall. When he deals with the problem of human freedom it is entirely within this presumption: he examines what difficulties are posed for the attempt to arrive at efficient causal generalizations or laws of a deterministic kind by human freedom – the potentially capricious character of human action. As we saw, he concludes that the only difficulty is one of complexity, the difficulty of identifying all relevant causes that govern human actions.

It will be clear that in this treatment of freedom Marshall most certainly does not recognize the implication of a subjectivist – interpretive methodology with a teleological mode of explanation for the human sciences which is carried by a fully adequate philosophical analysis of human freedom and subjectivity.[15] At the same time, however, it is clear from Marshall's various writings that he does not want to deny or even to denigrate human freedom of action. Hence we may conclude that the methodological precept which is espoused by Marshall is a 'superficial methodological monism', that is to say, the third variant of objectivism which holds that man may indeed be a free and self-conscious being but that this does not generate any significant or radical difference of method between the natural and human sciences hence that the human sciences should follow closely the methods of natural science and in particular its efficient-causal mode of explanation.

Having clarified Marshall's methodological precepts, let us now turn to a brief examination of his practice. Marshall was the first systematic exponent of a comprehensive corpus of economic theory along marginalist lines. He himself tells us that the central explanatory principle of all branches of his theorizing is the 'principle of substitution at the margin'. By this Marshall means in effect what I have called the optimization principle. For the principle of substitution refers to the notion of making small adjustments at some margin until an optimal solution is reached, and its mathematical formulation is the differential calculus of (constrained) maximization, which was widely used by Marshall.[16]

I have already shown in Chapter 5 that explanations based on the optimization principle are clear-cut instances of the subjectivist – interpretive methodology and involve a teleological mode of explanation. Since the optimization principle is indeed central to Marshall's economic theorizing (as can be seen from his theories of the utility maximizing consumer, profit maximizing firm, and so on) it follows that in practice Marshall has been using an unmistakably subjectivist methodology with a teleological mode of explanation which is radically distinct from the methodology of natural science with its efficient-causal mode of explanation.

Thus we are led to the conclusion that in Marshall, as in Mill, there is present a serious methodological gap between precept and practice. On the one hand, Marshall exhorts economists to follow as closely as possible the methods of natural science and in particular to adopt an efficient-causal mode of explanation and, on the other hand, in his own actual theorizing Marshall uses a subjectivist – interpretive methodology with a teleological mode of explanation which is radically distinct from the methods of the natural sciences.

9.3   John Neville Keynes

No survey of economic methodology in the last century would be complete without a reference to John Neville Keynes' work *The Scope and Method of Political Economy*.[17] Since this was a book devoted entirely to questions of methodology and the underlying philosophical issues which they raise, Keynes could hardly be guilty of superficiality. Nevertheless, throughout the whole of the book Keynes never once raises the fundamental question of whether or not the human sciences should adopt a subjectivist – interpretive methodology which with its teleological mode of explanation is radically distinct from the methods of the natural sciences. In fact Keynes touches only briefly on the whole question of methodological differentiation (in his discussion of the 'historical school') and the whole work is pervaded by the presumption that there should be a strict unity of method among the sciences and in particular that the human sciences should follow the efficient causal modes of explanation of the natural sciences.

Since at no point does Keynes give a systematic statement of the reasons for adopting a methodological monism, his views on the topic must be inferred from various remarks and presuppositions that occur at other stages of the work. There are two places were Keynes' implicit sympathy with methodological monism become fairly evident: first, in his discussion of the 'historical school' of economists and, secondly, in his discussion of induction and deduction in the human sciences.[18] We shall now consider each of these parts of Keynes' work in turn.

The Historical School of economics was an offshoot of the wider romantically inspired hermeneutical approach to the human sciences which was prevalent in Germany in the nineteenth century. Arising from Dilthey's humanism, there were two fundamental tenets in the historical school's methodology.

First, since the starting point of this approach is a forthright assertion of human subjectivity – that man is a free and self-conscious being, the responsible author of his own actions – it follows that to understand a human action we must understand the goal or intention of the agent involved. In other words the hermeneutical movement gives an early expression to the imperative of a subjectivist – interpretive methodology of the human sciences and insists, moreover, on the radical differentiation of this approach from the methodology of the natural sciences. (This was a direct reaction to Comte's reductionist objectivism in the human sciences.)

Secondly, since each human action is freely chosen it is, strictly speaking, unique and partakes of the character of a work of art. Hence any attempt at generalization regarding human activity is found to be distortive and each human action is to be interpreted and understood singly. Human science becomes hermeneutics – the art of interpreting individual actions in their historical setting – and resembles history or literary criticism much more than the natural sciences.

What is most interesting from my point of view in Keynes' discussion of the Historical School is that his criticisms are directed entirely at the second tenet while he completely ignores the first. Thus Keynes' discussion focuses exclusively on the possibility of generalization in human science given the convergence of human agent's preferences and on the practical and theoretical importance of such generalizations, while at the same time he does not deny the value of historical studies in economics. As regards the first tenet of the Historical School's position, the imperative of a subjectivist – interpretive methodology Keynes simply remains silent.

One possible reason for this surprising silence is that although it undoubtedly derives its inspiration from Dilthey's wider hermeneutical approach to the human sciences, in which the imperative of a subjectivist methodology occupies a central position, the Historical School of economists laid a great deal more emphasis on the second tenet of the hermeneutical position, namely that the human sciences should adopt a method of historical case-by-case study rather than trying to construct generalizations. Another possible reason for Keynes' complete silence on the subjectivist – interpretive question is perhaps that he simply took methodological monism for granted as having been already well established by John Stuart Mill[19] and so saw no good reason for raising the whole question of methodological differentiation between natural and human sciences yet again.

This latter interpretation, that Keynes simply took methodological monism for granted, is well supported by the tenor of his discussion of induction and deduction in economics in Chapters 6 and 7. This whole discussion is carried out entirely within the presumption of a strict unity of method between the natural and human sciences and Keynes envisages quite explicitly that the human sciences should adopt an efficient causal mode of explanation. Like Mill and Marshall he examines the implications of human freedom purely in terms of the problems it poses for a correct identification of all relevant causes and effects and for the accuracy of causal generalizations in human science. He also recognizes the problems of making controlled experiments in human science but points out that as in the natural science of astronomy, controlled statistical observation is a fully adequate substitute for experiment. Thus human freedom does not, for Keynes, pose any problem for the assertion of a strict unity of method among all of the sciences.

From these considerations we may, I think, quite safely infer that on the question of methodological differentiation Keynes adopts, just like Mill and Marshall, a position of 'superficial methodological monism'. I say the 'superficial' variant because at no point in the work does Keynes seek to deny human freedom or to suggest that man is merely an object in the eyes of the scientist. Rather he suggests explicitly that human freedom gives rise only to minor differences of degree between the natural and human sciences; and far from giving any recognition to the implication of a subjectivist methodology with a teleological mode of explanation that follows from human freedom, Keynes explicitly advocates an efficient – causal mode of explanation for the human sciences in Chapter 6. Hence we may conclude that although he never sets out the position in a forthright and systematic manner, a superficial methodological monism is a clear-cut presumption that underlies and pervades the whole work.

Unlike his son Maynard, John Neville Keynes was not an outstanding contributor to original economic theorizing and so his work in the field of economic theory is not as well known as is that of Mill and Marshall. None the less, we know that Keynes expounded and approved of the mainstream Anglo-Saxon economic theory of his own day. In the course of *The Scope and Method of Political Economy*, for instance, Keynes quotes with approval examples from the economic theorizing of Mill, Cairnes, Senior and even from the then new-fangled marginalist approach to economics of Jevons and Menger.[20] Since classical economics contains large areas of subjectivist – interpretive theory,[21] and since marginalist economics, being based on the optimization principle, adopts a subjectivist approach with a teleological mode of explanation throughout, it follows that in Keynes just as in Mill and Marshall there is a methodological gap between precept and practice.

Since Keynes had written a comprehensive treatise on economic methodology it is much more surprising than in Mashall's case to find such a serious inconsistency between his monistic precepts and a subjectivist – interpretive practice. This is particularly so when we bear in mind that Keynes had examined the historical school's approach to methodological issues. Perhaps the explanation lies in the fact that while Keynes was hardly guilty of superficiality in methodological matters, he was not by any means an original philosophical thinker. Thus on a number of issues and in particular on the question of a monism of method, rather than presenting any new approach of his own, Keynes simply repeats John Stuart Mill's position – Mill's 'Logic' being regarded as the most authoritative contemporary exposition of the philosophy of science.

We have now looked at the views of some of the leading nineteenth-century economists who have commented on the question of methodological differentiation between natural and human sciences and have found those methodological comments or precepts to be seriously at variance with the bulk of actual economic theorizing in the century. This same methodological gap between a superficial monist precept and subjectivist-interpretive practice may, moreover, be found in almost all of the other leading nineteenth-century economists as well, so the above sample (Mill, Marshall and Keynes) may be taken to be an accurately representative one. Before leaving the nineteenth century one brief aside may be made. The latter part of the century marked the high tide, at least in English philosophy, of a dogmatic positivism and of an incredible faith in the power and hence in the methods of inquiry of the successful natural sciences. English political economy, which more or less represented the mainstream of economic thought at the time, was caught up in this positivist enthusiasm for and faith in natural science. Considering this, it is not so surprising after all that despite the clearly subjectivist character of so much of economic theory so many leading economists should have assumed, almost as beyond discussion that the human sciences should follow strictly the methods of natural science.

9.4   Milton Friedman

Coming now to examine the typical methodological views of economists in the present century we encounter in the 1930s an interesting and very much exceptional standpoint in the writings of the so-called 'Austrian School' of economists, represented for example by Hayek, von Mises and Robbins. Since the Austrian viewpoint is exceptional and has never commanded anything like universal assent among mainstream economists I shall pass over it for now in order to show how, if we exclude the Austrian episode, there is a direct continuity between the typical methodological views of nineteenth- and twentieth-century economists. I shall, however, be returning in the next chapter to take a closer look at the Austrian approach to methodology.

Since 1945 the *locus classicus* of economic methodology has been Milton Friedman's article 'The Methodology of Positive Economics'.[22] Mark Blaug has even suggested[23] that together with some short articles by Nagel and Samuelson critical of Friedman, Friedman's article is the only piece of methodology which a great many modern economists have ever bothered to read. We may, therefore, commence our review of the methodological precepts and practice of modern economists with Friedman's article.

Although Friedman does not devote much of his article to the question of methodological differentiation between the natural and the human sciences he quite clearly espouses a position of superficial methodological monism on this issue which is identical in all essential points with the views of Mill and Marshall. Friedman does not want to deny human subjectivity, that man is a self-conscious and free being, but he argues quite explicitly that subjectivity does not give rise to any essential difference of method between the natural and human sciences. He points out first that although human freedom means that controlled experiment is generally impossible in the human sciences there are natural sciences such as astronomy which equally cannot carry out laboratory experiments and that in all such cases controlled statistical inquiry may be substituted for controlled experiments.

Secondly, he concedes that since human sciences deal with human relationships, and often directly with the value judgements of agents, it will be a great deal more difficult to preserve a strict value neutrality in human science. However, he argues that it is none the less possible to develop a value-neutral human science, and indeed he argues that such a value-free human science is an indispensable prerequisite for the formation of well-informed norms of policy and reform.

Friedman even goes so far as to recognize that in virtue of self-consciousness the human scientist may draw inspiration from his own actions when formulating theories. However, he insists that this introspection has only a heuristic role and hence is but a minor difference between the natural and human sciences. He most certainly does *not* draw out the implication that explanation of action in terms of motives of the agent involves a teleological mode of explanation which is radically distinct from the efficient causal mode of the natural sciences.

As a result of these deliberations Friedman concludes that:

Positive Economics is or can be an objective science in precisely the same sense as any of the physical sciences. Of course the fact that economics deals with the interrelations of human beings and that the investigator is himself part of the subject matter being investigated in a more intimate sense than in the physical sciences raises special difficulties in achieving objectivity at the same time that it provides the social scientist with a class of data not available to the physical scientist. But neither the one nor the other is, in my view, a fundamental distinction between the two groups of sciences.[24]

It will be clear, therefore, that Friedman espouses a superficial methodological monism. He does not deny human subjectivity but argues that it does not give rise to any essential difference of method between the natural and human sciences. Indeed, since he does not recognize that explanation in terms of motivation is teleological when he mentions the minor heuristic role of introspection, we may say that he implicitly envisages an efficient-causal mode of explanation for the human sciences.

Turning to look at the methods adopted by Friedman in his own work in economic theory we find that as in all mainstream economists the optimization principle is a centrepiece of his theorizing. Friedman has, for example, been a staunch defender of the profit maximization hypothesis in the theory of the firm while in his essay 'The Quantity Theory of Money, A Restatement'[25] where he seeks to outline a theoretical foundation for the neo-quantity theory of money he does so by deducing the characteristics of the demand for money of a utility maximizing wealth-holder. Since explanation in terms of the optimization principle is the epitomy of a subjectivist-interpretive approach to the human sciences it follows that in his own theorizing Friedman has been adopting a subjectivist-interpretive methodology with a teleological mode of explanation which is radically distinct from the methodology of the natural sciences with their efficient causal mode of explanation.

Hence we find in Friedman, as we have already found in Mill, Marshall and J. N. Keynes in the last century, a serious inconsistency between methodological precepts and practice. On the one hand Friedman has preached a monism of method urging that there is no essential difference in the methods of explanation of natural and human science, while at the same time in his own theorizing he has adopted a subjectivist-interpretive methodology with a teleological mode of explanation that is radically distinct from the methods of the natural sciences.

Friedman's article gave rise to one of those occasional and brief periods of internal methodological self-examination and debate among mainstream economists. The controversy was not concerned with the problem of methodological differentiation between natural and human science, so I shall deal with it only briefly here. It was concerned with what has come to be known as the 'Friedman twist' or simply the 'F-twist'.

The bulk of Friedman's article was devoted to a defence of the view that the assumptions of a scientific theory may be entirely unrealistic (that is, blatantly false) provided the theory predicts accurately. This amounts to an assertion that scientific theories, since they are not to be assessed directly for their truth value, are mere fictions devoid of any cognitive significance and to be assessed purely on such pragmatic criteria as their simplicity and 'predictive power for the class of phenomena they are designed to explain'.[26] Friedman leaves us in no doubt regarding the fictional character of theories when he says that we may prefix our most clearly unrealistic hypotheses with the words 'as if'.[27]

In an important article[28] surveying the controversy which arose over Friedman's strictures concerning assumptions and their realism Wong has shown that Friedman is here implicitly adopting a position known in philosophy of science as instrumentalism – the view that scientific theories are instruments of prediction devoid of truth value. In the same article, Wong also discusses the leading criticism of Friedman's view coming from within economics in a number of articles by Paul Samuelson.[29] Samuelson accuses Friedman of having taken the valid point that all scientific theories involve some degree of abstraction from reality and having twisted it into the much different and challengeable assertion that theories may be completely unrealistic (and so fictional)

– thus the term 'F-twist'. In order to achieve a decisive rebuttal of Friedman's position, Wong shows how Samuelson espouses a view of scientific theory known as descriptivism, and he goes on to show clearly that descriptivism involves a view of scientific theory which is as extreme and philosophically as crude and untenable as Friedman's instrumentalist view.[30]

Oddly enough, Wong does not propose any alternative view of scientific theory which would steer a *via media* between the descriptivist and instrumentalist extremes adopted by Samuelson and Friedman respectively. Indeed a later article by Lawrence Boland builds upon Wong's work characterizing Friedman definitively as an instrumentalist and shows how instrumentalism arises within modern post-positivist philosophy of science from a reflection on the problem of induction.[31] Boland concludes his article in a manner even more surprising than Wong with the assertion that 'no-one has been able to criticize or refute instrumentalism.'[32] Moreover, since any adequate reply to the F-twist must involve a decisive rebuttal of the instrumentalist conception of scientific theory, he holds that to date no decisive refutation of Friedman's methodological position has been offered. Elsewhere[33] I have argued that a decisive rebuttal both of the instrumentalist and the descriptivist conceptions of scientific theory can be achieved by adopting a 'realist' conception of scientific theory such as I have already outlined in Chapter 3. This view preserves the explanatory role of theories while insisting against the instrumentalist that, first and foremost, theory must achieve a true insight into the processes and generative mechanism which underlie and give rise to natural phenomena or into the motivations which underlie human actions.

In this chapter, however, I am not mainly concerned with the details of such a proposed resolution of the debate over the F-twist. Rather there are two general features of the controversy upon which I should like to focus here. First, it is notable that the whole debate was carried out entirely within the presupposition of a strict unity of method among the sciences. Consistently, with their precepts of a superficial monism of method, Friedman, Samuelson and other economists never raise the possibility that there might be a difference in the character of explanatory theories between natural and human science.[34] Instead the controversy was but a mirror image of a wider debate in the philosophy of natural science between instrumentalist, descriptivist and other views of the nature of scientific theory.

Secondly, the debate among economists over the F-twist also illustrates again a general point which I made in Chapter 8, namely the crudeness and rudimentary character of mainstream economist's grasp and appreciation of philosophical issues and problems. Both descriptivism and instrumentalism involve epistemologically crude and unsubtle views of the character of a good scientific theory.

9.5   Paul Samuelson

I have mentioned Paul Samuelson already in discussing the F-twist controversy. Since he is another leading modern exponent of mainstream economic theory we may now turn to examine what are his precepts and his practice in regard to the question of methodological differentiation. Samuelson like Friedman devotes very little attention to this question, possibly because, as so many mainstream economists before him, he simply takes for granted the position of a superficial methodological monism that has remained unchallenged by mainstream economists since Mill (with of course the sole exception of the Austrians).

Samuelson's views on this topic may be gleaned from the methodological preamble to his major well-known textbook *Economics*. There Samuelson is fully prepared to admit that man is a free and self-conscious being but he denies that this generates any essential difference of method between the natural and human sciences. In the first place, Samuelson recognizes that human freedom gives rise to the possibility of wide divergence among individuals in the manner in which they react to various situations and hence that a question mark hangs over the possibility of achieving systematic generalized theories in human science. Against this he cites the law of large numbers, arguing that the effects of individual caprice will tend to cancel out if we cast our theories at a sufficiently general level; that is, if we develop theories of large group behaviour rather than of the details of individual actions. Secondly, Samuelson mentions the by now familiar points that absence of controlled experiment is a feature of certain natural sciences as well as of the human sciences, and that while value neutrality may be more difficult to achieve in a human science none the less it can and must be achieved as in the natural sciences.

Finally Samuelson, like Friedman, is prepared to recognize that in self-consciousness the human sciences have at their disposal a fruitful heuristic source for the formulation of hypotheses: by introspection regarding the motives of one's own actions one may get useful clues regarding the explanation of the actions of others. However, he does not recognize the further implication that explanation of action in terms of motives involves a teleological mode of explanation that is radically distinct from the efficient-causal mode of explanation of the natural sciences. Indeed, when Samuelson is discussing how the law of large numbers can overcome the problem of individual caprice he quite explicitly envisages generalizations of an efficient-causal type for the human sciences – generalizations which will differ only in degree of precision from the (efficient) causal laws of the natural sciences. As he says:[35] 'Economic events and statistical data observed are alas not so well behaved and orderly as the path of heavenly satellites. Fortunately our answers need not be accurate to several decimal places; on the contrary if the right general directory of cause and effect can be determined we shall have made a tremendous step forward.'

We may conclude, therefore, that Samuelson espouses in effect a precept of superficial methodological monism: man may indeed be a free self-conscious being but this does not give rise to any significant difference of method between the natural and human sciences. In particular Samuelson argues that the human sciences should follow the efficient-causal mode of explanation of the natural sciences.

Turning now to examine Samuelson's own work in economic theory we find a practice which is almost completely at variance with his methodological precept. In his textbook, *Economics*, Samuelson presents a comprehensive exposition of modern mainstream economic theory, which we have already seen in Chapters 5 and 6 is pervaded by the optimization principle and hence involves a subjectivist-interpretive methodology with a teleological mode of explanation. Also in his *Foundations of Economic Analysis* Samuelson has shown how the mathematical calculus of constrained maximization provides a formal analysis which is applicable to almost every branch of economic theory. Constrained maximization is the mathematical expression of the optimization principle and so again Samuelson is acknowledging the centrality of the optimization principle to economic theory. Thus we are led to the conclusion that in Samuelson we find once again the methodological gap between a precept of superficial monism which would entail in particular an efficient causal mode of explanation for the human sciences and a practice which adopts a subjectivist-interpretive methodology, with a teleological mode of explanation which is radically distinct from the efficient-causal modes of explanation of the natural sciences.

Before leaving Samuelson there is one most revealing episode in his career which deserves some attention: that is the 'revealed preference' episode. Inspired by his monistic methodological precepts which urged economics to follow exactly the methods of natural science Samuelson expressed some dissatisfaction with the theory of indifference curves, or more generally with the utility theory of choice on the grounds that this approach involved references to empirically unobservable subjective states. Such reference he held should have no place in a human science, which seeks to follow the hard natural sciences which are based firmly on the data of experience.[36] Following this criticism of utility theory Samuelson introduced his 'revealed preference' theory of consumer choice from which all reference to subjective states was banished and which dealt only with preferences as revealed by agent's behaviour in actually observed situations of choice.

This episode suffered a most remarkable fate, however. Houthakker showed[37] that revealed preference theory yields exactly the same set of predictions as the older utility (or indifference curve) theory in all possible situations and that the theories differ only in their terminology and mode of understanding or explanation of human choices. Once this had been demonstrated it is interesting to find that economists at large, and even Samuelson himself, abandoned revealed preference theory and reinstated the older Paretian utility theory and associated indifference curve approach: it is this latter which today provides the basis for the economic theory of choice in the mainstream. What is revealing about this episode from the point of view of this book is that when economists were faced with choosing between two alternative theories of consumer choice yielding an identical set of predictions, one of which was built directly on a natural science model and embodies a typical behavioural efficient-causal (stimulus-response) approach to explanation of human action and the other of which sought to explain action in terms of the purposive attempt to achieve their goals by self-conscious agents and which thus embodies a teleological mode of explanation, they came down quite unequivocally in favour of the latter. This suggests that despite the widespread precept of a superficial methodological monism, in practice economists manifest a decided preference for, and commitment to, explanation in terms of the optimization principle and hence to a subjectivist-interpretive methodology with its teleological mode of explanation of human actions.

9.6   Richard Lipsey

The last economist whom I propose to examine in this survey of economic methodology is Richard Lipsey, another leading exponent of the modern mainstream position who is well known for his widely used textbook *Introduction to Positive Economics*. In the first chapter of that textbook Lipsey devotes some time to discussing methodological issues, and in particular he deals with the question of differentiation of method between the natural and human sciences. On this issue Lipsey has nothing new to add and he defends again a superficial methodological monist precept. He does not wish to deny human subjectivity but he argues in a manner which will by now be all too familiar, that self-consciousness and freedom do not give rise to any significant differences of method between the natural and human sciences. In relation to the problem of capricious individual actions by free agents Lipsey cites the law of large numbers to argue that the effects of individual caprice will tend to cancel out in the aggregate and hence that systematic generalizations will be possible in human as in natural science. Moreover, Lipsey clearly envisages that the human sciences should adopt the same efficient-causal mode of explanation as the natural sciences for he conceives of the generalizations of a human science as efficient-causal laws or generalizations about stimulus and response.[38] As he sees it, the basic question about the significance of freedom for the possibility of generalization in human science is:[39]

> whether human behaviour does or does not show sufficiently stable responses to factors influencing it as to be predictable within an acceptable margin of error . . . Stated carefully, the above view [that free will eliminates the possibility of human science] implies that inanimate matter will show stable responses to certain stimuli while humans will not.

Invoking the law of large numbers Lipsey argues that human beings taken in large numbers or groups will indeed display stable patterns of response to stimuli and that efficient causal generalizations (of behaviourist type) are possible and should be developed in the human sciences.

Lipsey also mentions some other familiar points in defence of monism. Controlled experiment is ruled out by human freedom but can be quite adequately replaced by controlled statistical inquiry as in such natural sciences as astronomy. On the question of value neutrality he concedes the difficulty of achieving it in a human science but argues that the human sciences can in principle seek and should seek to achieve value neutrality. Moreover, he adds that the requirement that theories should be 'inter-subjectively' testable, that is, capable of passing rigorous tests carried out by any practitioner of the science, affords useful help in eliminating theories which are based on pure prejudice. As a result of these considerations Lipsey concludes that despite human subjectivity there are no essential differences between the natural and human sciences and he urges economists to follow in particular an efficient-causal mode of explanation of stimulus response type.

Yet again, however, Lipsey's own work in economic theory is completely at variance with his precept of a superficial monism. In the first place, his textbook presents a comprehensive statement of modern mainstream theory that is pervaded by the optimization principle and so is the epitome of a subjectivist-interpretive approach. Secondly, in such original work as that with Lancaster on the 'theorem of the second best'[40] Lipsey is examining what will be the formal properties of purposive maximizing activity when a 'first best' (optimal) solution is for some reason unattainable. Clearly, the focus of the analysis is on explanations of action in terms of the goals of agents (which they seek to realize to the maximum degree possible) and so involves a teleological mode of explanation of actions within a subjectivist-interpretive approach to the human sciences.

We can only conclude that there is a serious methodological gap between Lipsey's methodological precepts and his practice. On the one hand, he preaches a superficial methodological monism urging economists to follow closely the methods of natural science and to adopt in particular an efficient causal mode of explanation. On the other hand, in his own theorizing to which the optimization principle is central Lipsey adopts an unmistakably subjectivist-interpretive approach with a teleological mode of explanation which is radically distinct from the efficient-causal mode of explanation of the natural sciences, and which is the antithesis of the behaviourist stimulus response approach to explanation of human action with which Lipsey seemed to flirt in his precepts.

By now we have seen from our survey of a range of mainstream economists' methodological precepts that ever since the time of John Stuart Mill they have adopted in effect a superficial methodological monist position, and precisely the same precept can be found in a wide range of other economic methodological commentators as well – in Senior, Hutchison, Koopmans, Machlup[41] and Blaug, for example. At the same time, and certainly since the advent of marginalism in the 1870s, mainstream economic theory has, in virtue of the central role played therein by the optimization principle, been the epitome of a subjectivist-interpretive methodology of human science with a teleological mode of explanation which is radically distinct from the methodology of natural science with its efficient-causal mode of explanation. I conclude, therefore, that there is a serious gap or inconsistency between the methodological precepts and practice of economists.

9.7   The Influence of the Philosophy of Natural Science

The long persistence of this methodological gap between precept and practice in economics provokes the obvious question of how such a serious misunderstanding can have prevailed for so long. One leading reason for this is the positivist background and sympathies of many leading mainstream economists. Economics has from the beginning been a largely Anglo-Saxon or in this century Anglo-American science despite the fact that there have been also many illustrious continental European contributors such as Menger, Walras and Pareto. Since the beginning of the nineteenth-century, Anglo-American thought in general has been dominated by empiricist and the closely related positivist approaches to knowledge and philosophy and the central conviction of positivism is that the natural sciences are the paradigm of all valid cognition.

This positivist background has in particular made its influence felt in the methodological precepts of economics which, as noted, has been predominantly but certainly not exclusively an Anglo-American discipline. This influence may be seen at work

(1)   *Directly*: Positivism views the natural sciences as the very paradigm or exemplar of valid human cognition, hence positivist-leaning economists will automatically recommend that economics should follow as closely as possible the methods of natural science; they will preach a methodological monism.

(2)   *Indirectly*: Given that positivist-leaning economists will tend to view the natural sciences as the paradigm of valid cognition they may well turn (and in fact have often turned) to the works of various philosophers of natural science for inspiration in their methodological comments. Indeed, much of the methodological debate which has occurred within mainstream economics has been but an epicycle on certain controversies in the philosophy of natural science.[42] In the remarks of leading philosophers of natural science on what ought to be the methods of the human sciences, the economist will find considerable reinforcement of his view that there should be no essential difference of method between the natural and human sciences. This fact may also be a significant reason for the persistence of the methodological gap between precept and practice at least among positivist-minded economists.

Philosophers of natural science have not in general had much to say on

the methods of the human sciences and much of what they have said has
been quite derogatory. None the less it is quite clear that in almost all
cases where they do comment on the methods of the human sciences it
is within the presumption of a strict methodological monism, of a strict
unity of method between natural and human science. Many examples of
this tendency could be given but I shall refer briefly here to two
representative examples. In the last century in his major work *A System
of Logic*,[43] John Stuart Mill wrote extensively on the methodology of
natural science, seeking to defend at length an inductivist method. When
in that work he came to deal with the methods of the human sciences,
as we have already seen,[44] he argued that the human sciences should
follow as closely as possible the methods of natural science. In much more
recent times the works of Kuhn and Lakatos have been prominent in the
philosophy of natural science and their influence on economists is evident
in the methodological works of Ward, Latsis and Blaug for example.[45] In
the case of both Kuhn and Lakatos we find only the most cursory remarks
about any human science, but what is clearly common to both is an
explicit endorsement of the unity of method among all of the sciences.
Each of them applies criteria derived from their respective methodologies
of natural science in order to condemn the scandalously immature
condition of the human sciences as they see it. For Kuhn the persistence
of fundamental debates on methodology (such as is the topic of this book)
testifies to the pre-paradigmatic immaturity of the human sciences,[46]
while Lakatos berates the human sciences for the presence in them of
'degenerating' research programmes and for their failure to submit
theories to rigorous empirical tests. It is clear that these remarks are based
on a presumption of a monism of method between natural and human
science and this presumption has been taken over directly into the
methodological precepts of those economists who have looked to Kuhn
and Lakatos for inspiration.

In this chapter I have sought to document the assertion made in
Chapter 8 that there is a serious methodological gap between the precepts
and the practice of most mainstream economists. I showed (Sections
9.1–9.6) that, on the one hand, economists ever since John Stuart Mill
have been preaching a precept of 'superficial methodological monism',
that is to say, although man may be a subject this generates no essential
difference of methodology, hence the human sciences should follow
closely the methods of natural science and in particular its efficient-
causal mode of explanation. On the other hand, the bulk of mainstream
economic theory epitomizes (as we saw in Chapters 5 and 6) a
subjectivist-interpretive methodology with a teleological mode of
explanation which is radically distinct from the methods of the natural
sciences with their efficient-causal mode of explanation.

Having demonstrated clearly the existence of such a methodological gap
the question regarding its long persistence naturally arises. In Section 9.7,
I adumbrated one conjecture which could possibly explain the persistence.
Mainstream economics, being a largely Anglo-American science, has
come under a strong influence of broadly positivist ideas. These have

contributed to the persistence of the gap in two main ways: (a) directly, since positivism regards the natural sciences as the paradigm of all valid cognition and hence *a fortiori* of valid method for the human sciences and (b) indirectly, because economists, whose grasp of philosophical issues is at best superficial, have turned to the works of leading philosophers of natural science for methodological inspiration. Here they found considerable reinforcing support for their methodological monist precepts. Since the precept of monism has such influential support outside of economics it is perhaps not so surprising that economists have taken it more or less for granted and have thereby persisted in the inconsistency between methodological precepts and practice.

Notes

1 Always remembering that the Austrian School of Mises, Hayek and Robbins is the only exception (in methodology) (cf. Chapter 10).
2 Despite Mill's own rash assertion that everything important had already been said in economics. It is only in methodology that economists have been prepared to allow Mill to have had, in effect, the final word.
3 J. S. Mill, (1879) *A System of Logic* (London: Longman), bk 6, ch. 1, p. 419 and pp. 429–35.
4 J. S. Mill, *A System of Logic.*
5 Cf. Section 4.1 for the classification of the versions of the objectivist position in methodology.
6 A fuller account of the Comtean reductionist version of objectivism will be found in Section 4.1.
7 Both of these latter theories form part of Mill's synthesis of classical economic doctrines.
8 J. S. Mill (1962), 'On liberty', in *Utilitarianism*, ed. M. Warnock (London: Fontana).
9 Marshall was not a pioneer, however. Gossen, Jevons and Menger were the first marginalists but Marshall is the first exponent of a comprehensive system of economics along marginalist lines.
10 A. Marshall (1962), *Principles of Economics* (London: Macmillan; 8th edn).
11 A. Marshall, *Principles of Economics*, p. 24.
12 It should be remarked that this particular argument put forward by both Mill and Marshall in favour of monism is seriously in error since it fails to recognize the key point that freedom is precisely the cancellation of all antecedents, determinants or causes (cf. the discussion of the central defect of all superficial monism in Chapter 4, and again in Part 3, Ch. 13, pp. 196–99).
13 A. Marshall, *Principles of Economics*, p. 36.
14 A. Marshall, *Principles of Economics*, p. 31.
15 Cf. Chapter 4, and again in Part 3 where the philosophical implications of subjectivity for human science are examined in length.
16 Often only in footnotes and appendices, however.
17 J. N. Keynes (1963), *The Scope and Method of Political Economy* (New York: Augustus Kelley).
18 J. N. Keynes, *The Scope and Method of Political Economy*, chs 6, 7.
19 It may be remarked that Keynes followed Mill quite closely on many methodological questions.

20 Cf., for example, ch. 4, p. 104, where he discusses Jevons and Walras' work and also the discussion of Jevons' theory of utility at p. 261.

21 For example, the theory of price formation or of wage differentials in competitive markets which focus on the optimizing activities of human agents.

22 M. Friedman (1953), 'The methodology of positive economics', in *Essays in Positive Economics* (Chicago: Chicago University Press).

23 Blaug, M. (1976), 'Kuhn v. Lakatos in Economics', in S. Latsis (ed.), *Method and Appraisal in Economics* (Cambridge: Cambridge University Press). It is worth remarking, however, that in the past seven years since I began writing this book, there has been a definite revival of interest in methodology by economists as evidenced, for example, by the appearance of books such as M. Blaug (1980), *The Methodology of Economics* (Cambridge; Cambridge University Press) and B. Caldwell (1982), *Beyond Positivism* (London: Allen & Unwin).

24 M. Friedman, 'The methodology of positive economics', p. 4.

25 M. Friedman (1969), *The Optimum Quantity of Money and Other Essays* (London: Macmillan), ch. 2.

26 M. Friedman (1953), *Essays in Positive Economics* (Chicago: Chicago University Press), p. 8.

27 That is, theories are not to give a true account of the world as it is but an 'as if' account of it.

28 S. Wong (1973), 'The F-twist and Samuelson's methodology', *American Economic Review*, pp. 312–25. Cf. also my discussion of instrumentalism in Chapter 2, pp. 32–35.

29 P. Samuelson. See notes on this question in *American Economic Review Papers and Proceedings*, vol. 52, 1963, pp. 231–36; vol. 53, 1964, pp. 736–9; vol. 54, 1965, pp. 1164–72.

30 Descriptivism in regard to scientific theories in the view that scientific theories are mere elegant redescriptions of data in precise language. *Inter alia*, they deprive theory of any strictly explanatory role, and certainly of any relationship of generality to particularity in relation to empirical data, which is how the explanatory role of theory is usually conceived in philosophy of science. For a descriptivist, it will be clear that false assumptions cannot be part of a good theory. (Thus Samuelson refutes Friedman.)

31 L. Boland (1979), 'A critique of Friedman's critics', *Journal of Economic Literature*, vol. 17, pp. 503–22.

32 L. Boland, 'A critique of Friedman's critics', p. 521.

33 P. J. O'Sullivan (1984), 'Friedman's methodology revisited: a proposal for a definitive resolution of the F-twist', *Explorations in Knowledge*, vol. 1, no. 2, pp. 32–49.

34 Admittedly there is no difference between the theories of natural and human science on this score; but it is significant that nobody rxises the possibility.

35 P. Samuelson (1967), *Economics*, 7th ed. (New York: McGraw-Hill), p. 7.

36 Samuelson was also pushed towards this conclusion by the description which as we saw he took up in his critique of the F-twist. Descriptivism holds that scientific theories should contain no more than a direct description of the data of experience in exact language and nothing more.

37 H. Houthakker (1961), 'The present state of consumption theory', in *Econometrica*, vol. 29, pp. 704–40.

38 Cf. Chapter 4 where I show that the efficient-causal mode of explanation in human science means in effect use of the behaviourist stimulus-response model of human behaviour.

39 R. Lipsey (1983), *Introduction to Positive Economics*, 6th ed. (London: Weidenfeld & Nicholson), p. 10.
40 R. Lipsey, and K. Lancaster (1956–57), 'The general theory of second best', *Review of Economic Studies*, vol. 24, no. 1, pp. 11–32.
41 The work of Fritz Machlup on methodology can best be described as perplexing. In the course of a considerable amount of writing on methodological matters in economics which probes rather more deeply than does that of most other economists, Machlup does make occasional bows in passing to subjectivist approaches, mentioning Weber and Schutz, but despite these he ends up espousing quite clearly a most unsatisfactory version of 'superficial methodological monism'. See F. Machlup (1978), *Methodology of Economics and Other Human Sciences* (New York: Academic Press), especially the essay 'If matter could talk'.
42 Cf. above, this chapter, p. 141, where I discuss the debate over the F-twist, for example.
43 J. S. Mill, *A System of Logic*, op. cit.
44 Cf. p. 131 and the quotation from Mill there.
45 B. Ward (1972), *What's Wrong with Economics?* (London: Macmillan); also see S. Latsis (ed.) (1972), *Method and Appraisal in Economics* (Cambridge: Cambridge University Press) and M. Blaug (1980), *The Methodology of Economics* (Cambridge: Cambridge University Press).
46 For a fuller account of Kuhn's (anti-) philosophy of science see above Chapter 2, pp. 30–32.

10

The Austrian Exception

In the course of the preceding chapters I have made reference to the fact that there has been one exceptional group of economists who have not been involved in a methodological inconsistency between their precepts and practice. This group, known as the Austrian School, has consistently argued that the human sciences and economics in particular should adopt a subjectivist-interpretive methodology. In this chapter I propose to examine the position espoused by this exceptional school of mainstream economists and to see why it has had such a limited influence on the rest of the mainstream despite the accuracy of its characterization of the practice of economic science.

10.1 The Origins of Austrian Methodology

Continental European thought and philosophy has, since Descartes' time at least, accorded pride of place to human subjectivity, to man's self-consciousness and freedom and hence distinctness from any other object in nature. It is thus not surprising to find that the Austrian School, in which the adoption of a subjectivist-interpretive approach is a key methodological principle, is of continental European origins. Its founding father was Carl Menger, one of the early exponents of marginalist economics, who also devoted considerable attention to methodological issues.

Menger was in fact deeply involved in the *Methodenstreit* which occurred mainly in continental European economics in the last century. This *Methodenstreit* was the debate on methods between the German Historical School and the advocates of a systematic economic science such as Menger. The Historical School had held that in view of the fact that man is a self-conscious, freely choosing being:

(1) No systematic generalizing science of human action is possible since each human action is unique and must be understood on its own terms.
(2) Action can only be adequately explained in terms of the goal of the agent, that is teleologically, and never in an efficient-causal manner.

(3) Just as we can know the contents of our own conscious states (e.g. our intentions) in reflection so also we can by means of a 'sympathetic' or 'empathetic' intuition know *a priori* the content of other persons' conscious states. Human science thus becomes much more akin to 'hermeneutics', the interpretation and appreciation of literary texts rather than to the natural sciences; and *inter alia*, the interpretive theories of human science do not stand in any need of empirical testing.[1]

Menger developed his own methodological position in a dialectical interaction with the Historical School's position and the influence of the latter is felt not only in Menger but also in all of the later Austrians. For we shall find as we unfold the Austrian position that while it rejects the Historical School's view that no systematic generalizing science of human action is possible, it takes over both the assertion of a subjectivist-interpretive approach and the notion that the interpretive theories of human science are somehow true *a priori*.

Carl Menger was himself a professor at Vienna and such later leading lights of the Austrian approach as Ludwig von Mises and Friedrich von Hayek were students there – whence the label 'Austrian' for this school of thought. However, there have also been British, American and Italian members of this broad school: Lionel Robbins, Frank Knight, and more recently Israel Kirzner, Gerald O'Driscoll and Stefano Zamagni to name but a few leading examples. It would be beyond the scope of this work to engage in a detailed survey of the methodological precepts and practice of each of these leading Austrians and so I shall confine myself in this chapter to a synopsis of those points of Austrian methodology which are typical of all members of the school and which are relevant to this work. In outlining those typical points I have probably presented them in a manner more systematic than they are to be found in any one of the Austrians, but I have supported the presentation with ample quotations drawn in particular from Mises, Hayek and Robbins.

10.2   The Subjectivist Tenet of Austrian Methodology

There are just two typical tenets of Austrian methodology which are of relevance to this work, but these are probably also the two most pre-eminent tenets of that position. These are the subjectivist tenet and the *a priorist* tenet. I shall deal now with each of these in turn.

All of the Austrian economists have argued that in view of the fact that man is a self-conscious being, freely choosing his courses of action, the human sciences must adopt a subjectivist-interpretive methodology. Human action cannot be explained along the efficient causal lines of the natural sciences; any kind of stimulus-response behaviourist account of action portraying it as the effect of some antecedent independently identifiable stimulus as cause is ruled out. Rather, the Austrians argue, to explain human action we need to grasp or understand the intention or motive of the agent. Such explanation of action in terms of the agent's goals is teleological in character and so radically distinct from the efficient-causal mode of explanation of the natural sciences. Hence the Austrians have spoken of a 'dualism of methods' in contrast to the methodological monism championed by so many mainstream economists.

There are a variety of arguments in the various Austrians leading them to the imperative of a subjectivist-interpretive approach with its teleological mode of explanation for the human sciences. Mises, for example, in the long methodological introduction to his treatise on economics[2] argues that just as we cannot make any sense of the natural world in everyday life unless we make use of the categories of cause and effect, so also in our everyday understanding of human actions we understand them teleologically: that is to say, we render the action of others intelligible to us by asking what the motives and intentions of these actions are. There is a decidedly Kantian flavour to Mises' deduction of the subjectivist imperative here: he seems to be arguing that just as we cannot possibly make any sense of the natural world except by imposition of the category of efficient causality upon it, so also we cannot possibly achieve an understanding of the human world of interacting, communicating, purposive beings except by imposition of the category of teleology. As Mises says:

> There are only two principles available for a mental grasp of reality, namely, those of teleology and causality. What cannot be brought under either of these categories is absolutely hidden to the human mind . . . Daily experience proves not only that the sole suitable method for studying the conditions of our nonhuman environment is provided by the category of causality; it proves no less convincingly that our fellow men are acting beings as we ourselves are. For the comprehension of action there is but one scheme of interpretation and analysis available, namely that provided by the cognition and analysis of our own purposeful behaviour.[3]

Hayek adopts a somewhat different line of argument in defence of the subjectivist imperative in his work *The Counter-Revolution of Science*.[4] He is severely critical of what he calls the 'scientistic attitude', a viewpoint which quite dogmatically regards the natural sciences as the paradigm of all valid cognition (because of the practical successes of theoretical physics) and which has been a cornerstone of positivist thought. Having exposed the dogma that underlies scientism Hayek goes on to examine with an open mind the question of whether or not the human sciences can follow the methods of the natural sciences strictly. He argues that since the human sciences must inevitably deal with various entities such as actions, social institutions and even tools, they must of necessity make reference to various conscious states of human agents, in particular to the beliefs and intentions of agents. The motives and intentions of agents are thus essential to the explanations of a human science and these cannot be observed empirically nor can they be encapsulated in an efficient-causal mode of explanation of action: they require teleology. Hence Hayek concludes that there is a 'methodological dualism', a radical disjunction between the subjectivist-interpretive methods of explanation of the human sciences and those of the natural sciences.

Lord Robbins also puts forward a forthright argument for a dualism of method and a subjectivist-interpretive approach to the human sciences in his well-known essay.[5] That essay is most famous for the highly succinct and influential definition of economics as a science of choice in the face of scarcity which Robbins outlined there. Robbins also went on later in the essay to examine some of the methodological implications of this definition. He made a scathing attack on all kinds of behaviourist approaches to economics, arguing that the stimulus response type of explanation, being efficient-causal in character, was completely inappropriate to the explanation of freely chosen actions. Consequently, argued Robbins, economics requires a mode of explanation quite distinct from the efficient-causal mode of the natural sciences; and although he says very little to elaborate on this alternative mode it is quite clear that what he has in mind is a subjectivist-interpretive approach such as is advocated by other leading Austrians. Robbins' espousal of methodological dualism and implicitly of the subjectivist imperative may be seen from remarks such as the following: 'The argument that we should do nothing that is not done in the physical sciences is very seductive. But it is doubtful if it is really justified.'[6] And he goes on to say (p. 89):

> It follows then that if we are to do our job as economists . . . we must include psychological elements [i.e. subjective states such as intentions of agents which are unobservable]. It seems indeed as if investigating this central problem of one of the most fully developed parts of any of the social sciences we have hit upon one of the essential differences between the social and the physical sciences . . . It may be suggested that if this case is at all typical . . . then the procedure of the social sciences which deal with conduct which is in some sense purposive can never be completely assimilated to the procedure of the physical sciences.

It should be remarked that in addition to arguing for the imperative of a subjectivist-interpretive methodology in the human sciences each one of the Austrians has clearly recognized the subjectivist character of actual economic theory, in particular from the advent of marginalism onwards. Menger himself was a founding father of marginalism, while Mises emphasizes the teleological character of explanations in economics. Robbins equally regarded economic theory as subjectivist in character and Hayek remarks at the end of an exposition of the subjectivist-interpretive approach to methodology,[7]

> All this [subjectivist-interpretive approach to methodology] stands out most clearly in that among the social sciences whose theory has been most highly developed, economics. And it is probably no exaggeration to

say that every important advance in economic theory during the last hundred years was a further step in the consistent application of subjectivism.

10.3   *The* A Priorist *Tenet: Its Different Meanings*

The second leading tenet of Austrian methodology which we shall consider here is that for which it has become best known: *a priorism*. Although a pervasive theme in Austrian thought, the arguments which have been put forward in its defence are seriously confused, and indeed it is not even clear that all Austrians have meant the same thing when speaking of *a priorism*: for *a priorism* can seemingly mean anything from an assertion that there are serious difficulties involved in testing subjectivist theories empirically to the view that the theories of a human science are true *a priori* and hence in no need of any empirical tests. Consequently, in expounding the *a priorist* tenet of the Austrians I shall first of all present a distillation of what seem to be the main lines of argument for *a priorism* in the school as a whole, together with some criticisms: and I shall then go on to examine what a number of specific Austrian theorists have actually said on the topic.

There are three main lines of argument towards the *a priorist* methodological conclusion which may be detected in the various Austrian writings. The first holds that the theories of the human sciences are systematic deductions towards conclusions from a set of axioms or initial assumptions which are regarded as obvious or self-evident in some way. Since the axioms are taken thus to be true (on the basis of introspection or everyday experience, or whatever) and, in no need of any empirical test, it follows that the conclusions and predictions of a theory deduced from such premises will be true *a priori*, provided the deduction is logically valid. Sometimes this line of argument seems to be little more than a claim that the human sciences are deductive in character[8] while the natural sciences are inductive. This rests on a misconception of the methods of natural science which Popper has clearly exposed and in any case the argument is not sufficient to establish the *a priorist* tenet, unless in addition to the deductive character of theory the *a priori* truth of the premises is assumed. Consequently, this first line of argument for *a priorism* is incomplete unless supplemented by some sort of argument (such as the third line of argument noted below) for the *a priori* truth of the axioms or premises of a human science.

The second line of argument points to some serious difficulties in testing the theories of an interpretive human science and concludes that in view of these problems the theories of the human sciences must be taken to be true independently of any empirical tests. The alleged difficulties of testing cited by the Austrians are familiar: the impossibility of carrying out controlled experiments, the much lesser degree of precision in the predictions of the human sciences and the danger that falsifying empirical tests will be rejected by means of recourse to various *ad hoc* stratagems[9] which are particularly easy to find given the vagueness of the predictions. In the first place, none of these arguments show that empirical testing is completely impossible and indeed there are some well-established natural sciences in which controlled experiment is impossible (and replaced by controlled statistical observation), while all of the natural sciences are susceptible to '*ad-hoccery*' from time to time. There is no essential difference, therefore, between the natural sciences and sub-jectivist human sciences regarding the possibility of carrying out empirical tests. In any case even if empirical testing were difficult or impossible this would not be sufficient to establish that the theories of a human science are true *a priori*. Once again some argument to show that the human sciences can begin from axioms which are true *a priori* and in no need of empirical testing would also be required.

The third line of argument for *a priorism* provides just the underpinning which the first and second need in order to be conclusive. It is held that the insight achieved by a human science regarding the motives and intentions of agents are true *a priori* in virtue of *empathy*. Just as we can intuit with certainty the contents of our own conscious states in introspective reflection upon them so also we can, upon careful and sympathetic reflection, grasp the contents of the conscious states of other persons. Upholders of the notion of empathetic intuition point out that in our everyday lives we constantly impute motives and feelings by analogy with our own to other people and that without such empathetic understanding human interaction in general and communication in particular would be well nigh impossible.

The influence of the Historical School and especially of hermeneutics is clearly evident in these views; and indeed if correct they would constitute a conclusive case for *a priorism* in the human sciences. However, as with all versions of 'empathy' theories there remains the philosophical problem of 'other minds': we cannot intuit with certainty the contents of other persons' conscious states because we cannot be directly acquainted with them in the manner in which we can know our own conscious states directly in reflection. Empathy may be vitally important both in everyday life and in science as a source of conjecture about other people's motivations and feelings but to claim *a priori* certainty for those intuitions (in either science or everyday life) is impossible. Consequently, this third line of argument for Austrian *a priorism* – an argument which, as we saw, is vital to the support of the first two lines of argument is also found seriously wanting on philosophical grounds.

The conclusion which emerges from the above discussion is that the Austrian arguments to the effect that economic theory is true *a priori* and in no need of empirical testing fail completely to establish their case. We may wonder, however, whether or not there is anything at all to be said for the Austrian aversion to empirical testing and whether or not there may be some more 'moderate' version of *a priorism* which deserves our attention. I shall now suggest that there *is* such a moderate *a priorism* which can make a valuable contribution to economic methodology; and while there are hints of this in some of the Austrian writers most of them have argued in the end for an extreme *a priorism*.

The hint regarding a more 'moderate *a priorism*' is to be found in the passing concession by a number of Austrians, notably Hayek and Robbins, that empirical testing might have a minor role to play in economic methodology. The suggestion is made that empirical testing may be important in order to establish whether or not the initial conditions and assumptions of a theory are realized in a particular situation and hence whether or not the theory is *applicable* to that situation for policy or other purposes.

This fact leads on to a most significant reflection of which only the barest hints can be found among the Austrians. In view of the fact that human preferences and hence goals will always be evolving and changing through time, as also will the social and economic institutions founded upon them,[10] it follows that the theories of a subjectivist-interpretive human science will always be historico-relative, that is to say they will be true – or, rather, as I shall say, *applicable* – only for as long as people's goals and preferences remain the same. In a new era with different goals the old theories would be inapplicable. We *cannot* say, however, that in the era of new goals and institutions the old theories are somehow *false*: there is no reason why in a subsequent era in which the old goals and institutions were to recur or be revived for some reason or other the old theories should not come into their own again and be readily applicable to practical problems.

Thus from the hints which are contained in the Austrian discussion of empirical testing and its role in the human sciences we can reach a most interesting new conclusion. In view of the historico-relativity of any interpretive theory in human science an empirical test (whether of its assumptions or of its conclusions) can *never* show that theory to be definitely false, nor of course could it ever show the theory to be true (because of the problem of induction). Unlike in the natural sciences where empirical testing is taken to give some indication of the 'truth value' of a theory (whether it is true or false for all time),[11] in the human sciences empirical testing can *only* tell us whether or not a theory is applicable to some currently prevailing (or past) situation.

It follows therefore that empirical testing plays a much less significant role in the human sciences than it is supposed to play in the natural sciences. But because, according to this view, empirical testing still plays some role in the human sciences, it is somewhat of a misnomer to call the view 'moderate *a priorism*': no *a priori* truth is being claimed for theories in the human sciences. The view might better be labelled therefore as the '*applicability* thesis'. I should hasten to add that although I have developed this thesis from certain hints contained in the Austrian discussion of empirical testing, no such thesis has been expounded systematically by any of the Austrians. Indeed many Austrians have argued for the more extreme view that the theories of human science are true *a priori* and in *no* need of any empirical testing.

Above I have given a distillation of the various lines of argument in defence of an 'extreme *a priorism*' drawn from a range of Austrian writers. This is because the arguments for *a priorism* are in almost every single

Austrian writer put forward in a much less systematic and more jumbled manner than in the above presentation of the case. None the less it will be useful to take a quick look at what some leading Austrian writers have had to say on the topic of *a priorism* and this will reveal how firm is their commitment to an extreme *a priorism*, whatever may be their arguments for it.

Mises is perhaps the strongest proponent of all of extreme *a priorism*. In the first four chapters of his *Human Action* he puts forward a number of arguments in defence of *a priorism* and leaves us in no doubt that for him empirical testing has no place in the interpretive human sciences. He points to the difficulty of controlled experiments and to the important point that the so-called 'hard facts' which are to serve as tests of theories in human science are invariably impregnated already with other human science theories in the way they are presented and selected. He emphasizes the formal and deductive character of a human science contrasting it with history as a description of particular events and he goes on to assert that:

> The sciences of human action differ radically from the natural sciences. All authors eager to construct an epistemological system of the sciences of human action to the pattern of the natural sciences err lamentably . . . The real thing which is the subject matter of praxeology,[12] human action, stems from the same source as human reasoning . . . That reason has the power to make clear through pure ratiocination the essential features of action is a consequence of the fact that action is an offshoot of reason. The theorems attained by correct praxeological reasoning are not only perfectly certain and incontestable like correct mathematical theorems. They refer, moreover, with the full rigidity of their apodictic certainty and incontestability to the reality of action as it appears in life and history.[13]

Thus we see in Mises a variety of the typical Austrian arguments for *a priorism* reaching a very definitive assertion of the extreme *a priorist* position as conclusion.

Lord Robbins at least in his 1935 essay[14] has also been a firm advocate of an extreme *a priorism*. He puts forward the conception of economics as a purely deductive theoretical science which proceeds from certain basic axioms to reach conclusions which are true *a priori*. The truth of the conclusions is guaranteed by the truth of the axioms, and for Robbins those axioms are entirely obvious as a matter of everyday experience or at least can be seen to be obvious through the most cursory reflection on human motivation. Of these axioms Robbins says for example: 'We do not need controlled experiments to establish their validity: they are so much the stuff of our everyday experience that they have only to be stated to be recognized as obvious.'[15]

On the basis of such axioms we can develop theories whose conclusions will be true *a priori* (for if a deduction is valid, truth is transmitted from premises to conclusion) and Robbins states this quite clearly:

To recognize that economic laws are general in nature is not to deny the necessity of the realities they describe or to derogate from their value as a means of interpretation and prediction. On the contrary, having carefully delimited the nature and scope of such generalizations we may proceed with all the greater confidence to claim for them a complete necessity within this field.[16]

The forthright statements of an extreme *a priorist* position have been re-echoed by many present-day representatives of the Austrian School. Rothbard devoted a whole article[17] to the defence of the position while Kirzner has repeatedly cast the gravest of aspersions on the usefulness of empirical work as a test of economic theories. Kirzner for example says that:

Austrian economists are subjectivists; . . . they are deeply suspicious of attempts to apply measurement procedures to economics; they are sceptical of empirical proofs of economic theorems and consequently have serious reservations about the validity and importance of a good deal of the empirical work being carried on in the economics profession today.[18]

Hayek, one of the most famous exponents of the Austrian approach, is somewhat more difficult to pin down on the question of *a priorism*. On the one hand, there are a number of indications that he subscribes to the extreme *a priorist* view. He thoroughly approves of Mises' methodology of the human sciences,[19] and he draws comparisons between the theory of evolution which he argues must be treated as true *a priori* in effect by biologists, and economic theory.[20] Like other Austrians, he emphasizes the value of human self-consciousness as a source of *a priori* intuitions regarding motivation of agents for an interpretive human science. He says. 'The physicist who wishes to understand the problems of the social sciences would have to imagine a world where he knew by direct observations the inside of the atom.'[21]

On the other hand, there are also indications that Hayek does not want to banish empirical testing altogether and that what he has in mind is a much more moderate *a priorism* which amounts in effect to the applicability thesis. He seems to suggest on occasions that the empathetic intuitions made possible by human self-consciousness are only of heuristic value and that the interpretive theories of a human science can be subjected usefully to empirical tests:

they [generalized theories of an interpretive human science] scarcely ever enable one to predict the precise outcome of a particular situation; and one could never verify them by controlled experiment although they might be disproved by the observation of events which according to one's theory are impossible.[22]

Moreover, Hayek seems to recognize that such empirical tests cannot establish the truth or falsity of an intepretive theory but rather can tell us whether or not a theory is applicable to a certain practical situation. He says:

> the important question usually is not whether the hypotheses or laws used for the explanation of the phenomena are true but whether we have selected the appropriate hypotheses from our store of accepted statements [*a priori* theories] and have combined them in the right manner . . . The problem will not be whether the model as such is true but whether it is applicable to [or true of] the phenomena it is meant to explain.[23]

Given this wide variety of remarks it is difficult to know just what version of *a priorism* Hayek ultimately wants to advocate; the extreme version or some kind of more moderate 'applicability thesis'. Suffice it to say here that like all of the Austrians he too incorporates some sort of *a priorism* as a key tenet of his methodology and regards this tenet as an important point of contrast between the human sciences and the theoretical natural sciences.

Finally, I wish to mention the very recent work by O'Driscoll and Rizzo[24] as an example of Austrians who shy away from a more extreme *a priorism* and seem to espouse some version of the applicaibility thesis. On the question of empirical testing they say: 'We try to steer a middle course between pure *a priorism* and pure instrumentalism.'[25] Since instrumentalism is a position which makes of empirical tests the *sole* criterion for adjudicating among scientific theories, while pure *a priorism* rules out any role whatever for empirical testing, then presumably the middle course which O'Driscoll and Rizzo wish to steer on the question of empirical testing will be some version of the applicability thesis as briefly sketched out by Hayek. As with Hayek and others, however, O'Driscoll and Rizzo do not spell out precisely what they mean by this 'middle course' on testing and one is left simply with hints and suggestions such as the above quotation.

10.4   Austrian Methodology of Economics: A Summary

From the point of view of this work there will be no need to take our discussion of the Austrian School any further for I have by now isolated and expounded at some length the two principles or tenets of the Austrian position which are most relevant to the debate between the subjectivist and objectivist approaches to the methodology of the human sciences.

We have seen in the first place that all of the Austrians subscribe to a subjectivist-interpretive approach to the human sciences with a teleological mode of explanation and see this as radically different from the efficient causal mode of explanation of the natural sciences. Since we have seen in Chapters 5 and 6 that such a methodology is epitomized by mainstream economic theory it follows that the Austrians have in this respect had a much more accurate conception of the methods actually employed by economists in their theorizing than the bulk of mainstream economists, whom we saw in Chapter 9 have advocated a 'superficial methodological monism' which is completely at variance with their practice. In Part 3 I shall be going on to argue that not only is the subjectivist-interpretive approach epitomized by economic theory, but that it is also the only philosophically defensible approach to the human sciences.

The second leading tenet of the Austrian position which is of relevance is the *a priorist* tenet. For a variety of reasons, most Austrians have argued that the theories of a subjectivist-interpretive human science cannot or do not need to be submitted to empirical tests and may be taken, therefore, to be true *a priori*. I have already shown that there are some serious shortcomings in each of the arguments for extreme *a priorism* and in Part 3 a fuller philosophical discussion of the appropriate role of empirical testing in a subjectivist-interpretive human science will be presented.[26] I shall show that the Weber–Schutz version of an interpretive methodology, such as I have briefly outlined in Chapter 4, recognizes the philosophical 'problem of other minds' and reaches the conclusion that interpretive theories must therefore be submitted to empirical tests even if those tests can only establish applicability rather than truth value.[27] For now, however, I only wish to draw attention to the important fact that even as a description of what economists actually do *a priorism* is not plausible. For while it may be true that economists have been somewhat lax in the matter of empirical testing as we shall see in the next chapter, they have not in general treated their theories as true *a priori* and have been prepared to submit them to empirical testing.

Thus we may conclude that while the Austrian School marks an important advance over the rest of mainstream economists in so far as it has correctly grasped the subjectivist-interpretive character which economic theory embodies (and ought to embody), most Austrians have at the same time advocated an extreme *a priorism* which is both philosophically challengeable and is not even an accurate description of the general practice of economists.

The only qualification which one might want to make to this conclusion is to recognize that there has been one small sub-group within the Austrian School which seems to shy back from an extreme *a priorism* to argue that empirical testing has a minor role to play in economics in establishing whether or not a theory is applicable to a particular situation in the actual world. This is the view of empirical testing which I have labelled above as the 'applicability thesis'. Such a view is not expounded systematically by any Austrian economists and there are at most only hints of it within the school. Even in the case of Hayek, who comes nearest to espousing such a view clearly, we have seen that it is very difficult to pin down what precisely is his position on *a priorism*.

In devoting a full chapter to the Austrian School, I have given an amount of attention to Austrian methodology which is quite disproportionate to the influence which it has had on the methodological precepts of most mainstream economists. My main reason for doing this has been to differentiate the typical Austrian position from the Weber–Schutz version of a subjectivist-interpretive methodology which I have sought to defend in this work, both philosophically and as an accurate description of what economists actually do. For while the Austrian and the Weber–Schutz approaches agree wholeheartedly on the imperative of adopting a subjectivist-interpretive approach with a teleological mode of explanation in human science and see economics as the epitome of such a science, they diverge sharply on the question of empirical testing of interpretive theories in human science, at least in the case of that majority of the Austrian School who have espoused an extreme *a priorism*. It is only in the case of that small exceptional sub-group within the school who have been groping rather confusedly towards the applicability thesis that there could be said to be a convergence between the views of certain Austrians and the Weber–Schutz version of a subjectivist-interpretive methodology on the question of empirical testing. Finally it may be remarked that there is in any case a sharp contrast in the modes of philosophical deduction of and hence arrival at subjectivist conclusions as between Austrian and Schutzian versions of the subjectivist-interpretive methodology. (It may be recalled from Chapter 1 that the critical foundations of any methodology can only be laid by philosophy, hence this contrast is significant.) The Austrians have argued their case mainly on the basis of an examination of the concept of action and modes of explanation of action such as we commonly use in everyday life. By contrast I shall be following Schutz in Part 3 of this book by attempting to deduce the imperative of a subjectivist-interpretive methodology from a basis in existentialist phenomenology.

Notes

1 For a further discussion of the hermeneutical and Historical School's positions, see Chapter 4, p. 61 and Chapter 9, p. 136.

2 L. von Mises, (1949), *Human Action* (London: Hodge).

3 L. von Mises, *Human Action*, p. 25.

4 F. Hayek, F. (1955), *The Counter Revolution of Science* (Glencoe: The Free Press), ch. 3, *passim*.

5 L. Robbins, (1935), *An Essay on the Nature and Significance of Economic Science* (London: Macmillan).

6 L. Robbins, *An Essay on the Nature and Significance of Economic Science*, pp. 87, 89.

7 F. Hayek, *The Counter Revolution of Science*, p. 31.

8 Popper's methodology of conjecture and refutation conceives of science as a process of attempted theoretical insight (hypothesis), the deduction of predictions from this and the empirical test of predictions, in short, the hypothetico-deductive model of scientific explanation (cf. Chapter 3, pp. 42–45).

9 For a discussion of '*ad-hoccery*', cf. Chapter 3, pp. 47–48.

10 The Austrians view social institutions as the resultant of purposive human actions: as the intended and sometimes unintended consequences of myriad human actions.

11 Recall that natural science theories aim at strict universality in space and time

(cf. Chapter 3). On the whole question of the role of generalizations in scientific explanation, see Chapter 3, pp. 42, 43, 47, 48.

12 That is, the sciences of human action, in Mises' jargon.
13 Mises, L. von, *Human Action*, p. 39.
14 L. Robbins, *An Essay on the Nature and Significance of Economic Science.*
15 L. Robbins, *An Essay on the Nature and Significance of Economic Science,* p. 79.
16 L. Robbins, *An Essay on the Nature and Significance of Economic Science,* p. 121.
17 M. Rothbard (1957), 'In defence of extreme *a priorism*', *Southern Economics Journal*, vol. 23, pp. 314–20.
18 I. Kirzner (1976), 'On the method of Austrian economics', in E. Dolan (ed.), *The Foundations of Modern Austrian Economics* (Kansas City: Sheed & Ward).
19 In which we saw the strongest version of extreme *a priorism* occurs.
20 F. Hayek (1967), *Studies in Philosophy, Politics and Economics* (London: Routledge & Kegan Paul), pp. 11–13. See especially s. VI of the first essay.
21 F. Hayek, *The Counter-Revolution in Science*, p. 41.
22 F. Hayek, *The Counter-Revolution in Science*, p. 42.
23 F. Hayek, *Studies in Philosophy, Politics and Economics*, p. 7.
24 G. O'Driscoll, and M. Rizzo, (1985), *The Economics of Time and Ignorance* (Oxford: Basil Blackwell).
25 G. O'Driscoll and M. Rizzo, *The Economics of Time and Ignorance*, p. 5.
26 Cf. Chapter 14, pp. 211–13.
27 Cf. my discussion of the 'applicability thesis' (p. 157).

11

The Twofold
Methodological Gap

The burden of the foregoing chapters has been that there is a serious inconsistency between economists' methodological precept of a superficial methodological monism and their practice of a subjectivist-interpretive methodology with a teleological mode of explanation. Some recent methodological work in economics has also made the suggestion that there are wide gaps between precepts and practice, but this work has not been concerned with the above-mentioned inconsistency which I have been discussing. Rather it has identified a quite different methodological gap between economists' precept and practice in the matter of empirical testing. In this chapter I shall review this second sort of inconsistency and argue that there is indeed a twofold gap between economists' methodological precepts and their practice; and I shall indicate how I would argue that these gaps should be closed.

11.1 Economists' Precepts and Practice
in the Matter of Empirical Testing:
A Second Gap

Economics, unlike many of the other social sciences, has not been much troubled by methodological debates or doubts in the course of its development. Such debate as there has been has largely been concentrated at the periphery of the science, being concerned with the challenge to the whole mainstream approach offered by various radical schools of protest such as the Historical School, the Marxists or the institutionalists. In the case of the Marxists the debate has, moreover, been as much about fundamental issues in political philosophy as about economic methodology.

Although the bulk of such methodological debate as there has been has been concentrated in these heated controversies with peripheral schools of dissent, mainstream economists have occasionally engaged in brief bursts of critical appraisal of their own methodology. Examples of this are John Neville Keynes' work in the last century, and the debate over the need for 'realism' in economic theories that was sparked off by Friedman's article in the 1950s.[1] The past ten years have witnessed another such burst of methodological 're-tooling' in which mainstream economists have turned to carry out a serious reappraisal of the way in which they practise their science.

To date all of this discussion of methodological matters by mainstream economists has been carried out within the presumption that there is a strict unity of method among the natural and human sciences. Mainstream theory has been defended against radical dissent by arguing that the mainstream approach alone follows the methods of natural science. Furthermore, when internal methodological reappraisals have occurred they have been fairly obvious shadows, imitations, or epicycles of certain wider debates in the contemporary philosophy of natural science. The Friedman–Samuelson debate over the F-twist was a reflection of the wider controversy over instrumentalist and other conceptions of the nature of scientific theory and the recent reappraisal has been no exception. It is a clear epicycle of the general warfare in the philosophy of natural science among Kuhnians, Lakatosians and Popperians and has been sparked off in particular by suggestions from Lakatos that some advances in the overall war might be achieved by a campaign in the boggy terrain of the human sciences.[2]

The central theme of this recent warfare in the philosophy of natural science has been the logic and epistemology of empirical testing of scientific theories. This has sparked off an interest in the question of the degree to which various human sciences submit their theories to serious empirical tests. In the case of economics there can be no doubt that as part of their overall methodological monist position, mainstream economists have preached that economic theories should be carefully tested empirically, just as theories of natural science are tested by experiment or controlled observation.[3] But what of their *practice*? The upshot of the recent methodological reappraisal in economics has been to show that economists have actually been extremely lax in the matter of seriously testing their theories and have thus fallen far short of their precepts in this matter. A number of contributors to the Latsis volume[4] have commented on this while in his recent work on methodology[5] Mark Blaug has gone to some length to show how wide is the gap between precept and practice in the matter of empirical testing. As Benjamin Ward has also commented: 'The desire systematically to confront the theory with the fact has not been a notable feature of the discipline.'[6]

In the course of his book Mark Blaug has identified a number of manifestations of economists' failure to live up to their precept of empirical testing. In the first place, he points out that economists have always preferred abstruse debates over the finer logical points of pure theory to any kind of empirical work designed to test pure theory. He notes also that the research field which holds highest prestige in the profession is probably that of the refinement of pure general equilibrium theory, an area which, though important, is the most abstract and the furthest removed from any kind of empirical work or testing.[7]

Secondly, Blaug points out that although economists have been prepared to submit their theories to empirical test on occasions, they have rarely taken such testing seriously. In some cases empirical testing has consisted simply of the most casual appeals to supposed everyday observations. More often, however, when an attempt has been made to collect proper empirical evidence, economists have sought to use the evidence in order to confirm their theories at any cost. To guarantee this they have been prepared to use a variety of stratagems; a narrowly selective approach to evidence has been taken with economists paying attention only to those data which confirm their theory while ignoring inconvenient evidence. Furthermore economists have been prepared to resort to all manner of *ad hoc* stratagems in order to defend their theories against possible falsification and to saying that the data are defective, initial conditions unfulfilled or importing some kind of purely *ad hoc* auxiliary hypothesis into the theory. This sort of attitude to empirical testing is perhaps best illustrated by the contortions through which economists have been prepared to go in order to defend the Hecksher–Ohlin theory of international trade flows and Samuelson's corollary theorem of factor price equalization against clear-cut falsifying evidence.[8] It should be clear that whether or not one is a Popperian to adopt this sort of attitude is in effect to fight altogether shy of seriously testing theories: it is to regard empirical data as relevant or useful only in so far as it happens to back up one's theory, otherwise to be ignored. Empirical evidence is not to be admitted to be a potential falsifier of economic theories.

The charge that economists have been lax in the matter of empirical work might perhaps be challenged by pointing to the vast amount of econometric work which has been carried out in the past twenty years. Blaug argues that unfortunately this work has not provided any kind of serious testing of economic theories and this for two reasons: first, as already noted because so much empirical work, with its blatant 'confirmationist' bias, has amounted merely to incidental theoretical-prejudice corroboration rather than to serious testing. In econometrics, this manifests itself in the incredibly selective approach to data whereby those data which will give the best fit for a regression equation are taken automatically as the most appropriate evidence in testing; in the readiness of econometricians to blame inadequacy of data for poorness of fit of regressions; and above all in the fact that when a single econometric confirmation of a theory is achieved that this somehow stands for all time and does not stand in need of repeated checking (as the natural sciences continually replicate their experiments.)[9]

Much more important has been the fact that a great deal of econometric work proceeds entirely independently of economic theory and so offers *no test at all* of any theory. Blaug argues that even a cursory survey of the journals will reveal how much econometric work, far from setting out to provide a test of some piece of mainstream economic theory, involves simply the presentation of some supposed empirical correlation which has been 'discovered' in the course of empirical work and for which some purely *ad hoc* theoretical rationalization may be offered at the end of the article, as an afterthought (if one is lucky). This afterthought usually bears little or no relation to the main corpus of economic theory and so any semblance of such work providing a serious test of mainstream theory disappears. Of such work Blaug remarks that 'it is like playing tennis with the net down'.[10]

It is worth remarking that the development of econometrics along lines that often bear no relation at all to mainstream theory may be readily explained as the influence of Friedman's methodology with its explicit espousal of an instrumentalist position. Beginning usually from a reflection on the fact that to any finite set of empirical data an infinite number of hypotheses, all of which could predict the data set, could be fitted instrumentalism holds that all theories are only fictions, and that therefore in choosing a theory to explain some set of facts we should choose that fiction (theory) which can predict the data and which is aesthetically the most pleasing or simple. It is clear, therefore, that for the instrumentalist what is of paramount importance in science is to achieve wide-ranging correlations among empirical data and that the construction of theories is demoted to the secondary role of constructing aesthetically pleasing fictions which can serve to 'codify the facts', or to rationalize the correlations which have been presented. It will be readily obvious that this kind of methodological position which was explicitly adopted by Friedman has had a direct influence on those large areas of modern econometric work which have been developed entirely independently of established mainstream theory and which proceed by presenting all manner of correlation among empirical data while giving these only the barest of theoretical rationalization as an afterthought – usually an afterthought which is entirely *ad hoc* and which bears little or no relation to established theories, let alone providing an empirical test of any such theory. Blaug has commented that this sort of econometrics 'quickly degenerates into a sort of mindless instrumentalism and it is not too much to say that the bulk of empirical work in modern economics is guilty to that score'.[11]

Not only does this type of econometric work devoid of a theoretical basis fail to test any economic theory (properly so-called); in the light of the arguments which I have put forward in Chapters 2 and 3, it also involves an instrumentalist view of the nature of scientific theory which I have shown to be untenable because it deprives theory of any explanatory role. Elsewhere I have even suggested that such econometric work proceeding under the banner of instrumentalism to correlate anything with anything in complete isolation from the insights offered by explanatory theories amounts to little more than 'economic astrology'.[12]

We may reach an important conclusion from our review of the recent round of methodological debate among mainstream economists: it has revealed a definite gap between economists' precepts and practice in the matter of empirical testing. Blaug and others have identified this gap within the presupposition of a superficial methodological monism. That is to say that while economists as part of their injunction to human scientists to follow closely the methods of natural sciences have held that economic theories should be submitted to careful empirical testing (just as the theories of natural science) they have in practice been extremely lax in this matter, fighting shy of any kind of serious empirical testing.

It is to be remarked that exactly the same gap between precept and practice would be identified by a Weber–Schutz version of the subjectivist–interpretive methodology since in that version empirical testing of interpretive theories plays an important role. Hence if economists were to adopt, as I will urge, a Weber–Schutz type of interpretive methodology (which would square much better with the character of mainstream theory based on the optimization principle), the failure to engage in serious empirical testing would *still* involve a clear inconsistency between methodological precepts and practice.

Thus although Blaug and others have reached the conclusion that there is a gap between precept and practice in empirical testing from the standpoint of a superficial methodological monism (which I have held to be wholly inadequate methodology for economics), since the same conclusion would be reached from the Weber–Schutz standpoint, which I shall advocate in Part 3 should replace monism, we may assert definitively and unambiguously that there is a serious inconsistency between what economists preach and what they practice in the matter of serious empirical testing.

11.2   Two Inconsistencies of Precept and Practice and How They Should be Overcome

The inconsistency between methodological precepts and practice which has just been discussed is clearly quite distinct from the inconsistency between a superficial methodological monist precept and a subjectivist interpretive practice which I have identified in the course of Chapters 5 to 9 of this work. Hence it transpires that economic methodology is characterized by a *twofold methodological gap* between precepts and practice. At the risk of some repetition but for purposes of clarity I shall now restate precisely wherein this twofold gap consists and shall indicate how the inconsistencies involved should be overcome.

There is, in the first place, a serious gap between the methodological precepts of economists regarding empirical testing and their practice. Most economists espouse a superficial methodological monism urging human scientists to follow closely the methods of natural science. Since empirical testing of theories is a central feature of all natural sciences economists have urged that despite such minor problems as the absence of controlled experiment in human science, economic theories should be submitted to careful empirical tests. At the same time, we found that in practice economists fight extremely shy of actually testing their theories: where possible they simply avoid testing or where some tests have been made they have not been taken at all seriously since they seek confirmation at all costs. Morever, a large proportion of econometric work being devoid of any theoretical underpinning cannot serve to test any theory.

While Blaug and others have identified this gap from the standpoint of a methodological monism I have shown that the same inconsistency would also arise within a Weber–Schutz version of the subjectivist-interpretive methodology in which the precept of empirical testing also occurs. Hence from the critical standpoint of a Weber–Schutz methodology such as I defend in this work we may say that this methodological gap on the score of empirical testing in economics ought to be closed off by bringing *practice* into line with *precepts*. Economists ought to take the imperative of empirical testing of their theories more seriously.

In the course of Chapters 8 and 9 we saw that the bulk of mainstream economists have in their brief discussion of methodology espoused a position of 'superficial methodological monism'. This position holds that the only problems posed by man's subjectivity (self-consciousness and freedom to choose) for the methods of human science are minor ones of degree (such as the need to adopt controlled observation rather than controlled laboratory experiment) and hence that the human sciences should follow closely the methods of natural science and in particular that they should adopt the efficient-causal mode of explanation of the natural sciences. At the same time we found in Chapters 5 and 6 that mainstream economic theory is the shining exemplification of a Weber–Schutz type of subjectivist-interpretive methodology[13] of human science with its teleological mode of explanation, a methodology which is radically distinct from that of the natural sciences with their efficient-causal mode of explanation.

It follows that there is a second clear-cut methodological gap in economics quite distinct from that we identified on the score of empirical testing. Since this second gap involves a complete misunderstanding of the nature of their own theorizing on the part of economists it is from a philosophical viewpoint considerably more serious than the first gap. Once again, from the critical standpoint of the Weber–Schutz version of a subjectivist-interpretive methodology which I adopt and seek to defend in this work, we may say that this second methodological gap ought to be closed off by bringing *precept* into line with *practice*. Economists ought to adopt a subjectivist-interpretive methodological precept.

In making the above suggestions as to how the two methodological gaps between precept and practice should be overcome I have explicitly invoked as my critical instrument of methodological appraisal the Weber–Schutz version of a subjectivist-interpretive methodology. This immediately raises the question of what grounds I have for advocating a Weber–Schutz methodology as the appropriate approach to the human sciences and hence for using that methodology as the basis for a critical appraisal of the actual practices of the human sciences.

Since we have seen in Chapter 1 how any such critical methodology of science must be grounded in philosophy we are thus led, at the end of this long case study of economic methodology in Part 2, to resume the purely philosophical argument which was left off at the end of Part 1. I hasten to emphasize once again that this long case study of economics was *illustrative* in character. By itself it could not possibly provide any kind of conclusive grounds for the subjectivist-interpretive approach to the human sciences and I introduced it only to bring the abstract methodological discussions of Parts 1 and 3 to life by showing how in the practice of a mature human science the subjectivist-interpretive approach with its teleological mode of explanation is clearly seen successfully at work.

Hence, since the main aim of this book is conceived as an attempt to provide a conclusive defence of the Weber–Schutz version of a subjectivist-interpretive methodology and thereby to make a contribution to certain current debates in the methodology of human science, I shall in Part 3 return to the plane of pure philosophy in order to complete the main tasks of the work. In addition to adducing what I take to be the conclusive philosophical grounds in defence of a Weber–Schutz version of the subjectivist-interpretive approach with its teleological mode of explanation, I shall also in virtue of having so grounded the Weber–Schutz methodological position, have shown why the two methodological gaps which I have identified in this chapter must or ought to be closed off in the precise manner which I have suggested above.

Notes

1   M. Friedman, 'The methodology of positive economics' in *Essays in Positive Economics* (Chicago: University of Chicago Press). Cf. also Section 9.4 of this book for a brief indication of what the debate was about.

2   S. Latsis, (ed.), *Method and Appraisal in Economics* (Cambridge: Cambridge University Press) which sparked off much of the recent reappraisal was the result of a conference on economic methodology which had been suggested by Lakatos (cf. Latsis' introductory preface).

3   In Chapter 8 I showed how economists have insisted on empirical testing as part of their superficial methodological monist position and how such problems as the absence of controlled experiment are held not to render empirical testing impossible in economics (cf. pp. 125–26).

4   S. Latsis (ed.), *Method and Appraisal in Economics* (Cambridge: Cambridge University Press).

5   M. Blaug (1980), *Methodology of Economics* (Cambridge: Cambridge University Press).

6   B. Ward (1972), *What's Wrong with Economics?* (London: Macmillan). See p. 173.

7   Cf. M. Blaug, *Methodology of Economics*, ch. 8 and ch. 15, p. 256.

8   Discussed by N. de Marchi in 'Anomaly and the development of economics: the case of the Leontief paradox' in S. Latsis (ed.), *Method and Appraisal in Economics*, and also in M. Blaug, *Methodology of Economics*, ch. 11, especially pp. 211–12.

9   Cf. M. Blaug, *Methodology of Economics*, p. 261, where he quotes Mayer with approval on this last point.

10   M. Blaug, *Methodology of Economics*, p. 256.

11   M. Blaug, *Methodology of Economics*, p. 257.

12   P. J. O'Sullivan (1984), 'Friedman's methodology revisited' in *Explorations in Knowledge*, vol. 1, no. 2, pp. 32–49.

13   Mainstream theory epitomizes a Weber–Schutz rather than an Austrian *a priori* version of the subjectivist-interpretive approach because, although lax in the matter of empirical testing, economists have in practice been prepared to do at least *some* testing.

PART 3

The Philosophical Deduction

Introduction to Part 3

The ultimate aim of this work is to provide a defence of the subjectivist-interpretive approach to the methodology of the human sciences against the objectivist-behavourist approach. Part 2 consisted of an exhaustive case study of a leading rigorous human science – economics – and reached the conclusion that despite what economists themselves have often said, economics is a shining exemplification of the subjectivist-interpretive methodology in practice. To have shown this is *not*, however, to have provided any conclusive rational defence of the subjectivist-interpretive approach; it is only to have suggested that the approach can definitely be turned into practice in the human sciences and is not merely an abstract possibility.

In Chapter 1 I showed at some length that a conclusive rational foundation for the methodology of any science can only be provided on the plane of philosophy. For a genuinely rational critique of the procedures of a science raises questions concerning the conditions for the possibility of valid knowledge and of the nature of the objects under study in any field: it raises, that is to say, questions of an epistemological and of a metaphysical character that can only be adequately answered by philosophy. I also showed in Chapter 1 that in order to be able to carry out this role of providing a critical-rational foundation for the methodology of the sciences philosophy itself must ultimately be based on a set of reflexively self-justifying propositions which cannot possibly be doubted and which thereby cut off the need for any further rational probing as to their validity or foundation.

Consequently in Part 3 I shall be returning to the plane of pure philosophy in order to carry out a twofold task. First, I propose to indicate briefly how philosophy can in my view attain a core of absolutely true propositions which may serve as the critical foundation of all human cognitions. I shall suggest that the method of phenomenology provides the key to discovering the absolutely certain propositions which we seek. Since this is not a work on epistemology I shall not devote much attention to this theme here.

Secondly, I propose to show how the subjectivist-interpretive methodology can be deduced from and thus given a critical-rational foundation in pure philosophy. I have already given a very brief indication of the philosophical linkages of the subjectivist-interpretive methodology in Chapter 4, showing that it has been deduced both from existentialist phenomenology and from the very different philosophy of linguistic analysis. Since I believe that only in phenomenology is the basis of absolute certainty which can provide the critical-rational ground of all human cognitions to be found I shall be focusing the bulk of my attention on the deduction of a subjectivist-interpretive methodology from existentialist phenomenology. Only a very brief indication of the parallel and less satisfactory deduction of the position by the linguistic analysts will be given.

12

The Existentialist Deduction of a Subjectivist Methodology

Returning now to the philosophical argument which was left off at the end of Chapter 4, my first task in this chapter must be to give some indication of how philosophy may be able to achieve the core of absolutely true propositions which are to serve as the foundation of all human cognition. I shall then go on to indicate how a subjectivist-interpretive methodology for human sciences may be deduced from such a philosophy.

12.1 The Phenomenological Method

In Chapter 1 of this book I argued at some length that if any science is to remain true to the spirit of rational critique and probing, the spirit of relentless quest for truth in dissipation of dogma and superstition which has been the mainspring of Western civilization, it must *inter alia* turn a critical eye on its own methods. But in order to carry out a critique of the methods of any specific science we must look to a discipline which lies beyond and transcends the sciences. For if any specific science is used as the basis of methodological critique of any of the sciences (including of itself) the critique will be involved in a vicious circularity and will therefore get nowhere. To base the critique of scientific method on science itself is only to adopt a dogmatic and hence uncritical attitude to the sciences.

In seeking to develop a rational methodological critique, therefore, we are led to raise questions which point beyond the sciences towards some discipline which transcends them. We are required to raise questions concerning the conditions for the possibility of valid knowledge and concerning the ultimate nature and knowability of the objects of science, questions which belong very clearly to the province of pure philosophy – of epistemology, logic and metaphysics. Yet at the same time in this turn to philosophy we must insure that philosophy itself will not be involved in the same kind of vicious circularity as the sciences if and when we turn to make a critical assessment of its methods.

For the turn to pure philosophy to provide a critical-rational ground for the methods of the sciences does not *per se* put an end to the possibility of further rational critique or probing: it does not *per se* absolve us of the need to submit the methods of philosophy itself to rational criticism. Since, however, there is no further discipline which lies beyond or transcends philosophy and which could therefore possibly provide a critical foundation in turn for the methods of philosophy we are led to impose on philosophy the following stiff condition: any philosophy worthy of the name must be capable of *providing its own ground*, that is to say, philosophy as the ultimate or final critical discipline must be capable of cutting off the need for further rational probing by endeavouring, in principle at least, to provide its own critical-rational foundation.

In Chapter 1 I showed how this formal requirement of providing its own ground could only be met by philosophy if it put forward propositions which in the moment of enunciating or reflecting upon them must be seen immediately to be true, that is to say propositions which are reflexively self-justifying. The very act of enunciating or of reflecting upon such propositions reveals or demonstrates their truth. When we have reached such a set of reflexively self-justifying propositions which provide their own grounds we shall be in the presence of a set of propositions which cannot possibly be doubted without becoming involved in a performative contradiction, and so we shall have achieved in effect a core of absolutely true propositions which can serve as the critical-rational foundation for all human cognition. We shall have developed the philosophical trunk of Descartes' tree of knowledge.

This conception of the task of philosophy arises directly from any attempt to evolve a rational critique of the methods of science and so it could be said to follow an essentially epistemological impulse or to involve an epistemologically inspired approach to philosophy. It conceives the first task of philosophy as the provision of a reflexively self-justifying critique of cognition. Such an approach to philosophy is epitomized, for example, by Descartes and Kant and even, I would suggest, by Plato and Hegel.[1] But its foremost exponent in recent philosophy has undoubtedly been Edmund Husserl.

Husserl conceived the task of philosophy very much along the lines which I have just outlined. He followed Descartes in recognizing that philosophy must seek to provide a core of utterly indubitable and hence absolutely true propositions which would serve as the critical-rational foundation of all human cognition, and so among other things of all of the sciences. Although he was the first to recognize the sad record of past philosophy with its speculative excesses in living up to this fundamental task, he repeatedly pointed out that philosophy cannot avoid or shirk the task. Thus against the anti-philosophy of positivism, which naively takes the natural sciences as the paradigm of valid human cognition and proposes to dispense with philosophy, Husserl points out that it is involved in a hopelessly uncritical attitude to science as well as being self-contradictory in any case. Against the even more radical anti-philosophy of epistemological relativism which holds that there are no absolute truths at all and thus no possibility of ever giving a conclusive rational justification of any human cognition, Husserl argues in his *Logical Investigations*[2] and elsewhere that such a position is either self-contradictory or else totally absurd and nihilistic (regarding the very possibility of rational discussion and argument). The arguments used by Husserl in disposing of the anti-philosophies of positivism and relativism are broadly similar to the lines of argument which I have already outlined against them in Chapters 2 and 3 of this work and so need not be repeated again here.

In order to carry out the first task of philosophy, the provision of a core of reflexively self-justifying and so absolutely true propositions, Husserl developed a rigorous new method for philosophy which he called the phenomenological method, or simply phenomenology. The inspiration for this new method came very clearly from Descartes since the very first principle of phenomenology is that we can attain the absolutely certain propositions which we are seeking only within the field of self-consciousness, that is in reflecting upon our own conscious states. For when we reflect on our own conscious states they are, *qua* conscious states absolutely given, absolutely transparent and so beyond doubt. Thus, for example, if in the course of thinking I reflect upon the fact that I am thinking, that fact is absolutely indubitable and so absolutely true. Similarly, if when laughing I reflect on the fact that I am laughing, or when watching a film I reflect on the fact that I am having a visual experience of some kind, I cannot possibly be mistaken. These facts are given to me with absolute certainty because if I tried to deny them I would be involved in a performative contradiction, that is a contradiction between the activity in which I am engaged and the proposition (a denial that I am engaged in the activity) which I assert.[3]

Descartes had been the first to exploit the field of self-consciousness in order to achieve a core of absolute truths for philosophy and he put forward the famous *cogito ergo sum*, the conclusive proof of his own existence as a thinking self from the undeniable fact of his activity of thinking. Husserl proposes to go a great deal further than Descartes in exploiting the field of consciousness present and transparent to itself in reflection. Following the lead of his teacher Brentano, who had emphasized that consciousness is always a relational or intentional activity, that is consciousness is always consciousness *of* something, Husserl proposed to examine in detail the objects for consciousness of various conscious acts. Where Descartes had produced the *cogito* Husserl proposes to examine the *cogitatum* or *phenomenon*.

In order to carry out this examination of the *cogitatum* – of the object – for consciousness Husserl proposes two steps.[4] The first is the *phenomenological reduction*. In the search for absolute certainty we have turned to the field of consciousness present and transparent to itself in reflection, to the field of self-consciousness or of the pure immanence of consciousness. Thus when we examine the 'object' of a conscious state in order to see what can be said about it with absolute certainty we must in the first place abjure any attempt to say anything about the object of a conscious state as a materially existing object. For both the features of the external object-in-itself, as well as the very fact of its material existence can always be called into question or doubted (in virtue of the unreliability of sense perception). All that is absolutely given is the fact that I am having a consciousness of something or other and the character or features of that conscious state *qua* conscious state. Thus, for example, when I have the visual experience of a sparkling long golden-hired maiden that is half a fish, I may be watching a movie, or I may be hallucinating or I may have discovered a real mermaid. All that we can lay down with certainty is *that* I am having a visual experience of a mermaid and the main features of that visual experience such as the vision of lustrous golden hair fluttering lazily in the sea breeze are undeniable. In other words we can say with certainty that I am having an 'experience of a mermaid' and can describe the mermaid as an object for consciousness. I can thus make an absolutely true statement about the phenomenon that I am experiencing but not about the material existence of its object.

Thus for Husserl the first step of the phenomenological method in its endeavour to examine what can be laid down with certainty about *cogitata* is what he calls the 'phenomenological reduction'. By this he means that we must suspend all judgements regarding the material existence of the object of a conscious state and any attempt to grasp the 'real' nature of such things in themselves.[5] We must, as he says, 'bracket' the existence of things and concentrate on the *pure phenomenon*, the object-for-consciousness or, to be more precise, the 'thing as it appears to consciousness'.

The second step of the phenomenological method is what Husserl calls the *eidetic reduction*.[6] In order to carry through our examination of the phenomenon as the absolutely given object of a conscious state we must achieve more than a mere description of the pure phenomenon. For Husserl, like Plato and other rationalists before him, recognized that all human cognition is cast at the universal level. We always think in terms, that is, of notions which are universal rather than particular, and nothing can ever be grasped in all its particularity. In other words, we think and know always by means of subsumption under the universal.[7] In examining the pure phenomenon, therefore, what we must aim at is not merely a description of it as a particular phenomenon, we must aim at an elucidation of the *form* or *essence* of the phenomenon.

It should be immediately remarked that Husserl is not here saying that we should seek to grasp the real essence of the thing-in-itself, or the materially (or otherwise externally) existing object. He is saying only that we are to elucidate the essence of the pure phenomenon. Moreover, Husserl follows an approach to consciousness and to thinking which had begun with Kant and had been continued through Brentano and which regarded all consciousness and thinking as essentially active in character. No cognition is for Husserl purely passive, rather consciousness is always active in the organization of pure phenomena, and in particular in subsuming them under various general notions. Hence the essence or form of the phenomenon is as Husserl puts it 'constituted by consciousness'. Put very simply, the way in which we organize the jumble of phenomena by ordering and subsuming them under general notions is the work of consciousness on its data, it is part of the creative activity of the mind. Human cognition is therefore always an 'activity'.

Given that the form or essence of phenomena is always constituted by each consciousness for itself there is no difficulty for Husserl in arguing that the essences of *phenomena* are absolutely given to consciousness and can be elucidated by a careful reflection on consciousness (once the first step, the phenomenological reduction, has been carried through). For to elucidate essence is only to elucidate the organizational activity of one's own consciousness in organizing phenomena under general notions, i.e. in constituting the essence of phenomena. But while the emphasis on the creative activity of the self, of the ego *cogitans*, in constituting essence allows Husserl to put forward the eidetic reduction as the second step of a philosophical method which will achieve absolute certainty (since each person can always elucidate his own conscious processes and hence constitutive activities in reflection), it poses another fundamental problem for the phenomenological method. For if each individual consciousness creatively constitutes essence how can we be sure that different people will constitute the essences of phenomena in the same way. If they do not then the absolute certainties achieved by the phenomenological method will be entirely personal or solipsistic and their philosophical value as absolute truths greatly diminished. There would also be a serious problem about inter-subjective communication of phenomenological insights.

It must be said that while Husserl recognized and grappled with this basic problem[8] he never resolved it at all adequately and it must remain the Achilles' heel of the phenomenological method. My own suspicion is that the problem can only be adequately resolved by the introduction of some idealistic notion of individual reason as a moment in the life of or as spokesperson of absolute Reason. But Husserl was determined to avoid any flirtation with such Hegelian notions and so the problem remains in effect unresolved in his work.[9]

As a matter of clarification, it should be remarked that a philosophy built up on Husserl's phenomenological method will not in any way conflict with or compete with the sciences. For the various sciences seek to grapple with various realms of the materially existing world, the world of real 'things-in-themselves', while philosophy in its quest for absolute certainty must, as we saw, bracket the material existence of things and suspend all judgements on the external world since these cannot be absolutely and indubitably grasped by consciousness; it must confine itself to the field of the activities of consciousness. Phenomenological philosophy and the sciences are thus concerned with two quite distinct fields and the only point of contact between them occurs when a rational critique of the methods of scientific inquiry, that is of the methods of cognition adopted by the scientific consciousness, is being carried out. I have already insisted repeatedly on the reasons why any such critique of scientific cognitions can only be carried out on the plane of a reflexively self-justifying philosophy.

12.2   Existentialist Phenomenology and the Analysis of Human Subjectivity

Since the first principle of Husserl's pure phenomenology is the turn to the field of self-consciousness in order to find a core of absolutely indubitable propositions it is clear that the notion of man as a *subject*, that is of man as a being who is aware of his own existence and freedom of choice, is central to Husserl's thought. But despite the centrality of subjectivity to his philosophy it can be said fairly that Husserl did not devote much time to exploring and elucidating in detail this notion of subjectivity. Nor did Husserl have much to say about the implications of man's self-consciousness and freedom for the methodology of human science.[10] Rather, Husserl devoted his life's work to the epistemological task of demonstrating the need for a philosophy which provides all human cognition with a foundation or springboard of absolute certainty and of providing a method whereby philosophy could hope to achieve this core of absolute truth. It was left to the school of Husserl's followers, known as 'existentialist phenomenologists' or simply as 'existentialists', to develop the themes of subjectivity and of its implications for the methods of human science in detail.

Existentialist phenomenology is a school of thought drawing a direct inspiration from Husserl which grew up in the period from 1930 to 1960. There is a definite continuity with Husserl since existentialism shares with him the view that the task of any rational philosophy is the quest for a core of absolute truths to serve as the foundation of all human cognition. Furthermore, existentialists turn to the field of self-consciousness and adopt indeed the method of phenomenology in order to achieve the certainty sought by philosophy.

Hence existentialist phenomenology must be seen as a change of focus or emphasis within the phenomenological programme for philosophy which had been laid down by Husserl. It is not a new school of thought that is opposed to Husserl. What all of the existentialists were perturbed about in Husserl's pure phenomenology was the bracketing of existence. While they accepted the reasons for this first step of the phenomenological method they feared that if the brackets were never to come off existence, phenomenology might achieve certainty but would at the same time be entirely irrelevant to the world of concrete material existence about which it could say nothing at all. Hence the basic goal of all existentialist phenomenologists is to see whether or not the method of phenomenology can ever get the brackets off existence and enunciate some absolute truths pertaining to the world of concrete material existence. In short they seek to develop a phenomenological philosophy that will be relevant to man's concrete existence, or a phenomenological philosophy of being or existence.

To achieve this goal the existentialist searches for a field where the phenomenological method, whose aim is to achieve absolutely certain and indubitable cognitions, can be applied but without any need to bracket existence. Drawing inspiration once again from Descartes the search does not take long: it is within the field of self-consciousness once again that we may discover some propositions pertaining to being or concrete existence which are absolutely true. Descartes himself had indeed presented the very first absolute truth of an existentialist phenomenology: the '*cogito ergo sum*', I think and therefore I am. For in the moment of reflecting upon the fact of my thinking I recognize as absolutely certain that I *actually exist*, for otherwise I could not possibly be thinking. As pointed out earlier, I cannot possibly deny my own existence without becoming involved in a contradiction between the proposition uttered ('I am not') and the very act of enunciating or even of thinking the proposition.

Drawing inspiration from this most fundamental proposition regarding existence enunciated by Descartes, existentialist phenomenology recognizes that when we turn the phenomenological method to focus on any conscious state or activity we do not have to bracket existence because the existence of that conscious state or activity is given absolutely to consciousness in reflection. Thus, for example, when I focus on my conscious activity of thinking, laughing, feeling sorrow or being excited, I am absolutely certain at least upon a careful reflection[11] that I am thinking or that I am laughing, that I am feeling sorrow or being excited (respectively). Hence when I reflect upon my conscious state or activities the actual existence of that conscious activity does not have to be bracketed. It is only the concrete existence of the *object* of my conscious state or act, but *not* the state or act itself whose existence may be doubted.

Husserl's pure phenomenology had concentrated exclusively on an elucidation of (the essences of) phenomena, of the intentional objects-for-consciousness and so existence had always to be bracketed. Existentialist phenomenology focuses instead upon the subject or self which has conscious experiences and on the conscious activities and experiences of the self; and neither the existence of the self nor of its conscious activities can be doubted since both are given absolutely to consciousness in reflection. Thus in the search for a field in which phenomenology can arrive at absolutely true propositions which are relevant to the world of concrete existence an important change of focus occurs. Where Husserl was concerned largely with phenomena, existentialist phenomenology gives pride of place to man, or more precisely to the self and to the elucidation in intimate detail of its conscious experiences. It is not surprising, therefore, that existentialist phenomenology should have spilled over into a broadly 'humanistic' type of philosophy.[12] Equally it is no accident that in the elucidation of man's conscious activities, existentialism should have turned to various art forms, but most notably to novels and dramas as a form of philosophical expression and comment. The works of Sartre, Camus, de Beauvoir and Marcel, for example, may be counted both as major literary and outstanding philosophical accomplishments.

Existentialist phenomenology thus proposes to examine and elucidate the nature or essence of various conscious states and activities without any need to take the brackets off the existence of those conscious activities since that is given absolutely to consciousness in reflection. Put another way, when we apply the phenomenological method to conscious states or activities we do not need to apply the first step of Husserl's method (the bracketing of existence) but may move immediately to the second step of the method, the eidetic reduction or intuition of essence. But this means that when we reflect carefully on our conscious states or activities (rather than on their objects) we shall be capable of elucidating the *real essence* or form of those conscious states. That is to say that in, for example, a careful phenomenological examination of what is involved when we laugh or choose or imagine we shall be able to elucidate the very essence of the act of laughing, the act of choosing or the act of imagining.

This is a powerful thesis which opens a most interesting field for existentialist phenomenology. For if in a careful reflection of our conscious activities we can elucidate *a priori* the real essence of those conscious acts, this will constitute a most valuable direct contribution from existentialist phenomenology to the human sciences. Sartre, for example, in his *Psychology of the Imagination*,[13] has shown how the first steps of any theory of the imagination in psychology may be laid by means of an existentialist phenomenological elucidation of the real essence of any act of imagination; and that real essence constitutes a foundation of absolute certainty upon which the psychology of imagination may build. Equally, in Chapter 5 (p. 87) I sought through an existentialist phenomenological examination of acts of deliberate choice to lay down with absolute certainty the real essence or form of all such acts. I suggested that any act of deliberate choice is aimed at optimization in the light of the information available to the agent. I went on to show how this formal 'optimization principle' provides the most fundamental building block of all mainstream economic theory.

To forestall any misunderstanding it should be emphasized that the potential direct contribution which an existentialist phenomenology can thus make to the human sciences is a very limited one. For what can be given with absolute certainty to consciousness in reflection is only the real essence, the *form* of a conscious activity which will be common to every individual instance thereof. There is no question of being able to know with certainty and *a priori* the detailed contents of each particular instance of a conscious activity, except of course in the case of the thinker's very own conscious activities. Thus, for example, when I laid down in Chapter 5 the formal optimization principle as the real essence of any act of deliberate choice, there and then the direct contribution of existentialist phenomenology to the economic theory of choice ended. Thereafter the purely formal optimization principle had to be fleshed out with refutable conjectures regarding the detailed goals or objectives which different human agents pursue in a variety of situations. Hence the *a priori* contribution of existentialist phenomenology to economics can be seen to be a useful but limited preliminary.[14]

The notion of human subjectivity is brought to centre stage and given the full spotlight of philosophical attention by existentialist phenomenology. I shall now examine the main features of subjectivity which have been elaborated by the existentialists and which are of direct relevance to the methodology of human science. Rather than going through the ideas of leading existentialist thinkers singly, I have presented a notion of man as subject which emerges as common ground among these thinkers relying most heavily on Satre and Schutz, and to a lesser extent on thinkers such as Camus and Merleau-Ponty.

The first principle or step of all phenomenology, existentialist or otherwise, is to turn to the sphere of self-consciousness, that is to say to the field of consciousness present and transparent to itself in reflection. The existentialists argue that in such moments of reflection on ourselves and our activities we can always come to know with certainty:

(1) *that* we are doing something,
(2) *what* we are doing,
(3) *why* we are doing it,
(4) *that* we are always *free to choose* otherwise than what we are doing at present.

All of this can be realized with absolute certainty by the agent if only he or she reflects carefully on his or her activities. What emerges, therefore, is the picture of man as a being who is capable of becoming aware of his own activities and who is indeed the freely choosing and hence responsible author or initiator of his various courses of action. In other words existentialist phenomenology leads us to a notion of man as *subject*, and to an emphatic rejection of the notion of man as a mere passive object, as another thing-in-nature. This is the point which Sartre is trying to drive home when he says with characteristic dramatic exaggeration that man is 'nothingness at the heart of being'. Man is nothing – he is not an object, but rather a self-conscious subject who initiates courses of action in the world. Man is the fulcrum of subjectivity which 'constitutes' the known world in which he lives.

Possibly the most important implications for the methodology of the human sciences are generated by the notion of freedom which is built into the existentialist conception of man as subject. It should be emphasized that upon a careful phenomenological reflection this freedom of choice is revealed to be all-pervasive and inescapable, and that it brings with it a heavy burden of responsibility. For no matter what course of action of our own that we reflect upon we cannot deny that we could always have chosen to do otherwise than we decided to do, even if it might have been extremely difficult to have decided to do otherwise. *In the moment of decision all antecedent determination of whatever kind is transcended and cancelled and we become the fully responsible authors or initiators of our own courses of action.*

Sartre in particular[15] has emphasized how radical this realization of freedom must be, at least if we are honest with ourselves, that is if we refrain from being 'in bad faith' with ourselves. He has insisted, for example, that even the refusal to make choices or decisions (rather like the dice man) is itself a choice – a choice of systematically refraining from choice. He has also pointed out that because of freedom we are left 'without excuse' for the courses of action we take, we bear the full burden of responsibility for them. Thus we may not have recourse to the argument that various of our past experiences, traumatic or otherwise, have somehow or other determined the course of our present actions. For however difficult it may sometimes be to blot out, that is to transcend and cancel, those past experiences and their influences upon us today, nevertheless it *is always possible* for us to make the effort to do so. Thus in the moment of deciding upon a course of action we inexorably become the author or initiator of the action: since we could have chosen otherwise, no matter how great the difficulty of doing so, we simply are not determined by past experiences.

I have dwelt on the radical character of human freedom as presented by Sartre in particular because it is of the utmost significance for the methodology of the human sciences as we shall see below. But I should hasten to add now that although the notion of freedom put forward by existentialist phenomenology is a radical one, it is *not* an absolute freedom. Man's freedom is not a freedom to do just anything at all which he pleases, as might God: it is rather a limited freedom.[16]

In a careful reflection by consciousness upon itself man becomes aware not only of the freedom of the act of decision or choice: equally inexorably he becomes aware of the *limitations* on that freedom. We become aware that far from being in a position to choose just anything at all we live in a world of other things and of other people. The brute presence of the material world constraining and limiting the scope of our choices is ever present, and has been dramatically expressed by Sartre in his novel *La Nausée*, for example.[17] Merleau-Ponty and Schutz for their part have emphasized the inescapably inter-subjective character of a wide range of our experiences. Thus, for example, in any genuinely interpersonal relationship where we come to know the other person intimately, we cannot possibly deny the existence of the other person without becoming involved in a performative contradiction. We cannot, for example, love or have intimate sexual relations with a mere figment of our imagination. In love or sexual relations the presence of another subject, that is of an independent self-conscious being who initiates his or her own courses of action, is absolutely and undeniably given to our consciousness. We experience that other person precisely as the limit of our own freedom of action, as an independent fulcrum of subjectivity which is not subject totally to our own will and which cannot therefore be purely a creature of our own imagination.

These limitations upon our freedom of choice and action which are given absolutely to consciousness in reflection also allow existentialist phenomenology to make further progress in removing some of the brackets upon existence which Husserl's pure phenomenology had left untouched. For now we recognize that we cannot, without becoming involved in the performative contradiction (of asserting an absolute god-like freedom of action which cannot possibly square with our experience of the limitations on our choices) deny the actual existence of an external material world, nor can we deny the actual existence of other subjects, of other persons. It should be clear, however, that since the existence of other things is given to consciousness precisely by the experience of limitation that all we can establish in phenomenological reflection is the *brute presence* of other things-in-themselves, and persons – sheer otherness. When we say that the existence of other things-in-themselves and persons is given absolutely to our own consciousness we are *not* claiming that we may then proceed to elucidate the real essence of those other things and persons by means of the usual 'eidetic' reduction. All we are saying is that our own consciousness and specifically our own freedom of action is exorably *bounded*; and what lies beyond that boundary or limit we cannot either know in essence by means of phenomenological reflection nor can we subjugate it to the absolute control of our wills. One is reminded again of Sartre's hero, Roquentin, in *La Nausée*, when he sits gazing at the trunk of a tree in a park realizing its brute otherness, inscrutability, and absurdity.

Having emphazised that human freedom is always a limited one, I should like to forestall immediately a possible misapprehension to which this emphasis might give rise. What we have been saying in effect is that man always finds himself in a situation in the world where his freedom of action is limited by the external material environment and by the presence of other selves like himself. This does not mean that the situation of the agent somehow determines or may be cited as an efficient cause of his courses of action. For although limited by his situation man still retains the freedom to choose various courses of action in any given situation and is therefore the fully responsible author and initiator of the course of action which he eventually chooses. Put another way, in any given situation there are always a variety of possible *re-actions* which may be *chosen* by the agent and so the particular course of action which eventuates cannot be seen as somehow determined by the situation but rather as a freely chosen reaction to that situation.

This point will be familiar to economists who have always been concerned with the analysis of choices within constraints. For the economist it must seem banal if not trivial to insist that human choices are always limited or constrained by the situation in which man finds himself. Equally, however, the economist would be surprised if it were held that the constraints somehow determine the courses of human action so that man has no freedom of choice at all. For that would be tantamount to saying that in analysing the activities of consumers, for example, it would be sufficient simply to define the constraint functions in order to be able to analyse and predict consumer actions.[18] No reference whatever to utility functions (or to preferences) would be needed.

Since I shall be examining the implications of the human situation in a limiting world for freely chosen actions at greater length in Chapter 14, when I come to deal with Schutz's discussion of the motivation of human action ('because' motives and 'in-order-to' motives), I shall defer further treatment of this topic until then.

12.3   The Fundamentals of a Subjectivist Methodology Deduced

Existentialist phenomenology brings, as we saw, the notion of subjectivity to the very centre of the philosophical stage and proceeds to develop an indepth examination of the character of subjectivity. It is now time to see what general implications the resulting detailed notion of man as subject generates for the methodology of the human sciences. Existentialist phenomenologists have not been slow to draw out these implications and Alfred Schutz in particular has outlined a detailed subjectivist-interpretive methodology of the human sciences that is based explicitly on phenomenology.[19]

If man is a self-conscious being who knows or can know in reflection what he is doing, why he is doing it and that he is always free to do otherwise, then to explain or understand a human action will require that we grasp the *intention* or *goal* of the agent. Since in the moment of free choice all antecedent determination is transcended and cancelled and man becomes the responsible author and initiator of his courses of action it follows that there can be no question of explaining the action in terms of any antecedent event or experience as its stimulus or cause; rather to understand a responsibly chosen course of action will require that we should grasp the goal or end of the agent to which the action is directed. Schutz and Weber both call the goal or intention of action its *subjective meaning* for the agent.

Such explanation of action in terms of the goal of the agent involves a teleological mode of explanation in the very strictest sense. Broadly speaking, we mean by teleological explanation any explanation of an event or action in terms of some end-state or goal, in terms of some *telos* towards whose eventual realization the event or action is a step. The notion of teleological explanation is perhaps most closely associated with Aristotle who developed a whole physics using teleological explanations, or explanations in terms of 'final cause' or *telos*[20] as opposed to efficient causal or mechanical causal explanations. Aristotelian physics has long since been discarded in favour of natural sciences which adopt an efficient-causal mode of explanation, and this is not entirely surprising since there is something problematic about imputing goals and a tendency to strive to achieve them to inanimate natural objects. Strictly speaking, goal-directed activity implies necessarily a self-conscious agent to choose the goal and to direct the activity. In fact, both Aristotle and his latter-day scholastic followers seem to have been aware of this point since they saw God as the self-conscious agent who provides the goals of the natural world and directs inanimate objects towards realization of those goals.

But while teleological explanation is problematic when applied to the natural world of objects there is nothing problematic about the notion of a teleological explanation of men's actions in terms of their goals. For the implication of human subjectivity as outlined by existentialist phenomenology is precisely that men, *qua* self-conscious responsible authors of their actions, choose the goals to which their actions are directed and in that moment cancel all antecedent determination of their actions. Hence the explanation of the freely chosen actions should be teleological in the very strictest sense: that is to say an explanation of the action of a self-conscious and freely choosing being in terms of the purposes, the intentions, of that being as agent.

Having established the imperative of adopting a teleological explanation of human action in terms of the goals of the agent for the human sciences we may immediately make another important methodological point. Since a strictly teleological mode of explanation is quite definitively distinct from an efficient-causal mode of explanation, it follows that on this score there is an important differentiation of method between the natural and the human sciences. The slogan of 'methodological monism' is discredited and we have to recognize a dualism of method between the natural and the human sciences. Various attempts have been made to conflate efficient-causal and teleological explanations but I shall defer treatment of these until Chapter 15 in order not to interrupt the main flow of the philosophical argument. Suffice it to say here that I shall show that such attempts at conflation are seriously confused and that at least since the time of Plato and Aristotle the radical contrast between 'efficient causal' and 'final causal' or teleological explanation has been clearly recognized by philosophers (cf. Chapter 15, pp. 229–36).

Thus we can see how the main features of a subjectivist-interpretive methodology of the human sciences may be deduced directly from the notion of human subjectivity which has been elaborated with certainty by existentialist phenomenology. The notion of man as a self-conscious freely choosing purposive actor, the author and initiator of his courses of action, is made into an absolute starting point for the human sciences: and from this the imperative of adopting a teleological mode of explanation of human action in terms of the goals or intentions of the agent is deduced. Such explanation is strictly teleological in character and so radically distinct from the efficient-causal mode of explanation of the natural sciences. Thus we may also deduce that there is an important differentiation of method between the natural and the human sciences.

These implications of existentialist phenomenology and of the conception of man as subject which it lays down with absolute certainty by using the phenomenological method have been brought out by a number of leading thinkers. Husserl himself was severely critical of the positivist assumption that all sciences and hence the human sciences should be based on the methods of natural science and he was specifically critical of the behaviourist approach to psychology which ignores the subjective dimension of consciousness and treats man purely as an object – the 'reification' of consciousness as Husserl puts it.[21] Sartre has also drawn out the implications by developing a phenomenological approach to psychology which he opposes both to behaviourist and to Freudian psychology. Again the basis of Sartre's rejection of these latter approaches to psychology is that they have a seriously inadequate grasp of what the subjectivity of man means and entails for the human sciences.[22] Other psychologists have taken up Sartre's lead and developed in more detail an 'existentialist psychology' – notably R. D. Laing.

But by far the most systematic outline of the implications of existentialist phenomenology and of its conception of man as subject for the methodology of the human sciences is presented in Alfred Schutz's work *The Phenomenology of the Social World*. I shall leave the discussion of this detailed blueprint of a subjectivist-interpretive methodology for treatment in a later separate chapter (Chapter 14). Having given a summary of the main implications of an existentialist phenomenology for the methodology of the human sciences in this chapter I shall, in Chapter 13, indicate (for completeness) how existentialist phenomenology equally rules out in principle the objectivist-behaviourist approach to the methodology of human science in all of its versions.

Notes

1   Plato's whole philosophy may be seen as a relentless critique of common sense and a search for absolute truth. Hegel's *Phenomenology of Mind* is in my opinion one of the most unusual and interesting works on epistemology-critical theory of knowledge ever to appear. It is interesting to note that Hegel himself thought of the *Phenomenology* as an introduction to the method which he was to use in his later works in philosophy, hence as providing in effect the critical justification of his philosophy.

2   E. Husserl (1970), *Logical Investigations* (London: Routledge & Kegan Paul).

3   It may be of interest to remark that what is involved here is not a logical contradiction, for although I may be laughing it would be quite possible to imagine my not laughing at this very moment. Thus the contradictory of these absolutely true propositions is conceivable. Propositions which are enunciated as absolutely true in virtue of reflection by consciousness on itself are, therefore, *not* logically necessary propositions (since the contradictory is conceivable) and so are not subject to the charge of being tautologous. They are absolutely true but contingent propositions. This point disposes of a common positivist line of objection of the phenomenological quest for absolutely certain proposition.

4   See E. Husserl (1964), *The Idea of Phenomenology* (The Hague: Martinus Nijhoff) for a concise outline of what Husserl intended by the phenomenological method.

5   Husserl is here using the distinction current in philosophy since Kant between the 'thing-in-itself' (noumenon) and the 'thing-for consciousness' or 'object as it appears to consciousness', the phenomenon.

6   'Eidetic', from the Greek word *eidos* meaning form or essence.

7   The only apparent exception is in the cases where ordinary proper names are used to speak of specific particulars. But Russell suggested that even these are only 'definite descriptions' in terms of some universal notions upon closer examination, and the only strictly logically proper names would be words such as 'this', 'that'. Cf. B. Russell, (1972), *The Philosophy of Logical Atomism*, D. Pears (ed.), (London: Fontana), ch. 6, pp. 99–112.

8   E. Husserl (1960), *Cartesian Meditations* (The Hague: Martinus Nijhoff) Meditation 4 and especially 5 deal with this issue. For a useful commentary see P. Ricoeur (1967), *Husserl: an Analysis of His Phenomenology* (Evanston, Ill.: North University Press), ch. 5.

9   We may note that in his last great work, *The Crisis of European Science and*

Transcendental Phenomenology, there are hints of a quasi-Hegelian teleology of reason in human history. They are, however, only hints and Husserl never adopted a Hegelian absolute idealism.

10 The theme of 'subjectivity' is of course present in Husserl: the point is that he does not explore subjectivity in the same depth as Sartre or Merleau-Ponty, for example. Also Husserl did recognize that the notion of man as subject rules out the objectivist approach to the human sciences, as we shall see below. This theme was peripheral in Husserl, however.

11 I say upon reflection because often we may not be sure off-hand what we are feeling (for example, is it sorrow or pity, and so on) but must reflect in order to establish what is our conscious state. But on reflection our conscious state can be established with absolute certainty.

12 J. P. Sartre (1948), *Existentialism and Humanism* (London: Methuen) gives a very brief and readable introduction to existentialism which emphasizes the anthropocentric humanist theme.

13 J. P. Sartre (1972), *The Psychology of the Imagination* (London: Methuen), part I, especially pp. 1–2.

14 Indeed, even this limited contribution has a question mark hanging over its alleged 'certainty'. For existentialist phenomenology just as much as Husserl's pure phenomenology is bedevilled (in the step of eidetic reduction) by the problem of inter-subjectivity. If all essence is constituted by consciousness the problem arises that my constitution of essence may differ from yours, in which case the 'real essence' constituted in reflection by me may not coincide with yours for any given conscious state. Joy for me may be different from joy for you, for example. As I noted above (p. 179) no satisfactory resolution of this problem is offered by Husserl, nor indeed by any existentialist phenomenologist. Also I indicated how I believe this problem would have to be resolved.

15 J. P. Sartre (1969), *Being and Northingness* (London: Methuen), pt 4, ch. 1, and many other Sartrian works.

16 There seems to be some ambiguity in Sartre on this point. In the collection of essays on Descartes (Paris, 1946) Sartre seems to suggest that man's freedom is the absolute freedom Descartes attributed to God. Elsewhere, notably in *Being and Northingness* Sartre speaks of human freedom as strictly limited by the constraints of the material world. For an interesting discussion of this theme see the article by D. Follesdal (1981), 'Sartre on freedom' in *The Philosophy of Sartre*, P. Schilpp (ed.), (La Salle, Ill.: Open Court).

17 J. P. Sartre (1965), *La Nausée* (Paris: Gallimard, 1938); R. Baldick (trans.) *Nausea* (Harmondsworth: Penguin).

18 Utility functions are specifications of the goals of self-conscious agents. Hence if we were to analyse human choices as entirely determined by situation there could be no question of using any kind of 'goal function' as maximand. We could only have constraint functions.

19 A. Schutz (1972), *The Phenomenology of the Social World* (London: Heinemann), *passim*.

20 *Telos* in Greek means some ultimate goal or end. When Aristotle speaks of 'final cause' by this he very clearly means *telos* and distinguishes it carefully from the notion of 'efficient cause'.

21 E. Husserl (1965), *Phenomenology and the Crisis of Philosophy*, Q. Lauer (trans.) (New York: Harper), pp.79–122, especially p. 103.

22 Throughout his life, Sartre insisted on the absolute transparency of consciousness or itself in reflection, that is the first step of phenomenological philosophy. Hence he always resolutely opposed the Freudian notion of an

'unconscious', a realm of consciousness which cannot be given to the self in reflection. (If it cannot be given to the self, how can anybody else come to know it?)

13

The Existentialist Refutation
of
an Objectivist Methodology

In Part 3 of this work concerned with the philosophical grounding of a subjectivist-interpretive methodology of the human sciences I am adopting, as in Part I, an essentially dialectical strategy of argument. I build up the philosophical defence by considering first the broad positive arguments in favour of the subjectivist approach (thesis stage), then I move on to consider what methodologies of human science are definitively ruled out as invalid by those same basic philosophical arguments (the antithesis stage) and finally I return to reassert and to present in detail the principles of a subjectivist-interpretive methodology. The strand of unity running through this dialectical discussion of methodology is provided by existentialist phenomenology with its notion of human subjectivity which I have outlined at length in the last chapter, along with a preliminary indication of how it points to the imperative of a subjectivist-interpretive methodology.

In this chapter I shall be concerned with the antithesis stage of the above strategy, that is, I shall be considering how existentialist phenomenology leads to a decisive refutation of all versions of an objectivist-behaviourist approach to the methodology of the human sciences. I shall show why the reductionist, instrumentalist, and superficial monist variants of the objectivist-behaviourist approach are all untenable once we grasp the full implications of human subjectivity.

13.1 The Philosophical Presuppositions of the Objectivist Approach Rebutted

In developing this critique of the objectivist-behaviourist approach to methodology of human science the first step should be to direct our critical attention to the philosophical underpinning of that approach. In Chapter 4 I pointed out that the typical philosophical inspiration of the objectivist approach which emphasizes a unity of method among natural and human sciences comes from empiricist and positivist approaches to philosophy, or in some cases from the latter-day descendent of positivism, relativism.

Empiricism is the conviction that all valid human cognition must be based on sense-experience, that is on empirically observable data. Positivism, which grew out of empiricism, is the assertion that the natural sciences provide the paradigm of all valid human cognition, and more specifically that the only propositions which are meaningful are either tautologous identity statements or else empirically verifiable propositions.[1] These philosophical views lead directly towards a conviction that the human sciences should follow strictly the methods of the successful natural sciences which are regarded as the exemplar of human cognition; and the empiricist premise in particular points towards a banning of all reference to human subjectivity, since conscious states and activities are not empirically observable.

Since positivism becomes involved in manifest contradictions when the principle of verifiability is turned upon itself[2] it has given way to a relativist position in much Anglo-American thought. The relativist recognizes the difficulties involved when we seek to enunciate as a universal truth that the sciences are to be the paradigm of valid human cognition and so he holds that there are no absolute truths at all and that to look for conclusive rational justification of any proposition is pointless. The relativist does argue that on pragmatic grounds, such as usefulness to mankind, the natural sciences have a definite claim to being regarded as the paradigm of useful human cognition and hence they conclude that if the human sciences are to prove similarly useful they ought to follow closely the methods of natural science.

Existentialist phenomenology has presented a decisive critique of each one of these philosophical positions along lines which are very similar to the exhaustive critiques of positivism and of relativism which I have already given in Chapters 2 and 3. It will be sufficient, therefore, to mention only the main points of these lines of criticism here. Against positivism, as well as challenging its underlying assumption of an unreflecting common sense empiricism, all phenomenologists have relentlessly pointed out that positivism becomes involved in hopeless self-contradiction. Husserl in particular went on to show that a central difficulty with all positivist thought is its adoption of a naively uncritical and even dogmatic attitude towards the methods and achievements of the natural sciences. Not only is such faith in the natural sciences unwarranted when we consider some of the horrors such as nuclear weaponry which it has brought with it as well as its benefits; but Husserl has also shown that no natural science could ever provide a critical-rational foundation for its own methods.[3]

Relativism has been given the roughest ride of all by phenomenologists, and in my view rightly so. By a line of argument very similar to that which I have given in Chapter 3, they have shown that the relativist position is either immediately self-contradictory (by enunciating itself as absolute truth) or else it is totally nihilistic regarding the possibility of any rational dialogue or exchange of views since there can be no rational standards for the appraisal of arguments. A consistent relativist (in good faith) should refrain from *all* further rational discussion or publication of reasoned academic work; he should try brainwashing or killing people in order to secure agreement with his point of view (if that is what he wants – he might alternatively become a recluse).

13.2   The Objectivist Behaviourist Methodology Rebutted in Detail

Having shown how existentialist phenomenology leads to a rebuttal of the typical philosophical underpinning of the whole objectivist approach we shall now turn to examine how existentialist phenomenology with its elaborate notion of human subjectivity leads to a decisive refutation in detail of the objectivist-behaviourist approach to the methodology of the human sciences. In Chapter 4 I have distinguished three different versions of the objectivist-behaviourist position and I shall now show how each of these versions in turn is ruled out by the existentialist phenomenology which I have outlined in the last chapter.

The first variant of the objectivist-behaviourist position is the *reductionist* variant. According to this position man *is* no more than another object in nature, he is *only* a complex organism. Reference to the human spirit or mind are only the relics of outdated religious modes of thought and, inspired by a thorough-going materialism, the reductionist looks forward to the day when every aspect of human life will be capable of being explained in terms of neuro-physiology of the brain in interaction with material stimuli upon it. If man is thus merely another object in the material world, no more than a highly complex organism, it follows immediately that the human sciences are to treat man purely as an object and that all reference to subjective conscious states or activities is to be banished from the human sciences, their place being taken if at all by references to various brain states. Furthermore, if man is only another object in nature it follows that there will be no significant difference between the methods of the natural and the human sciences, and indeed many reductionists explicitly look forward to the day when all of the sciences, natural and human, will be reducible to an all-embracing physics and/or chemistry.[4] Finally, since we are to follow the methods of natural science in human science and to treat man strictly as another object in nature (making no reference to any subjective conscious states), it follows that the human sciences should adopt an efficient-causal mode of explanation of human action. Human action is always to be explained in terms of some antecedent (or coinciding) independently observable event as stimulus or cause of which the observed behaviour (action) is the effect or response.

In the light of the existentialist phenomenology and in particular of the conception of man as subject which it laid down with absolute certainty this reductionist variant of the objectivist-behaviourist position is fairly evidently refuted. In the first place, it explicitly entertains a notion of man as mere object, mere complex organism which is directly at variance with the notion of man as a self-conscious subject which was revealed with absolute certainty in phenomenology. Following immediately from this we may recall that the further elaboration of the notion of human subjectivity in phenomenology led to a recognition that man is a being who in reflection can always come to know what he is doing, why he is doing it and that he is always free to choose to do otherwise. Since in this moment of choice or decision all antecedent determination of whatever kind is transcended and cancelled and man becomes the responsible author and initiator of his courses of action, it follows that any attempt at efficient-causal explanations of human action in terms of some antecedent observable event as cause is involved in a serious misunderstanding of human action and so must be definitively ruled out from a human science guided by the search for true insights regarding human affairs. Finally, the empiricist-inspired ban on all reference to subjective conscious states by the reductionist version of objectivism is emphatically rejected by existentialist phenomenology. Not only is the empiricist underpinning of this ban on references to unobservable conscious states and activities rejected: existentialist phenomenology holds that the *only* certainties which man can discover (in philosophy *and* in science) are to be found precisely in the field of self-consciousness, a field which can only be given to reflection and can never be observed empirically.

Thus existentialist phenomenology achieves a decisive refutation of the reductionist version of the objectivist-behaviourist approach to the methodology of human science. It may also be remarked that since we have refuted both the notion of man as object and the use of efficient-causal explanation in the human sciences, the notion of a strict unity of method among the sciences championed by the reductionist objectivist is also in a shambles. Indeed, we saw in the last chapter that if we follow through the full implications of subjectivity we shall be led to adopt a teleological mode of explanation in human science which is radically distinct from the efficient-causal mode of the natural sciences. Hence also on the score of a unity of method among all the sciences (methodological monism), existentialist phenomenology both undermines the positivist dogma from which such a view typically flows and shows in particular that the methodology of the human sciences cannot be equated to that of the natural sciences when the full implications of subjectivity for methodology are recognized.

The second major variant of the objectivist-behaviourist approach which I identified in Chapter 4 was the *instrumentalist* variant. This version of the objectivist position shies away from the outright denial of human subjectivity of the reductionist approach, and so avoids any head-on collision with the notion of human subjectivity as put forward by existentialist phenomenology. However, under the inspiration of positivist and of relativist approaches to philosophy which hail the natural sciences as the paradigm of valid (or useful) human cognition these objectivists hold that while man may indeed be a subject, for purposes of human science he is to be treated *as if* he were merely another object-in-nature, a mere complex organism. Once this step has been taken the details of this second version of the objectivist-behaviourist position will clearly be the same as the details of the reductionist version of objectivism. The human sciences in treating man as if he were an object are to follow strictly the methods of the natural sciences, and more specifically they are to adopt an efficient-causal mode of explanation of human actions.

Since we saw in Chapter 12 how existentialist phenomenology lays down with absolute certainty the notion of man as subject, that is man as a self-conscious and freely choosing being who is the responsible author and initiator of his courses of action, it follows that the fundamental notion (of man as object) of this second variant of the objectivist-behaviourist approach is most definitely revealed to be a *fiction*. Thus the second variant of objectivism which holds that we are to treat man for purposes of human science as if he were an object is in effect proposing that we should build up all of the human sciences on a fictional foundation. It is precisely because the whole edifice of human science would be shot through with an explicitly fictional notion of man, whereupon all of its theories would have a fictional character, that I have chosen the label 'instrumentalist' for this variant of the objectivist-behaviourist approach.[5]

Let us now see how an existentialist phenomenology can decisively rule out this second variant of the objectivist-behaviourist position. We saw at some length in Chapter 12 that the fundamental impulse which underlies all phenomenology is the search for truth. Phenomenology insists that the fundamental regulative criterion of all types of human inquiry must be truth, or the pursuit of truth, and any discipline which relinquishes or abandons the goal of truth cannot be regarded as valid knowledge, nor indeed can it be even regarded as rational, since for phenomenology it is ultimately human reason which demands that we should always relentlessly pursue the critical search for truth.[6] From this it immediately follows that instrumentalist approaches to science which explicitly renounce the search for truth and regard scientific theories as mere fictions are completely untenable: instrumentalist science by abandoning the search for truth has abandoned rationality and so cannot be regarded as valid human knowledge at all.

In addition to this basic criticism all of the other more specific criticisms of detail which existentialist phenomenology makes of the reductionist variant of objectivism apply equally well to the details of the instrumentalist variant. Thus, for example, the notion of man as freely choosing subject is completely incompatible with adoption of an efficient-causal mode of explanation: it demands rather a teleological mode of explanation which is quite distinct from the efficient-causal mode of the natural sciences.

We may conclude, therefore, that this second 'instrumentalist' version of the objectivist-behaviourist approach to the methodology of the human science, although it does not clash head-on with existentialist phenomenology by declaring that man IS only an object (as does the reductionist) is, nevertheless, refuted by existentialist phenomenology just as decisively as was the first 'reductionist' variant of the objectivist-behaviourist position. Indeed, I would also point out that since the instrumentalist variant of objectivism would lead to a body of theory permeated by instrumentalist fictions in the human sciences all of the criticisms which I have already made of the instrumentalist conception of science in Chapters 2 and 3 are pertinent here and would only serve to supplement the powerful criticisms of the position already offered by existentialist phenomenology.[7]

The third variant of the objectivist-behaviourist approach to methodology of human science which I distinguished in Chapter 4 was 'superficial methodological monism'. It is of particular importance to consider this variant of objectivism in this book since it has been a widely held methodological position among mainstream economists and in Chapters 8 and 9 we saw how a variety of leading economists have preached just such a methodological position in their usually brief excursions into the field of methodology. The hallmark of the superficial methodological monist position is that it does not want to make, or does not see any need to make, a philosophical commitment on the question of man's subjectivity. For the superficial monist holds that man may indeed be a subject but that does not generate any significant differentiation of method between the natural and human sciences.

It is important to realize straight away that this variant of objectivism is distinct from the two already considered. For it neither holds that man is only an object (as in the reductionist variant) nor does it hold that man is to be treated as if he were an object (as in the instrumentalist variant).[8] Superficial monism therefore retains the fundamental objectivist conviction that there should be a unity of method between natural and human science and specifically that both should adopt an efficient-causal mode of explanation while avoiding the more forthright and controversial tenets regarding the nature of man of the other two variants of the objectivist-behaviourist approach. By avoiding these more controversial aspects, superficial monism has therefore appealed to many practising human scientists and especially to economists as a seemingly more reasonable version of the objectivist approach. I shall show, however, that from a *philosophical* point of view superfical monism is hopelessly confused and so upon a critical examination turns out to be an even less acceptable position than either of the other two variants of objectivism already considered and refuted.

Superficial methodological monists typically examine a catalogue of the various possible implications which human subjectivity might have for the methods of the human sciences from which they conclude that human subjectivity does not give rise to any special problems of method in human science such as are not encountered in the natural sciences. Hence they argue that the human sciences can and should follow the methods of the well-established natural sciences in all essential details and specifically in the adoption of an efficient-causal mode of explanation.

The fundamental flaw or difficulty of the superficial methodological monist position may now be simply stated; it has overlooked what is by far the most important implication of human subjectivity in its catalogue of the methodological consequences of subjectivity. For we have seen at some length in Chapter 12 how a rigorous existentialist phenomenological examination of human subjectivity leads us towards a notion of man as a freely choosing self-conscious being who knows (or in reflection can come to know) what he is doing, why he is doing it and that he is always free to choose otherwise. In other words, we are led to a conception of man as the responsible author and initiator of his own courses of action in the world, from which it follows that there can be *no* question of explaining human actions in terms of some antecedent event or state of the organism as cause (for in the moment of choice all antecedent determination is transcended and cancelled). To understand and explain human action we must grasp the goal or intention of the agent and so the explanation of human actions must be strictly teleological in character. Since this strict teleological mode of explanation is radically distinct from efficient-causal explanation (and wholly incompatible with it in the explanation of human action) it follows that there should be a radical differentiation of method between the natural and human sciences.

Thus we see how the existentialist phenomenology of human subjectivity leads also to a definitive refutation of this third variant of the objectivist-behaviourist position. Indeed, it will now be clear that this third superficial monist variant is philosophically even less satisfactory than either the reductionist or instrumentalist variants. For once we have developed a philosophically adequate appreciation of human subjectivity in existentialist phenomenology we find that superficial monism overlooks what is by far the most important methodological implication of subjectivity: the imperative of teleological explanation. It is precisely because of this philosophical incompleteness of the position that I have chosen the label 'superficial methodological monism' for it.

Once the full philosophical implications of human subjectivity have been appreciated we may wonder if there is any way in which a methodological monist position maintaining a unity of method among the sciences could be preserved.[9] There are two further stratagems of desperation which a methodological monist might employ to preserve the unity of method among the sciences in the face of the existentialist elucidation of the full implications of human subjectivity, and I note these possible stratagems here briefly for completeness. A desperate monist could concede that human subjectivity leads to the imperative of adopting a teleological mode of explanation but he could argue that there is *still* a unity of method either

(1) because the mode of explanation adopted by a science is a matter of no methodological significance, or
(2) because teleological explanations are no different from efficient-causal modes of explanation.

Either of these stratagems could save the day for a unity of method among the sciences, although we may note, at the cost of a Pyrrhic victory. The sort of human science which is envisaged by this last ditch stand of the monists is one which adopts a teleological mode of explanation and does not treat man as an object in any way. It is therefore very far removed from the sort of human science modelled exactly on the natural sciences which is envisaged in the reductionist variant of objectivism and towards which positivism has looked forward since the time of Comte.

In any case neither of these defensive stratagems are philosophically permissible within the framework of an existentialist phenomenology, such as I have outlined in Chapter 12, whose overriding regulative criterion is the search for truth. The first stratagem which holds that the mode of explanation of a (human) science is a matter of no methodological consequence amounts to an assertion that the *content* of an explanatory theory is of no consequence at all provided the theory predicts well or passes some other such practical test. Thus, for example, whether we explain a man's actions as determined by such past experiences as the way his mother fed him as an infant or as being freely chosen courses of action, it is alleged that which way we choose to explain the actions is a matter of no consequence provided the explanation we adopt can predict a man's behaviour reasonably well.

It will be immediately obvious, therefore, that this first stratagem relies once again on an *instrumentalist* conception of scientific theories and indeed could not possibly be pressed unless on an implicit appeal to instrumentalism. I have already shown at length how, if the goal of human inquiry is to be the pursuit of truth, instrumentalism (which abjures the quest for truth in science) is a completely untenable position. Since this first further stratagem for defending superficial monism cannot be put forward without at least implicit invocation of instrumentalism, I have thereby shown it to be untenable.

The second defensive stratagem which could be adopted by the superficial monist is again to concede that the human sciences shold adopt a teleological mode of explanation (given human subjectivity) but to argue that this does not give rise to any significant difference of method because teleological explanation is after all no different from, or only a species of, efficient-causal explanation. I shall postpone a fuller treatment of this question until Chapter 15, but I may give a brief indication here of why I believe this line of argument to be seriously erroneous.[10] Ever since the time of Plato and Aristotle philosophers have seen an important distinction between the efficient-causal and the final-causal modes of explanation. An efficient-causal explanation typically answers a 'how' question, such as how an internal combustion engine works. A teleological explanation by contrast typically answers a 'why' question. It is an answer to the question 'to what purpose', and hence always makes implicit reference to the goals of some self-conscious purposively acting agents. Furthermore, the relationship between efficient cause and effect is very different from the relationship of the goal of an agent to the action which seeks to realize that goal.

In the light of the general indications just given we may say that this second defensive stratagem of the superficial monist is also quashed. We may thus in general conclude that the third variant of an objectivist-behaviourist methodology, which I have called a superficial methodological monist, is decisively refuted by an existentialist phenomenological philosophy which upholds the goal of pursuing truth in science and which has laid down with absolute certainty the notion of man as subject and which from that has drawn the implication of a teleological mode of explanation for the human sciences.

By this stage of the discussion I have shown how from a starting point of philosophical certainty in existentialist phenomenology we may deduce:

(1)   The imperative of adopting a subjectivist-interpretive approach to the human sciences with its teleological mode of explanation which is radically distinct from the efficient-causal mode of explanation of the natural sciences (the thesis stage of the dialectical strategy of argumentation, in Chapter 12.)

(2)   The decisive refutation of each variant of the opposing objectivist-behaviourist approach to the human sciences (the antithesis stage of the dialectical argumentation, carried out in this chapter).

It would be difficult to imagine a more comprehensive argument in defence of the fundamental principles of the subjectivist-interpretive approach. I shall now move on, therefore, to the synthesis or consolidation phase of the philosophical argument. In Chapter 14 I shall examine in much more detail the central features which a subjectivist-interpretive methodology deduced from a basis in existentialist phenomenology and its conception of human subjectivity should incorporate.

Notes

1   For a fuller discussion of positivism, see Chapter 2.

2   Cf. the critique of positivism, Chapter 2, pp. 18–23.

3   Cf. Chapter 1, p. 11 and Chapter 12, p. 175 for a similar line of argument.

4   This will be readily recognizable as the Comtean and positivist type of dream of an eventual unified science. More recently reductionism has been championed by the sociobiology school. See for example the work by A. Rosenberg (1981) *Sociology and the Pre-emption of the Social Sciences* (London: Routledge & Kegan Paul), where he argues that the human sciences should all be reduced to and expressed in terms of socio-biology forthwith. Rosenberg bases his argument on transparently positivist philosophical premises and on a conception of man as mere object (see his Chapter 2) and so it will be evident from the existentialist phenomenological discussion of reductionist objectivism which just follows in the main text why I would regard Rosenberg's position as completely untenable.

5   We may recall from Chapter 2 that instrumentalism is the view that all scientific theories are mere fictions (pp. 33–34).

6   I have already shown in Chapters 1 and 12 how for phenomenology it is the demand of reason to criticize and dissipate the mists of dogma and superstition which gives rise to the relentless search for absolute truth. We may note that here we have an interesting new approach to the tricky question 'what is truth'. Truth, I would suggest, is achieved only in the moment when reason can no longer harbour any possible doubts about a

proposition (truth as absolute evidence, if you like). This has the interesting corollary that it makes reason and not truth into the ultimate 'primitive term'. Moreover, since reason is an activity upon which consciousness can reflect there is no difficulty about taking it as a primitive. Finally, I would suggest that we then define knowledge after the manner of Plato's *epistime* as the (absolutely) true proposition thus grasped by human reason (cf. my discussion of the critical activity of reason whose *telos* is truth in Chapter 1, pp. 7–10).

7   Cf. Chapters 2 and 3, p. 34 and pp. 39–40, where I argue that instrumentalism has misunderstood the relation of theory to data and would be quite incapable of distinguishing science from sorcery, and so on.

8   Otherwise they would probably champion the reductionist or instrumentalist versions of objectivism.

9   This is obviously an important concern from any positivist-minded thinker.

10 Cf. Chapter 15, pp. 236–39. I have also noted a third possible defensive stratagem for superficial monism which would argue that even if the human sciences are teleological this does not amount to a difference of method because certain natural sciences such as biology also sometimes use teleological explanations. Apart from being a Pyrrhic victory for monism once again, since the subjectivist character of human science is conceded. I shall show in Chapter 15 that this argument is in any case confused and mistaken.

14

The Central Principles of a
Subjectivist Methodology:
Alfred Schutz

This chapter will complete the dialectical strategy argument in defence of a subjectivist-interpretive methodology which I have been carrying out since the beginning of Part 3. I shall present now in much greater detail than in Chapter 12 the central principles of a subjectivist-interpretive methodology which may be deduced from existentialist phenomenology. In doing so I shall be drawing heavily on the work of Alfred Schutz, although some of the ideas presented draw their inspiration from other thinkers, in particular from Sartre.

14.1   The Details of a Schutzian Subjectivist Methodology:
Subjective Meaning and Objective Meaning

Alfred Schutz was inspired to write his *magnum opus*[1] by a discontent with what Max Weber had said on the question of methodology in human science. It is clear enough from Weber's rather brief and sketchy remarks on methodology that he definitely favoured some sort of interpretive methodology, insisting that the most basic task of human science is to interpret the meaning of actions, by which he meant the goal of the agent. Schutz, however, found that Weber's work stood in need of considerable elaboration and clarification and this on two main fronts.[2] First, he felt that Weber's methodology was devoid of any rigorous philosophical foundation. Schutz sought to provide this by drawing on existentialist phenomenology. Secondly, he believed that Weber had left some hopeless ambiguities in his presentation, notably on the questions of subjective and objective meanings of actions – as well as on the whole question of the motivation of action. Again drawing on existentialist phenomenology and its notion of subjectivity, Schutz seeks to clarify where exactly a subjectivist-interpretive methodology must stand on these questions. Given the wide variety of versions of the interpretive methodology which have appeared in the past one hundred years Schutz's assertion that Weber left some serious ambiguities in his presentation is far from fanciful.

Weber's methodological sketches are therefore the foil against which Schutz develops his presentation of the subjectivist-interpretive methodology and they can explain the structure of Schutz's work with its seemingly inordinate emphasis on certain themes (such as subjective meaning as distinct from objective meaning) and its almost cursory treatment of the question of teleological explanation and its contrast with efficient-causal explanation. But Schutz's work is not simply a critical evaluation of Weber. On the contrary, it is perhaps the single most systematic statement of the principles of a subjectivist-interpretive methodology with a rigorous philosophical foundation in existentialist phenomenology which has ever been written, and it is precisely for this reason that I have based this chapter directly on Schutz. It is also worth remarking that while Schutz presents a critique of the ambiguities left by Weber he is in full agreement with the fundamental principles of an interpretive methodology as stated by Weber.

Schutz deduces all of the central principles of his methodology from existentialist phenomenology, and in particular from its notion of man as subject. Drawing direct inspiration from Husserl he insists that man is a being who can reflect upon himself and in so doing can come to know what he is doing, why he is doing it and that he is always free to choose otherwise. Schutz laid particular emphasis on the constitutive role of consciousness, on the fact that the form or essence of phenomena is always constituted by consciousness and he turned this to account by showing how in particular the 'meaning' of any course of *action* is always constituted by the agent. This is simply another way of saying that the goal or purpose of any activity is always freely chosen by the agent, thus that man is always the sole responsible author and initiator of his courses of action in the world.

From this Schutz deduces that to understand or explain a course of action we must grasp the intention or goal of the agent. To use Schutz's own terminology, to understand an action requires that we should grasp its *subjective meaning* for the agent involved, where by the subjective meaning of action Schutz always means (by definition) the goal of the agent. Furthermore, such explanation of action in terms of the agent's own goal is strictly teleological in character and so is radically distinct from the efficient-causal mode of explanation of the natural sciences. Schutz also briefly but quite explicitly rules out any sort of efficient-causal explanation from the human sciences since it cannot possibly be consistent with the notion of man as a self-conscious freely choosing subject who is the author of his own actions.[3] I shall not delay over these fundamental principles of the subjectivist-interpretive methodology as presented by Schutz since I have already dealt with them at some length in my own deduction of the subjectivist approach in Chapter 12.[4] Instead I shall pass on to the distinctively Schutzian contribution to the subjectivist-interpretive approach which consists of his clarification of the notions of subjective and objective meaning and of the whole question of the motivation of actions.

Schutz approaches the question of subjective and objective meaning from a most illuminating phenomenological treatment of the act of communication, in particular inter-subjective communication by means of language. Every speech act is an attempt at communication of the conscious states or experiences of the speaker to some other person (and in some mood or other such as the indicative, imperative or interrogative). The goal of any speech act is therefore the communication of the agent's conscious state in all its fullness and the speaker attempts to do this by means of language. Thus language is for phenomenology nothing more and nothing less than an instrument for the communication of thoughts.[5]

Having introduced this notion of language and the speech act Schutz examines the question of the 'meaning' of a speech act. He insists that there are always two quite distinct levels of meaning in a speech act (communicated in language). First, the objective meaning of a speech act. By this Schutz means the everyday common sense meaning of a statement as it would be interpreted by any listener who spoke the speaker's language. If there is any lack of clarity about this objective meaning of a speech act it can readily be resolved by having recourse to a dictionary which is in effect a catalogue of the objective meanings of words in a language.

Secondly, the subjective meaning of a speech act. By this Schutz means the deeper personal meaning of a statement with all of its nuances, the conscious state which the agent is seeking to communicate in all of its personalized richness. For, as Schutz points out, in addition to the 'objective' everyday meanings which words possess, there is for many words used by a speaker also an aura of entirely personal or 'subjective' meaning; and if we are to appreciate in all its fullness the conscious state which an agent is trying to communicate to us we shall have to be able to appreciate in addition to the objective meanings of the words he uses the nuance of personal 'subjective meaning' which attaches to them. That there is such an aura of subjective meaning surrounding many of the words used by an agent is undoubtedly the case, and indeed the artistic appreciation of outstanding works of literature in any language is especially concerned (among other things) with seeking to bring out in its full richness the aura of intensely felt subjective meaning which surrounds the core of everyday objective meaning in the works of any great poet, novelist or dramatist. Many examples of words which at the hands of some speaker or writer acquire a special force and thus a subjective meaning special to that author or speaker could be given: the word Piraeus for example can be vastly more resonant with meaning to a person who has studied classical Greek while a word as banal as 'anchor' may mean a mere piece of ship's chandlery to one person but to another may be a symbol of rock-solid stability in a world of chaos. The aura of subjective meaning which we thus attach to words may arise in a variety of ways; from all sorts of evocative associations to the manner or the circumstances in which we first learned how to use a word.

Having clarified the two different levels of meaning of any speech act or statement Schutz goes on to apply the same distinction to all actions. We may in the first place speak of the *objective* meaning of an action. By this

Schutz means that interpretation of the goal or intention of an agent which would be made by any everyday observer of his activity. Thus in our everyday lives we are constantly making interpretations of the intentions or goals of the activities of agents in a routine, common sense way. If, for example, I see a man's arm flailing, an axe falling, wood shattering, I will usually interpret this scene by saying that the man I observe is 'chopping wood'; that is to say that I will not interpret the scene before me as some entirely chaotic jumble of axe, excited man and wood but rather as a man who intends to chop some wood and is carrying out this project. In an equally common sense everyday manner, if I see pieces of coloured paper or bits of metal being passed around I will interpret this as the use of money as a means of payment of some debt.

These everyday common sense interpretations of the goals of the observed activities of agents are what Schutz means by the 'objective meanings' of actions. It should be fairly clear that when we speak of the task of a subjectivist human science as the interpretation of the intention or meaning of actions for agents that we are not suggesting that the human sciences should concern themselves exclusively with the interpretation of the objective meanings of actions. For that would reduce the subjectivist human sciences to being no more than a codification of common sense interpretations, to being little different from a sort of super-catalogue or 'dictionary' of the way in which we usually interpret the actions of other agents. Such a codification of common sense interpretations might be a useful preliminary to a human science but it could never amount to anything more than a largely descriptive exercise. We could hardly call such a human science explanatory.

Schutz contrasts with this objective meaning of an action the *subjective* meaning. Extending the distinction of subjective and objective meaning of words which he had already made Schutz defines the subjective meaning of action as the full personal intention or goal of the agent. This is not something which is given to everyday common sense interpretations of action since what we are examining here is the 'meaning' of action in its fully personalized richness. We are inquiring more deeply into the motivation of the agent seeking to discover of what more ultimate project some specific activity is a component part or means to its realization. The contrast of subjective and objective meanings of an action may be well illustrated by the example of the woodcutter. As we have already seen, the objective meaning of the activity or scene we observe is that there is a man who intends to cut some wood. If we inquire into the subjective meaning we are seeking to discover *why* he is cutting wood (for example, for a wage or for a weekend hobby), and we may then further inquire as to why he should want to earn a wage or why he should have such a hobby, etc. It is quite clear that these personalized subjective meanings are not given immediately to common sense but can only be conjectured by the observer.

Since we have seen in Chapter 12 that the aim of an interpretive human science should be to achieve a true insight into the intentions or goals of agents in an action it should be clear that in Schutzian language this amounts to saying that the task of the human sciences should be to interpret the full subjective meaning of action for the agent involved. Thus it becomes abundantly clear that an interpretive human science is not simply a codification of the objective meanings of actions. Such a science would not only be little more than a dictionary-like codification of everyday interpretations, it would not in any case be capable of getting to grips with the full subjective meaning of the actions of agents. For it is quite possible that the common sense interpretation of the intentions of an agent engaged in some activity fall far short of or are completely mistaken regarding the true intentions of the agent.

Before leaving the topic of subjective meaning there is a further point which may usefully be made. As I have already noted in the case of the woodcutter example, there are within the field of the subjective meaning of action, different levels or depths of motivation into which we may penetrate. Thus we may ask why the woodcutter is chopping wood; if for a wage, why he wants to earn a wage; if he wants general material well-being we may go on to question why this should be a component of his ultimate life project, and so on. There are, in other words, layers of subjective meaning and once we have successfully achieved an insight regarding one layer of subjective meaning we can always proceed and probe further by peeling back deeper layers of motivation. Thus, just as in the natural sciences where the resolution of one problem invariably sets the terms for some new and deeper investigation (as with the splitting of the atom, and so on) so also in the interpretive human sciences, once we have achieved some satisfactory interpretation of subjective meaning there will invariably be some deeper question regarding some more ultimate level of subjective meaning which then opens up. There is no question, therefore, of the human sciences quickly moving towards a complete and exhaustive account of the subjective meanings of actions: rather as in the natural sciences we have a human science which must seek to probe ever more deeply into the projects and ultimate goals which motivate human actions.[6]

Max Weber had left the question of subjective and objective meanings of actions in a seriously ambiguous manner, and in fact a number of commentators have held that when Weber spoke of interpretation of the meaning of action as a key part of the methodology of human science what he had in mind was only interpretation of everyday objective meaning. It was this confusion in Weber which prompted Schutz to write at such length on the question of objective and subjective meaning. I believe that Schutz's interpretation of Weber as having intended that the human sciences should seek to elucidate the full subjective meaning of actions for the agents involved is a correct one, since otherwise it is difficult to see why Weber should have laid such emphasis on the notion of *Verstehen*, the understanding of the intention of the agent. (As we have just seen, a science of objective meanings of actions would be a trivial descriptive exercise.)[7] In any case, whatever one may think of Schutz's exegesis of Weber, it is quite clear that, from an existentialist phenomenological philosophy and its analysis of human subjectivity,

what follows as an imperative for the human sciences is that in explaining human action they should seek to grasp the goal of the agent,
that is to say, the full subjective meaning of the action for the agent
involved.

14.2   *Schutz's Analysis of the Motivation of Action*

The second area where Schutz achieves an important clarification of the
details of a subjectivist-interpretive methodology is on the question of the
motivation of human actions. Weber and others have spoken loosely of
the interpretive approach to human science as the attempt to explain
human actions in terms of the 'motives' or motivation of the agent, but
as Schutz points out there are a number of different meanings which may
be attached to the notion of motivation. Schutz reviews these and seeks
to clarify what precisely is meant by the explanation of action in terms
of its motives within a subjectivist-interpretive human science.[8]

Schutz begins by defining the '*in-order-to* motive' of an action. By this
he means the goal or purpose of an agent to which some activity is
directed: we shall say that the agent's goal is the 'in-order-to motive' of
the action in question. It will be immediately clear that this in-order-to
motive is exactly the same as the 'subjective meaning' of an action for an
agent which we defined in the previous section. Furthermore, since the
main aim of a subjectivist-interpretive methodology is precisely to explain
human actions in terms of the goals of the agents involved, it follows that
the principal task of an interpretive human science will be in effect to
explain human actions in terms of their in-order-to motives.

Schutz goes on to point out that in everyday speech we often translate
propositions about in-order-to motives into a seemingly causalist or
'because motive' language. Thus for example instead of saying 'I opened
my umbrella in order not to get wet' – a clear instance of explaining my
action in terms of its in-order-to motive or goal, we may often express this
as 'I opened by umbrella because I did not want to get wet'. The latter
proposition seems to be conceiving of the goal of the action as analogous
to an antecedent efficient cause of the action, it seems to be expressing
the 'in-order-to motive' as a 'because motive' of action. Since teleological
explanation is radically distinct from efficient causal and the relation of
a goal to the action which realizes it quite distinct from the relation of
efficient cause to effect, Schutz argues that this translation of a
teleological explanation of action in terms of the agent's goal into
efficient-causalist language is involved in a serious distortion. Whatever
may be the usages of everyday speech in this matter, for purposes of
human science such a translation of in-order-to motivation into the
efficient-causal language of 'because motives' can only foment serious
misunderstanding and should therefore be banned from a rigorously
precise human science. This is why Schutz chooses the label 'pseudo-
because motive' for such translations and bans them from the human
sciences.

But is there any way in which we can speak of a 'genuine because motive' of an action? Schutz like many other proponents of existentialist phenomenology recognizes that while man is certainly free to choose he does not choose entirely *in vacuo*. As noted when dealing with the existentialist account of human subjectivity in Chapter 12, man not only comes to recognize his freedom and consequent responsibility for his actions in a careful phenomenological reflection, he also perforce recognizes the *limitations* of that freedom – that his freedom is not the absolute freedom of God. Man finds himself thrown (or 'abandoned' to use Sartre's term) in a certain situation in the material universe over which he has little or no control. This situation consists not simply of the various physical constraints, which men encounter in the material world: it also includes all of the *past* experiences of the agent which continue to have implications in the present but which today he is powerless to change even though many of them may have been freely chosen at some stage in the past. Schutz suggests that although the situation of an agent can never determine the course of his actions in the world (for that would be inconsistent with freedom of choice) we may say that an agent's situation *influences* the way in which he eventually chooses, and that we may therefore deepen our appreciation and understanding of a goal-directed action by examining the situation of the agent in which it arose and to which it is a reaction. Those aspects of an agent's situation which have influenced an agent's choice Schutz calls the '*genuine because motives*' of an action. They are quite distinct from the in-order-to motives of an action (unlike the pseudo because motives) as the following examples will show:

(1) *In-order-to* motive:
     'I opened by umbrella in order not to get wet.'
(2) Genuine because motive:
     'I opened by umbrella because it was raining.'

I should hasten to mention that prominent among the aspects of an agent's situation which exercise an influence on his choice are those aspects which constitute a constraint on his present freedom of action; but not all aspects of an agent's situation which influence his choices need be constraints. Thus, for example, my choice of what goods and services to buy is definitely constrained by the level of my income, more precisely, by the amount of leisure time I am prepared to sacrifice in order to earn an income to buy goods and services.[9] On the other hand, there are various past experiences or even physical aspects of my situation which may influence my choice without strictly speaking constraining it. I may or may not choose to take up in later life the games I played at school: or if I live in Rio de Janeiro, I may or may not be a regular visitor to the seaside. Yet one might well say that the games I played at school have influenced my choice of game to play in later life or that the sheer fact of living in Rio has influenced my predilection for beach life.

Thus while constraints are a very obvious type of influence on actions they are not the only way in which we can envisage an agent's situation influencing his freely chosen actions; they are not the only kind of 'genuine because motives' of action. Those aspects of an agent's situation in the world which exercise an influence on his choices we call then the 'genuine because motives of an action', and as already noted we may achieve a considerable deepening or enhancement of our understanding of an agent's course of action by an appreciation of these because motives of an action. There are two points of the utmost methodological importance which should immediately be made, however:

(1) The citing of the genuine because motive of an action as part of the explanation of an action does *not* and *must not* involve any kind of efficient causal mode of explanation of that action.

(2) The genuine because motive is always parasitic upon the in-order-to motive of an action and can only be intelligible once the in-order-to motive of an action has already been specified.

Taking the first of these methodological points, I have repeatedly emphasized that in a careful phenomenological reflection man can come to recognize with absolute certainty that he is always free to choose in various ways albeit within constraints. The moment of this awareness of freedom is the moment when all antecedent determination of whatever kind is transcended and cancelled and man becomes the fully responsible author and initiator of the courses of action which he takes. Consequently, when man finds himself in a certain situation there can be no question of that situation somehow determining the course of his action in a closed efficient-causal manner. Rather there is always a *variety* of possible ways of *re-acting* to the situation, and man is the fully responsible author of the particular reaction which he chooses.[10] Thus rather than the situation being somehow an efficient cause which determines the action as an effect, the situation is a background influence to which the chosen course of action is a purposive freely chosen reaction. This point may be readily illustrated from economic theory. For although economics is almost invariably analysing instances of constrained choice by agents, the economist most certainly does not conceive of the constraints as determinants or efficient causes of action. Rather, once we have specified what are the goals (in-order-to motives) of agents, the constraints are an important influence to be taken into account when deducing the course of action which an agent with the specified goals will be likely to take given his situation. Thus far from being efficient causes determining actions, the constraints, or more generally the 'because motives' of an action may be cited only within a wider explanation of action in terms of the agent's goals, that is to say within a teleological mode of explanation of action, and they serve to deepen our appreciation of why the agent should have chosen freely a certain course of action.

These considerations lead me to the second methodological point: that the because motive is entirely parasitic upon in-order-to motive explanation and may only be cited in conjunction with such an explanation. For given that man is always the responsible author and initiator of his actions and of his reactions to certain situations, it follows immediately that the primary requirement in explaining any action or reaction must be to specify the goal which the agent is seeking to achieve. In the case of purposive reactions to certain situations we may then supplement our appreciation of the goal or in-order-to motive explanation by citing the situation to which the action is a purposive reaction. But unless we have first specified what the goal of the agent's freely chosen reaction is, citing of the because motive will take us nowhere towards explaining the action of the agent precisely because there is always a wide variety of ways in which the agent could choose to react to that situation (cited in the because motive) in which he finds himself. For example, in the economic theory of the firm it would be quite pointless if in seeking to explain a firm's pricing policy we were simply to cite the constraints on the firm's choices, represented by cost curves and demand curves. We cannot make any head-way towards explaining price (or towards any non-trivial predictions for that matter) unless we specify the goal of the firm – the in-order-to motives of its actions – which might be profit maximization, sales maximization, entry prevention, and so on.[11]

We now reach the important conclusion that the primary aim of a subjectivist-interpretive methodology should be to achieve an explanation of action in terms of its in-order-to motive. The citation of the (genuine) because motives is entirely parasitic upon and supplementary to the grasping of the in-order-to motive. Moreover, it does not involve introducing any kind of efficient-causal explanation of human actions.

Schutz's treatment of the question of motivation and its precise meaning thus achieves another valuable clarification in the outline of a detailed subjectivist-interpretive methodology for the human sciences. I should now like to go beyond Schutz to suggest that his distinction of the in-order-to and because motives can offer a most illuminating way of demarcating the respective fields of sociology and economics.

Although both economics and sociology are today well-established human sciences they stand in a somewhat uneasy and often quite antagonistic relationship to each other. One reason for this is undoubtedly that the respective fields of the two disciplines are not at all well defined with the result that there is a large grey area over which it is not clear whether economic or sociological analysis would be most appropriate. I shall now suggest that Schutz's treatment of motivation offers a most interesting and clear-cut way of defining the respective fields of economics and sociology within the framework of a subjectivist-interpretive methodology of the human sciences.

In the course of Chapters 5 to 7 above I have shown at length that the centrepiece of all mainstream economic theory is the optimization principle, that is to say that economic theory seeks to explain any human action (that proceeds from deliberate choice) in terms of the goals of the agents. In doing so, the economist invariably takes the situation of the agent (his preferences and the constraints he faces) as given. Hence in the Schutzian terminology of motivation we may immediately say that economics is concerned with or focuses upon the in-order-to motives of actions, taking the (genuine) because motives for granted and as the concern of other disciplines.

It is a good deal more difficult to pin down the essential interests of a discipline as wide-ranging as sociology. However, I venture to suggest that a pervasive concern of sociological analysis is with the manner in which various social 'facts', conventions or institutions influence the actions of individual agents or groups of agents. In other words, a great deal of sociology is concerned with the influence of an agent's social situation on the course of his actions. Putting this in Schutzian language, sociology is essentially concerned with the because motives of action, while taking the in-order-to motives more or less for granted. Such a definition would not only clarify the appropriate fields of economic and sociological studies; it also emphasizes the complementarity of economics and sociology in the study of social problems (since the because motive is entirely parasitic upon the in-order-to motive of action).

If this proposed definition of the field of sociology and its demarcation from economics seems idiosyncratic, I would point out that it converges closely with the definition of sociology which has been put foward by at least one leading modern sociologist, Raymond Boudon. In his interesting work *La Logique du Social*[12] Boudon has suggested that whereas economics has always taken the provenance of constraints and of agents' preference for granted, that is to say as givens into which he would not inquire, sociology has by contrast made of these its central concern. Boudon surveys a wide range of sociological literature from Pareto and Durkheim up to the present day suggesting that a central theme of all sociology has been the manner in which various social 'facts'[13] or institutions exercise an influence over the actions of individuals, and often constitute significant constraints on their possible courses of action. Boudon goes on to insist at some length that we must not conceive of this influence of social situations on individual action in an efficient-causal determinist manner since that would involve a serious misunderstanding of human action and its motivation. He argues that we are rather to conceive of social 'facts' and institutions as background influences or constraints to which action is a purposive and freely chosen reaction. Having surveyed a number of specific areas of sociological theory such as Durkheim's theory of suicide and anomie and the theory of participation levels in education and having shown that a much more satisfactory understanding of these is achieved when we adopt an interactionist teleological rather than an efficient causal framework, Boudon concludes:

> Le fait que son (l'acteur individuel) action se déroule dans un contexte de contraintes, c'est-à-dire d'éléments qu'il doit accepter comme des données qui s'imposent à lui ne signifie pas qu'on puisse faire de son comportement la conséquence exclusive de ces contraintes. Les contraintes ne sont qu'un des éléments permettant de comprendre l'action individuelle . . . des relations de causalité que le sociologue décèle entre les propriétés des systèmes d'interaction et le comportement des individus n'est géneralement possible que si ces comportements sont concus comme des ACTIONS dotéés de finalité.[14]

Thus Boudon is quite clearly suggesting that the central concern of sociology is with the influence which various social situations exercise on individuals' courses of action, and that we are to conceive of this influence not on efficient-causal lines, but as an important element within a teleological mode of explanation of human action (that is, we are to conceive of the influence of the situation as a social 'fact' to which the agent reacts in a purposive freely choosing manner). It will, therefore, be evident that although Boudon does not seem to have been aware of Schutz's work, that his proposed definition of sociology may be immediately re-expressed in Schutzian language by saying that the central concern of sociology is with the 'because motives' of action within the framework of a subjectivist-interpretive methodology. Indeed, we may also remark that Boudon saw his proposed definition of sociology as providing a useful demarcation of the respective fields of sociology and economics. Where sociology is concerned with constraints and their influence, economics concentrates on the goals of action taking the constraints as given.[15] Again, this may be succinctly re-expressed in Schutzian terminology by saying that whereas sociology is concerned essentially with the 'because motives' of action, the central concern of economics is with the 'in-order-to motives' of human actions.

Schutz's treatment of motivation, and in particular his distinction of the in-order-to and because motives, thus allows us to achieve a most illuminating definition of sociology and a clearcut demarcation of the respective fields of sociology and of economics: sociology is the study of the because motives of action while economics is the study of in-order-to motives. Since I have also shown that within a subjectivist-interpretive methodology the because motive is parasitic upon the in-order-to motive of action this definition and demarcation has the great merit of emphasizing at the same time the *complementarity* of sociology and economics. Rather than being disciplines which stand opposed to each other and offer conflicting policy advice, if we follow the above definitions economics and sociology should complement each other in the analysis of social problems and in the resulting recommendations for policy.[16]

14.3   The Need for Empirical Tests of Interpretive Theories in Human Science

The final element of the Schutzian subjectivist-interpretive methodology with which I shall deal is the imperative (for Schutz) of subjecting the interpretive theories of a subjectivist human science to careful empirical testing. Although Schutz himself did not devote much of his time to discussing this imperative which he took to be fairly obvious, it will be appropriate to spell out the point clearly in this book because many economists when they hear of the subjectivist approach to the human sciences immediately associate such an approach with *a priorism* – that is to say with the quite distinct thesis that the theories of an interpretive human science can be known to be true *a priori* and hence do not stand in any need of empirical testing. Since there is a wide consensus that at least one essential ingredient for a discipline to be called a rigorous science is that it should subject its theories to empirical tests, this association by economists of the subjectivist approaches with *a priorism* has led them in general to recoil in horror from such approaches.[17]

Although Max Weber may not have been quite as clear as one could wish on the imperative of empirical testing in his methodological sketches, Schutz makes it abundantly clear that the theories of an interpretive human science must be subjected to careful empirical testing.[18] He recognizes that although each person can in reflection on his own consciousness come to know with absolute certainty what he is doing and why he is doing it, the conscious states and activities of *other* persons cannot be given absolutely to *that person's own* consciousness in the same way. We can only *conjecture* the details of the conscious states of other persons.[19] Since the aim of the human sciences is to construct explanatory generalizations which apply to myriad agents other than the human scientist himself it follows that the theories of an interpretive human science will be conjectural and hence stand in need of empirical testing against actually observed behaviour patterns and activities of agents in the world.

It will help to clarify matters if we contrast this Schutzian view of the imperative of empirical testing in interpretive human sciences with some of the counter-claims for the *a priori* truth of interpretive theories which have been made. It is these counter-claims which have led economists to associate automatically *a priorism* with subjectivist approaches to the human sciences, although we shall now see that there is no such necessary linkage. *A priorism* has been put forward in conjunction with a subjectivist-interpretive methodology both by the Historical and Hermeneutical Schools in the last century and also in the present century by many of the economists within the so-called Austrian School.

The Historical and Hermeneutical Schools, drawing their inspiration from Dilthey, argued that the aim of the human sciences should be to grasp the subjective meaning of action for an agent at its deepest and most uniquely personal level: and they believed that this deepest subjective meaning could be grasped with absolute certainty by another person by means of *empathetic intuition*, that is to say by a sympathetic projection of oneself into the position of the other person in order to imagine exactly what his or her conscious states are. Consequently the followers of the Historical and Hermeneutical Schools held that their interpretations of the subjective meanings of other persons' actions were true *a priori* and did not require to be tested empirically.

It is quite clear why Schutz rejects any such claim of the *a priori* truth of interpretive theories based on empathy. We simply cannot know with absolute certainty the detailed contents of other persons' conscious states and activities as we know our own. Hence while empathetic intuition may be of considerable heuristic use it cannot yield us interpretations of subjective meaning which are absolutely certain. Rather all such interpretations of other persons' motivations are conjectural in character and so stand in need of an empirical test which can provide an independent check on the accuracy of empathetic intuitions.

The Austrian School of economists has been a definitive exponent of subjectivist-interpretive methodology in the present century. But while they have rejected the Historical School's search for the deepest and uniquely personal level of subjective meaning of actions and championed instead systematic interpretive generalizations regarding the typical subjective meaning of large groups of agents, many of the Austrians have taken over from the Historical School the notion that interpretive theories regarding the motivation of other people's actions can be known to be true *a priori* in virtue of some sort of empathetic intuition. This is the view which I labelled as 'extreme *a priorism*' in Chapter 10 (p. 156), where we saw that it has been upheld by much of the school.[20] However, it will be clear that Schutz would reject any such extreme *a priorism* for exactly the same reasons (just given above) as he rejects the *a priorism* of the Historical and Hermeneutical Schools.

Before leaving the topic of *a priorism* in the subjectivist-interpretive human sciences there is one further point which I must clarify. When discussing existentialist phenomenology in Chapter 12 above I suggested, following Sartre, that there is a potential direct contribution which might be made by *a priori* phenomenological elucidations of the form or essence of various conscious states and activities to the human sciences. However, I may recall that I made it abundantly clear there that such an *a priori* contribution from existentialist phenomenology to the human sciences pertains purely to the *forms* of various conscious states (the essence of joy, of deliberate choice, and so on) and can tell us nothing about the detailed contents of other people's conscious states or activities. Hence the *a priori* contribution remains a strictly limited and preliminary one and is nothing more than a very minor qualification to the Schutzian insistence that the theories of a subjectivist-interpretive human science must be subjected to rigorous empirical testing.

We may conclude therefore that mainstream economists' widely held suspicion of a subjectivist-interpretive methodology on the grounds that if they adopt it they will be led off into some extreme hermeneutics or empathy-based *a priorism* (Mises-style) is completely unfounded. If it is a widely recognized requirement for a discipline to be worthy of the title of a science that it should submit its theories to rigorous empirical tests, then unquestionably an economics, psychology or sociology which is based on a Schutzian subjectivist-interpretive methodology will be a fully rigorous science.

Before closing this discussion of the scientific credentials of a Schutzian subjectivist-interpretive human science there is a further but much less important issue which I may mention briefly – the requirement that a rigorous science should be *value-neutral*. By value neutrality I mean that the scientist must, when developing his theories, divest himself of all prejudices and moral evaluations in order to be able to pursue and to discover truths, however unpalatable these truths may be to himself or to others. In other words, the requirement of maintaining a value neutral attitude in science is a direct implication of the adoption of *truth* as the ultimate regulative criterion of all human inquiry (which I have defended in Chapters 1 to 3). We must pursue the truth in science irrespective of what or whose moral and political pre-conceptions and prejudices we may upset.

The natural sciences have never had much difficulty in maintaining a strict value neutrality since so much of their theory is concerned with topics which are morally and politically uncontroversial. The human sciences by contrast, and especially economics and sociology are dealing with human affairs and man's social interaction in particular, an area which is the subject of heated and endless controversy in moral and political theory. Consequently, the risk of hidden evaluative premises or prejudices of various kinds obscuring the search for truth in the human sciences is much greater and the preservation of a strictly value neutral attitude by the human scientist is correspondingly more difficult.

It should be emphasized, however, that at least in a Schutzian human science, value neutrality can and must be maintained despite the difficulty. Both Weber and Schutz have quite explicitly said that, although an interpretive human scientist will often be dealing directly with other people's moral evaluations when seeking to elucidate the motivations of their purposive actions, nevertheless the human scientist must at all times maintain a strictly detached and unprejudiced attitude towards those values of others and towards his subject matter in general. Value neutrality does not mean that the human sciences should never look at people's moral and political evaluations; on the contrary they will often be of considerable relevance when we seek to explain the goals pursued by agents in some action or other – the central concern of a subjectivist-interpretive methodology. Value neutrality only means that the human scientist should avoid judging those moral evaluations of others and should treat them simply as further relevant facts when explaining human actions, in other words he should maintain a strictly detached attitude towards his subject matter. Consequently, while the subjectivist interpretive human sciences deal with a field which is a central concern of moral and political evaluations and controversy and while the human sciences must indeed often take some of these evaluations into account as facts, this does not mean that they cannot maintain a value neutral attitude.

Therefore on this further requirement of scientificity which is sometimes put forward, namely the preservation of a strictly value-neutral attitude, the subjectivist human sciences of the Schutzian variety again measure up well, and Schutz himself has insisted quite clearly that the subjectivist human sciences must maintain such an attitude.[21] Having thus demonstrated on this point as on the requirement of empirical testing the fully rigorous scientific character of a Schutzian subjectivist-interpretive human science, any lingering doubts or suspicions which are harboured by economists or other human scientists regarding the scientific credentials of a Schutzian human science should have been definitely laid to rest.

Notes

1   A. Schutz (1972), *The Phenomenology of the Social World* (London: Heinemann).

2   Cf. A. Schutz, *The Phenomenology of the Social World*, ch.1. On Weber's methodology see M. Weber (1978), 'Economy and Society', G. Roth and C. Wittich (eds) (New York: Bedminster Press), pp. 3–63, especially pp. 3–31.

3   Cf. A. Schutz, *The Phenomenology of the Social World*, pp. 229–30.

4   Cf. A. Schutz, *The Phenomenology of the Social World*, pp. 229–30.

5   This notion of language as secondary to thought and as mere instrument for communication of thoughts may be contrasted with the notions of language as the primary datum of philosophy in modern British philosophy, especially in works inspired by Wittgenstein.

6   A good example of a work which has probed systematically into the more ultimate motivations of human activity is M. Weber's (1970), *Protestant Ethic and the Spirit of Capitalism* (London: Allen & Unwin), where he shows how the behaviour of profit-maximizing entrepreneurs can ultimately be explained in terms of a Calvinist view of how eternal salvation in an after life can be attained. Hence, profit maxmization is seen as contributing towards this more (or most) ultimate goal of the agent.

7   W. Runciman (1972), *A Critique of Max Weber's Philosophy of Social Science* (Cambridge: Cambridge University Press) is an example of an exegesis of Weber which accords to interpretation in human science only the role of interpreting objective meaning. This interpretation of objective meaning is seen by Runciman as merely a classification preliminary to a human science which will adopt an efficient-causal mode of explanation of actions along objectivist-behaviourist lines. No doubt such an exegesis of Weber is possible given the ambiguity of his original presentation, but I doubt very much that it accords with what Weber really meant given his emphasis on human subjectivity and the subjectivist-interpretive character of a great deal of his actual work in sociology and economics. In any case, I am not so much concerned here with what Weber meant but rather with the kind of interpretive methodology that can be rigorously deduced from existentialist phenomenology.

8   Cf. A. Schutz, *The Phenomenology of the Social World*, pp. 86–96.

9   That is, ultimately by a time constraint.

10 This (rather Sartrean) way of looking at freedom and the implications of constraints generates some far-reaching implications for political philosophy. It will mean that man is always free, even under the most totalitarian of régimes: the crux of the matter is rather the degree of constraint on freedom of the individual which a state or community ought to impose. Of the many political philosophers who have spoken of freedom, only J. S. Mill in his essay 'On liberty', seems to have recognized this. Notice also that this way of looking at freedom means, further, that in some sense people only get the sort of régime which they deserve. One is always free to revolt or protest against state interference in and constraint of one's freedom.

11 On all of this, see Chapter 12, pp. 184–85 and Chapter 6, pp. 99–100.

12 R. Boudon (1979), *La Logique du Social* (Paris: Hachette), ch. 1, 8.

13 This term is due to Durkheim. It signifies any social situation which influences human action but which the individual agent *by himself* is powerless to remove. Thus, for example, laws, the political party system are social 'facts'.

14 R. Boudon, *La Logique du Social*, p. 33.

15 Cf. R. Boudon, *La Logique du Social*, pp.14–15.

16   One of the great scandals of human sciences is their failure to speak with one voice on urgent social problems. The proposed definition points the way towards an ending of the cacophony. It suggests that there is indeed everything to be gained from an interdisciplinary approach to dealing with such problems.

17   M. Blaug (1980), *The Methodology of Economics* (Cambridge: Cambridge University Press). See, for example, Blaug's discussion at pp. 46–9 and pp. 91–3.

18   Max Weber had rather confused matters by using the term 'causal adequacy' of interpretive hypotheses to describe the requirement that interpretive theories should have their predictions checked against actual behaviour patterns in the world. Schutz clarifies Weber's position and insists clearly on the requirement of empirical testing of interpretive theories in his book *The Phenomenology of the Social World*, pp. 229–34.

19   Unless we actually meet them personally and ask them to tell us about their conscious states. For the most part this will be impracticable if not impossible, however.

20   There is also a small sub-group within the Austrian School which eschews extreme *a priorism* and argues that empirical testing of interpretive theories has an important role to play in establishing the applicability or inapplicability of such theories to various practical situations. This I have noted in Chapter 10 is a most interesting view, but it remains exceptional within the Austrian School. For the most part Austrian economists have been extreme *a priorists*.

21   I have treated the question of whether or not a value-neutral human science is possible only briefly here (and suggested that it is possible). I am fully aware that there has been much debate on this question and on whether or not a *completely* value-neutral attitude is ever possible given the often value-laden character of language and the fact that any human science must choose specific areas for study (the problem of values in fact-selection). However, a full dress treatment of value neutrality would have been inappropriate in this work, not least because it is an issue on which objectivist behaviourists and subjectivists are fully agreed.

15

A Resolution of Some Notorious Sticking Points

In the last chapter I sought to show that a human science which adopts a Schutzian subjectivist-interpretive methodology would be a fully rigorous science. In this chapter I shall turn my attention to some often-encountered difficulties or sticking points within a subjectivist-interpretive methodology, seeking to resolve these and to clarify the position which the mature Schutzian version of a subjectivist methodology takes up in relation to these problems.[1]

Specifically I shall be dealing with:
(1) the principle of methodological individualism;
(2) rationality postulates;
(3) the distinction of efficient-causal and strictly teleological modes of explanation;
(4) the nature of such teleological explanations as are sometimes found in the natural sciences.

Apart from the obvious linkage between the third and fourth items there is no special connection between these themes: they are merely a selection of some notorious points of difficulty which often crop up in discussions of a subjectivist-interpretive methodology. The chapter is therefore somewhat of a ragbag but I have thought it important to include it in order to strike pre-emptively against certain fairly common but (as I shall seek to show) ill-grounded or confused objections to a subjectivist methodology at least in its mature Schutzian version.

15.1   The Principle of Methodological Individualism in a Subjectivist Human Science

There is no doubt that a subjectivist-interpretive methodology of human science carries with it a principle of methodological individualism. Not only Weber and Schutz but also a variety of other proponents of the subjectivist approach, such as Hayek and Boudon, have all properly recognized this. But some care should be taken in specifying precisely in what sense an individualist principle is implied by the subjectivist-interpretive approach.

Methodological individualism pertains to the question of social 'wholes' and how they are to be treated and understood within human science. By a social 'whole' we mean any kind of macro-level social phenomenon. This will include not only all sorts of social institutions and collective groupings but also Durkheim's social 'facts'; the latter are simply any macro-level features or 'facts' of a society over which the individual agent taken by himself has no power at all. Within a subjectivist-interpretive approach no attempt is made to deny the existence of such social wholes: but it is insisted that they have no existence apart from the individuals who make them up and are incapable of any action other than through the actions of those individuals. To be more precise, social institutions and any kind of social facts are regarded purely as the intended or often unintended resultant of myriad purposive individual actions: and institutions are incapable of 'acting' (or social facts of exercising any influence) other than through the actions of some individual agents who comprise the institution (or whose actions give rise to the social 'fact'). In other words, there can be no question of viewing social wholes as some kind of mysterious independent social force, still less of investing them with some sort of independent organic existence or even personality as has sometimes happened.[2] It may be mentioned in passing that the tendency to personify or otherwise to attribute independent existence to social wholes has often arisen from a failure to grasp the point that a macro-social phenomenon is often the *unintended* resultant of a variety of purposive individual actions. There are many instances where holistic phenomena are the 'resultant of human action but not of human design'. Hayek has written at some length on such phenomena[3] of which he believes that the market system is an outstanding example, and Boudon has shown how a wide variety of 'social facts' can readily be explained in this manner.[4] Once we grasp the simple notion that individual human actions often give rise to various unintended side-effects (or 'spillover' effects as they are known to the economist) there is nothing suprising or mysterious about such macro-level social phenomena that are not the intended goal of individual actions. To take an example: once we have understood how a market system of interaction will operate under conditions of perfect competition there is no need to invoke any mysterious 'invisible hand' or pre-ordained 'natural harmony' in order to explain why such a market system produces certain kinds of socially optimal results. These results are simply an unintended macro-level by-product effect of the myriad individual optimizing decisions made by individual agents.

In addition to insisting that social wholes are nothing apart from and incapable of acting except through the individuals who comprise them and their actions, the subjectivist/interpretive human scientist holds that while these social wholes exist and may be an important influence on individual actions they *cannot* be held to be efficient causes or determinants of human action. This point follows immediately from the conception of human subjectivity and human action put foward by existentialist phenomenology and which, I have argued,[5] provides the philosophical foundation of the whole subjectivist-interpretive methodology. We saw there that although human action always occurs within the constraints of the situation in the world in which man finds himself, none the less every human action is *freely chosen* within those constraints: and in the moment of free choice all antecedent determination of whatever kind is transcended and cancelled. Hence *inter alia* it will follow that there can be no question of seeing social wholes as somehow determining human actions in an efficient-causal manner. Social wholes do indeed exist but holistic determinism is definitively rejected by the subjectivist-interpretive approach.

That is not to say that macro-level social phenomena of all kinds may not be an important background influence on human actions: but this influence must be understood along the lines of the Schutzian 'because motive' of actions with which I have dealt in Chapter 14 (pp. 207–9). Thus social wholes form a fairly important part of the constraining situation in the world in which man finds himself and to which his actions are often a freely chosen reaction. Put another way, social wholes may be the 'because motives' of human action.[6] As I have already argued in Chapter 14, however, the reaction to the influence/constraints contained in the because motive is always a freely chosen reaction so that there can be no question of conceiving 'because motivation' along efficient-causal determinist lines. In the specific case here social wholes may indeed be important background influences to be taken into account as because motives within a subjectivist-interpretive human science; but they are not efficient-causal determinants of human actions.

Again, Raymond Boudon's work provides an ample illustration of the treatment of social wholes and their influence on human action within a subjectivist-interpretive approach.[7] Having argued that social wholes are nothing other than the intended or often unintended resultant of individual human actions he goes on to show how, when they have emerged, macro-level social phenomena become important elements in the social 'situation' in which men find themselves and to which many of their purposive actions will be a freely chosen reaction. Thus he is led to a conception of sociology as essentially a study of systems of interaction between purposively acting human agents. Social wholes are the intended or unintended result of certain individual actions; and those social wholes then become the background influences, the because motives, to which further human actions are again freely chosen purposive reactions. Boudon devotes most of his book to illustrating this theme which is an integral part of the methodological individualist principle of the subjectivist-interpretive approach. As he puts it:

les phénomènes auxquels le sociologue s'intéresse sont conçus comme explicables par la structure du système d'intéraction à l'intérieur duquel ces phénoménes émergent.
L'atome logique de l'analyse sociologique est donc l'acteur individuel.[8]

In the light of the preceding discussion we may say that a subjectivist-interpretive human science involves a principle of methodological individualism, and that this amounts to (a) an insistence that while such social wholes certainly exist they are incapable of any action other than through the action of the individuals who make them up, and (b) that while social wholes may be an important background influence (a because motive) of actions they can never determine actions in an efficient-causal manner.

It is of some importance to distinguish this methodological individualist principle of a Schutzian human science from certain other types of individualism which are much more challengeable than it. This is particularly so since it has often been assumed by critics that once the 'individualist' label has been pinned on the subjectivist approach that this by itself is a condemnation of the approach.

In a valuable article that does much to clarify the whole issue of individualism in the human sciences Steven Lukes[9] has distinguished a number of very different individualist principles. Of these the most important are ontological individualism, political individualism, and methodological individualism as defined already.

Ontological individualism is the view that only individuals actually exist or are real; and that social wholes do not actually exist in the world and are only mental constructs or fictions. It is sometimes further held that since social wholes of any kind are merely fictions they are empirically unobservable and so, for positivists, talk of them would be meaningless.[10] This is a rather extreme variant of individualism and as Lukes points out it is highly implausible. It would mean for example that no collective entity could be said to exist actually but that they are all mere fictions. Thus not only would actual existence be denied to 'the working class', the 'nation', and so on, reality would also be denied to crowds, flocks and forests. In any case it should be obvious that there is no attempt to maintain an ontological individualism in a Schutzian subjectivist human science. The actual existence of social wholes of various kinds is never denied.

Political individualism refers to a normative principle of ethical or of political theory to the effect that the individual agent ought to be the ultimate focus of all moral evaluation or of political values and arrangements. It has received striking expression for example in the moral philosophy of Kant which enjoins us never to treat another person as a mere means but always also as an end[11] and in the political philosophy of J. S. Mill's 'On Liberty'.[12] It amounts to the assertion that the well being of individual agents ought never to be sacrificed for the good of some social whole or collectivity and in political terms to the insistence that political legitimacy derives solely from the consent of the individuals governed.

There may well be much to be said in defence of ethical and political individualism, and some (but by no means all) exponents of the subjectivist-interpretive approach to the human sciences have been strong advocates of political individualism.[13] But it should again be clear that political individualism is completely distinct from the methodological individualist principle involved in a subjectivist-interpretive human science. Political individualism is a normative theory of how an ideal society ought to be constructed while methodological individualism is only a theory of how we should proceed in an explaining macro-level social phenomena and which neither denies their existence nor their influence on individual actions.

It will be clear, therefore, that the principle of methodological individualism which is involved in the subjectivist-interpretive approach to the human sciences is very different from either the ontological individualism or the political individualism described above. Hence when it is said that the subjectivist approach adopts an individualist standpoint it must be realized that what is meant by this is 'methodological individualism' and not either ontological or political individualism such as I have described above. Once this is recognized much of the sting is taken out of the charge of individualism against the subjectivist approach, and certainly it does not follow that having shown the approach to involve an individualist principle, that that is enough to condemn it.[14]

Indeed the methodological individualist principle which is involved in a subjectivist-interpretive human science is a fairly minimal innocuous one which would probably be acceptable to most human scientists. It makes no attempt to deny the existence of social wholes or their influence on human actions and it amounts to little more than a determination to avoid mysterious personification or attribution of independent organic existence to social wholes, and above all to avoid holistic determinism as a mode of explanation in the human sciences.

15.2 Rationality Postulates and the Subjectivist Approach: A Clarification

A second topic which has been the source of some confusion and controversy in relation to the subjectivist-interpretive methodology has been the question of rationality postulates. To be precise, there has been some dispute as to the assumptions about human rationality which are implicit in the subjectivist methodology.

I have already dealt at some length in Chapter 7 with the postulates of rationality which are involved in economic theory, and a number of important points from that discussion may usefully be recalled here in order to initiate the discussion of the role of rationality postulates in any human science which adopts an interpretive methodology. In Chapter 7 I followed Benn and Mortimore[15] in drawing a fundamental distinction between epistemic and practical rationality. Epistemic rationality is a property of thoughts and propositions, and we may say that an assertion is epistemically rational when we have an absolutely conclusive proof of it. I pointed out that to assume full epistemic rationality on the part of all human agents would mean attributing omniscience or perfect knowledge in all matters to them, and such an implausible postulate is not required by economic theory, nor indeed by any other human science.

For purposive goal-directed activity can readily be carried out by agents in a world of uncertainty where knowledge is imperfect: the countless purposive actions engaged in daily by human beings in the actual world testify to this. I did point out in Chapter 7, however, that goal-directed activity will only be possible when the level of agent's information in matters which pertain to their choices is of a fairly satisfactory kind – sufficient to give a reasonable chance of success in the execution of one's plans. Otherwise goal-directed activity would almost always fail miserably to attain its ends and would be quite pointless. Hence we may say that any interpretive human science (whose centrepiece is always the attempt to explain human action in terms of the agent's own goals) must always presume a reasonable level and quality of information pertaining to choices on the part of human agents.[16] This, however, falls very far short indeed of being a postulate of 'epistemic rationality' and hence no such postulate is implied by the adoption of a subjectivist-interpretive methodology.

The epistemic rationality of thoughts is contrasted with the notion of the practical rationality of actions. An action is said to be practically rational if it meets the following three conditions (a) the action must be directed to some goal, (b) the goal aimed at must be consistent with other goals pursued by the agent, (c) the action must be geared to achieve the maximum level of attainment of the goal to which it is directed subject to the constraints of the agent's situation and in the light of the information available to the agent. This notion of practical rationality is the exact logical equivalent of the optimization principle which I have shown to be central to all mainstream economic theory: an action which is practically rational is precisely an action which is aimed at optimization and vice versa. Since I have argued that economic theory focuses its attention exclusively on cases of deliberate choice, that is to say on actions that are preceded by a reflection and deliberation on alternatives available, and since I have argued that an existentialist phenomenological examination of the act of deliberate choice will reveal that any such choice will aim at optimization, it follows that economic theory adopts a universal postulate of practical rationality of actions.[17] Economic theory, in other words, focuses its attention solely on actions which are practically rational.

That much has already been established at some length in Chapter 7. What I wish to examine now is the role played by practical rationality postulates in human sciences other than economics which adopt a subjectivist-interpretive methodology. There can be no doubt that some human sciences will have to deal with actions which are not practically rational, not aimed at optimization. This is simply because there is in the actual world a wide variety of actions which are impulsive and unreflective, that is they are not preceded by any careful deliberation over alternatives by the agent and so will usually not be aimed at optimization. When an agent acts entirely on impulse and without thinking it is extremely unlikely that the action will turn out to achieve his goals in the maximum degree possible consistent with the constraints of his situation. Thus we cannot presume that impulsive actions are practically rational and I will speak of them from now on as non-rational actions. By this term I wish to suggest only that impulsive actions are not optimizing actions and so are not practically rational. (I am deliberately avoiding the term 'irrational' for such actions because of its pejorative connotation.)

The human sciences will undoubtedly have to get to grips with the field of non-rational actions since there are so many instances of impulsive actions in the actual world. But will a human science based on the subjectivist-interpretive methodology encounter difficulties when dealing with the field of non-rational actions? According to the existentialist account of subjectivity as outlined in Chapter 12 *every* human action is freely chosen by the agent and in the moment of free choice all antecedent determination of whatever kind is transcended and cancelled. The agent becomes the fully responsible author and initiator of his action, whether that action is purely impulsive or follows from a careful deliberation. Furthermore, every freely chosen action initiated by the agent must be directed to achievement of some goal or other by the agent, however vaguely or erroneously that goal and the means to attain it may be perceived, otherwise the agent would not have bothered to initiate the course of actions in question.

An existentialist-phenomenological examination of human action thus suggests that any human action, whether impulsive and so non-rational, or practically rational, will always be freely chosen and end-directed. Hence the explanation of any human action must be cast in terms of the goal of the agent involved, that is to say that the human sciences, in the explanation of non-rational impulsive actions as well as in the case of practically rational actions, should adopt a subjectivist-interpretive methodology with a teleological mode of explanation. Moreover, since all human actions are freely chosen and goal-directed there can be no question (*inter alia*) of giving an efficient-causal account of impulsive actions in which they are viewed as the behavioural effect or response to some antecedent external stimulus.[18] Indeed, the very simple fact that we often subsequently regret impulsive actions and speak of seeking to control our impulses in the future underlines the fact that impulsive actions are none the less freely chosen; and so cannot be understood along efficient-causal lines but rather teleologically. Hence in answer to the question as to whether or not a subjectivist-interpretive human science can get to grips with non-rational actions the answer is most certainly *yes*. Indeed, given the freely chosen goal-directed character of all non-rational as well as practically rational action a human science must adopt a subjectivist-interpretive approach in the explanation of all such actions.

Since the assertion that all impulsive and so non-rational actions are none the less freely chosen and end-directed may seem rather surprising or far-fetched to some I may pause briefly to give some illustration of the point. Examples of how non-rational actions may be interpreted as directed to some goal and of why they must be seen always as freely chosen abound in the literature of existentialist phenomenology, especially in existentialist-based psychology. But I shall confine my illustration of the existentialist approach to non-rational action to one outstanding and highly suggestive example which deals with the most wildly impulsive type of activity of all – Sartre's theory of emotion. Sartre has returned to the theme of emotion at a number of points in his life work, both in pure philosophy and in his literary productions. But the main essentials of his conception of emotion were already outlined in his early work, *A Sketch for a Theory of the Emotions*, and did not alter substantially thereafter.[19]

In that work, Sartre first of all rejects the various objectivist-behaviourist accounts of emotion as offering an inadequate understanding of emotion before turning to existentialist phenomenology as a method whereby an insight into the essence of any emotion or emotional activity can be achieved.[20] The main essentials of the theory of emotion which Sartre presents as a result of this phenomenological study are as follows:

(1) Emotion is always a freely chosen and end-directed activity of the agent. This follows from Sartre's radical notion of human freedom (and consequent responsibility) and from the simple consideration that if not freely chosen by the agent it can make no sense whatever to speak of controlling one's emotions.

(2) Emotion is, however, a very special type of end-directed activity. It arises when the agent finds it impossible to achieve some end which he strongly desires by means of the everyday practical instruments at his disposal; and finding his situation thereby intolerable he seeks to achieve his desired goal by a magical transformation of the everyday world in which the practical barriers to the attainment of his goal are wished away. Emotion is thus a sort of magical incantation designed to achieve some desired goal. This option is very well illustrated by a fit of anger for example where the agent strikes out blindly to achieve some desired end in the face of insuperable obstacles to its attainment. Sartre also illustrates it for a variety of other emotions such as joy, fear, shame, and so on.

(3) Emotion being merely a magical incantation is totally (or largely) ineffective in reaching the desired goal of the agent precisely because the insuperable practical obstacles remain. Emotion always involves, therefore, a self-deception and the person who allows himself to be carried away by emotion is in 'bad faith'. Emotion attempts to transform the everyday world by magic, but it succeeds only in transforming the subject involved in the emotional activity.

(4) Finally, it should be noted that Sartre makes a distinction between feeling and emotion. Clearly, there are many intense feelings which we experience which are not involved in any attempt at a magical transformation of the world and which are not involved in any self-deception. Unlike emotion, which for Sartre is always highly impulsive and unreflecting, feelings are the result of a reflection on our likes and dislikes. Being based thus on a reflection by consciousness on itself, feeling cannot (for Sartre) be involved in any self-deception; and activities which are motivated by feeling are activities which follow from a deliberate choice and so will be

practically rational. Such activities are contrasted by Sartre with emotional activities which are unreflective and so impulsive and non-rational. This distinction between feeling and emotion is an important one since it absolves Sartre's theory from a possible charge of excessive narrowness in his conception of emotion. The notion of emotion is not to be equated with the broader notion of feeling (or romantic sentiment) in Sartre's usage.

This theory of emotion offers I believe a powerful and radical insight into the real essence of emotion (at least emotion in Sartre's narrowest sense of the term as opposed to feeling), but I shall say no more about it here since I have introduced it merely as an illustration. What is important from my point of view is that Sartre has shown that even the most wildly impulsive type of activity represented by the emotions is always freely chosen and end-directed; hence in the explanation of this most impulsive type of action a subjectivist-interpretive methodology with a teleological mode of explanation should be adopted while efficient causal explanations of emotion along objectivist-behaviourist lines are quite explicitly ruled out.

We may now summarize the results of these discussions of the role of rationality postulates and assumptions within a subjectivist-interpretive methodology. I have shown that:

(1) A subjectivist-interpretive human science does not require a postulate of epistemic rationality of human agents, that is, it does not require an assumption of perfect information or omniscience on the part of agents.

(2) A subjectivist-interpretive methodology does not require a postulate of practical rationality of human actions either, for I have shown that impulsive non-rational actions can also be encompassed within a subjectivist-interpretive human science with its teleological mode of explanation. Indeed, I have argued that the only adequate explanation of non-rational actions will be achieved by a human science which adopts a subjectivist-interpretive methodology.

We may conclude, therefore, that a subjectivist-interpretive methodology does not carry with it any kind of necessary postulate of human rationality.

Having clarified this point quite definitively we may note a much less important point regarding practical rationality and interpretive methodology which has been made by both Weber and Schutz. This is that in the *heuristic* process of conjecturing interpretive generalizations in a subjectivist human science, it will be much easier to formulate promising conjectures about practically rational rather than about non-rational actions. The reasons for this are not far to seek. In the case of non-rational impulsive action the goal is often only vaguely defined and the means taken to achieve the goal will not be the most effective or efficient means, and may often be such that they would fail entirely to achieve the desired goal (cf. the complete ineffectiveness of the attempted 'magical transformation' involved in emotional activity). By contrast, in the case of practically rational actions the goal is clearly defined and the means taken are the most effective available, at least in the light of the agent's information whence it is much easier for the human scientist to conjecture correctly what is the goal being aimed at by agents in cases of practically rational actions than in cases of non-rational actions.

It is for this reason that Weber and Schutz have spoken of a heuristic preference for practically 'rational ideal types' in interpretive human science, that is a preference for the framing of interpretive 'course of action ideal type generalizations' which focus on practically rational actions. This most certainly does not mean that the interpretive human sciences will ignore the field of non-rational actions; indeed I have already shown that existentialist psychology which adopts an explicit interpretive methodology has investigated the field of the non-rational action in some detail. As Schutz puts the point:

> interpretative sociology, – but in this it is by no means alone [among human sciences] – prefers rational action types . . . But this does not by any means imply that interpretative sociology neglects irrational action. Weber has again stressed that the latter is part of the subject matter of sociology.[21]

Thus far I have shown that in the study of non-rational actions a human science can and indeed must adopt a subjectivist-interpretive methodology with its teleological mode of explanation, but at the same time any human science will find it easier heuristically to deal with and frame conjectures about practically rational courses of action.[22] I should now like to close the discussion of rationality postulates in an interpretive human science by pointing out that it would be easy to overstate the range of human actions in the actual world which are non-rational and that the range of practically rational actions is a good deal wider than is often imagined. In doing this I shall also be showing that the heuristic preference of interpretive human sciences for practically rational course of action types does not involve any very serious narrowing of focus (and in any case, as Schutz and Weber both emphasize, there is no question of neglecting non-rational actions altogether).

There are two important points or considerations which can show that the range of the practically rational as opposed to the non-rational type of action is much wider than is often imagined. First, there are certain categories of unreflective but not impulsive actions which are often erroneously conceived of as non-rational, and secondly there is a largely bogus dichotomy between reason and feeling or romantic sentiment. I shall deal with each of these points briefly in turn.

There are many human actions in everyday life which are carried out unreflectingly without any immediate forethought or deliberation yet which we would not want to call impulsive actions. The most important categories of such actions are *habitual* and traditional actions and it has often been held that in the absence of any immediately prior deliberation these types of action cannot be seen as optimizations and so are not practically rational. This conclusion involves a serious misapprehension, I would suggest, and I may illustrate my point for the case of habitual actions.

Habitual actions are those which are carried out by an agent regularly in the same way, based on some rule of thumb, and it is precisely in virtue of the rule of thumb that the agent can act immediately without deliberation although not impulsively. But to understand the goals aimed at by an agent in such an action we must examine the provenance of the rule of thumb which is guiding the decisions; we must in other words ask what end the rule of thumb is aimed at achieving if we are to achieve an adequate grasp of the intentions of the agent. Investigation of the provenance of the rule of thumb will require that we look back to some prior deliberation and choice which was carried out by the agent in reaching his rule of thumb; and the adoption of a rule of thumb based on a prior deliberation for all cases of action of a similar type is itself eminently rational, itself an optimization since it economizes the scarce decision time of the agent.[23] I would, therefore, argue that not only should we refer back to some prior deliberation and optimization by an agent in seeking to interpret the intentions of an agent in any habitual action based on a rule of thumb; the decision in principle by an agent to adopt certain rules of thumb rather than to engage in a careful deliberation in every instance of action in some well-defined type of situation is itself an optimization and so practically rational.

If there were any remaining doubts that habitual unreflective actions (being based on a rule of thumb) should be explained in terms of some prior deliberate choice in which the rule of thumb was formulated they may perhaps be put to rest by the following consideration. If a rule of thumb begins to yield persistently results which are very clearly non-optimal for the agent he will soon revise the rule of thumb, he will engage in a careful new deliberation with a view to working out a new rule of thumb which will yield him optimal results. People will not persist in habitual courses of action which they realize to be systematically bad or non-optimal for them, at least for the most part.[24]

All of these points may be amply illustrated by the mark-up theory of pricing in micro-economic theory. This theory recognizes that many firms arrive at their pricing decisions by habitually marking up by a certain proportion over cost (cost-plus pricing) rather than by any elaborate profit maximization (optimization) process of deliberation. This may well be the case but the crucial question for the economic theory of pricing is surely what governs the size of the habitual mark-up; how is the size of the mark-up arrived at in the first place. Inevitably the answer to this question must be sought in some prior deliberation by the firm on what is the 'profit maximizing' or otherwise optimal level of mark-up to use as a rule of thumb for pricing, and the rule of thumb is used thereafter precisely to save on scarce managerial decision time. Furthermore, if firms suspect that their regular mark-up is failing badly in relation to the profit maximizing or other goals which it was supposed to achieve they will quickly engage in a new process of deliberation with a view to revising the habitual mark-up so as to achieve optimal results in the new situation.

I conclude, therefore, that habitual actions although unreflective are none the less practically rational since they are based essentially on a prior deliberation by the agent together with an equally rational decision to save on scarce decision time. Moreover, an adequate understanding of habitual actions must refer back to the original deliberation from which the rule of thumb guiding habitual actions arose since only thus can the goals aimed at in habitual actions be elucidated.

The second major point which I should like to make in clarification of the range of practically rational as opposed to non-rational actions in the actual everyday world is simply that the fact that if an action is undertaken from a motive of feeling or from some romantic motivation this does not mean that it cannot also be a practically rational action. Indeed I would argue that a great many romantically motivated actions are at the same time practically rational. To see this point we may recur to Sartre's distinction between feeling, or as I would say, romantic sentiment in general and the narrower notion of emotion. An emotional activity (in Sartre's narrow sense) is always impulsive and wholly unreflective, that is to say that it does not follow or proceed from any deliberate choice but is entirely spontaneous. Although such actions are end-directed they involve a blindly impulsive striking out to achieve one's goals by magical means and so cannot be attempts at optimization (after deliberation); they cannot be practically rational actions.

But a great many actions which are inspired by feeling or romantic sentiment are not emotional actions in the sense described by Sartre: and Sartre's distinction of feeling and emotion is designed to recognize precisely this point. We engage in very many actions which have a highly romantic or sentimental inspiration only after a careful deliberation about ends and alternative ways to achieve them. Such actions, although sentimentally inspired, will none the less be attempted optimizations and so will be practically rational. I have already pointed out in Chapter 5 that there is no reason why the generalized utility function of one agent should not include among its variables or arguments the well-being of some other agent or agents in the economy and indeed this is arguably the very essence of the feelings of both love and hatred. Thus, if in the passionate pursuit of love for another person I decide after some deliberation to buy some lavish present as testament of my feeling, this action must be regarded as an attempted optimization. To the extent that my testimony of love succeeds in winning the heart of my loved one the action will achieve what for me is an undoubtedly optimal result: the fulfilment of a reciprocal love affair, and so the action, although supercharged and gilded with romantic sentiment and even perhaps with desperate passion, is none the less practically rational.

Exactly similar arguments apply to any sentimentally inspired actions which are undertaken after careful deliberation: they are optimizations in the light of an agent's goals and so practically rational. If I stop in the street to pick up an old lady's parcels or to help a blind person there is nothing irrational or non-rational about these actions (at least when deliberate); equally if I feel for the well-being of certain animals (so that their well-being becomes an argument in my utility function, that is to say an *end* which I would like to pursue) a deliberate action in defence of the well-being of such animals (such as a boycott of Canadian fish products in protest against the killing of baby seals) is practically rational.

These considerations lead me to a conclusion which I suspect has some very far-reaching implications. For although reason and emotion as defined in Sartre's narrow sense are diametrically and implacably opposed, the great classical opposition between reason and feeling or between reason and romantic sentiment which has so often been a theme of ethics, art and literature is an entirely bogus dichotomy. A great many of our human activities which are infused and inspired with romantic sentiment are none the less eminently rational for the manner in which they contribute to the quality of our lives, the quality of human existence. Indeed a human existence devoid of all romantic sentiment would be unbearably *ugly* while it is romance alone which can *beautify* man's pitiful existence. Can it then be irrational or non-rational to be romantic? Certainly some of the greatest rationalist philosophers were intimate with the great romantic movement of early nineteenth century thought and literature (Schelling and Hegel for example), and Hume may not have been far off the mark at all when he made the famous comment that: 'Reason is and ought only to be the slave of the passions.'

15.3   The Radical Distinction of Efficient-Causal and Teleological Explanations

I have repeatedly asserted without any further comment as yet in the course of this book that teleological explanations of human action in terms of the agent's intentions or goals are radically distinct from the efficient-causal explanations of natural science. Although most philosophers would agree with this distinction it has been held by a number of Anglo-American thinkers in recent years that teleological explanation is after all only a species of efficient-causal explanation. Davidson[25] and Aune[26], for example, have denied that there is any radical distinction between reason-giving (teleological) explanations of action and the efficient-causal mode of explanation of the natural sciences.

There is a second reason for paying some attention to this theme. In the course of Chapter 13 I argued that the version of the objectivist-behaviourist approach, which I have labelled as superficial methodological monism, is definitively ruled out by existentialist phenomenology. This was because when the full implications of human subjectivity (*inter alia* the imperative of an interpretive methodology with a teleological mode of explanation) are recognized there can be no question of saying that whether or not man is a subject the human sciences are to follow fundamentally the same methods as the natural sciences. It would be possible for the superficial monist to counter against my arguments in Chapter 13 that even if a teleological mode of explanation is conceded for the human sciences this still does not give rise to any radical differentiation of method between natural and human science because teleological explanations are after all only a species of efficient-causal explanation (Chapter 13, pp. 197–98). Even though this line of reply by the superficial monist would gain him at best a Pyrrhic victory in the methodological debate (since the substance of the interpretive methodology would have been conceded) I wish to show that it is in any case a mistaken line of reply.

The starting point of any discussion of the distinction between efficient-causal and teleological modes of explanation must surely look to ancient Greece, and in particular to Aristotle's classification of the four causes or types of cause. For Aristotle, to explain any event or phenomenon was to grasp its cause or causes but he distinguished four very different types of cause and so four different modes of explanation, the material cause, formal cause, efficient cause and final cause. The material cause and the formal cause need not concern us here since they belong strictly speaking only to the Aristotelian metaphysics of hylomorphism and have no modern counterparts. By the efficient cause Aristotle clearly meant something very similar to the modern notion of the mechanical cause as used in physics and other natural sciences. To explain an event in terms of its efficient cause was to cite some antecedent independently identifiable event or process which produces the event (under study) in a regular or law-like manner as its effect. Hence efficient-causal explanation is essentially an answer to the question 'How?' How, or by what process, did some event come to happen? I shall not delve any further into the intricacies of what is involved in efficient-causal explanation here, that is, into such questions as whether or not efficient causation amounts (as Hume argued) to nothing more than contiguity, priority, and constant conjunction. For purposes of drawing the contrast between efficient-causal and teleological explanation, which is my sole purpose in this section, the above sketch of the notion of efficient cause and effect is quite sufficient.

Finally, Aristotle distinguished the notion of final cause by which he meant the end or goal to whose realization some event is a stepping stone. To explain an event in terms of some goal towards whose realization it is directed must always, strictly speaking, involve an implicit reference to some self-conscious agent in whose plans or projects the event is a means to the realization of its goals. To speak of purposive goal-directed behaviour necessarily implies a purposively acting being who, as Schutz put it, 'fantasises the goal of the activities in question in the future perfect tense'. To speak of beings devoid of consciousness as behaving purposively is simply nonsensical. For Aristotle and the ancient Greeks, this final causal mode of explanation was an answer to the question 'Why?' Why, or for what purpose, did events happen in a certain way? Furthermore, this explanation of events in terms of purpose was for the Greeks a more ultimate form of explanation than the efficient causal, for it offers a more final type of answer to the demands of inquiring human reason than efficient-causal explanation ever can. One is reminded here of the famous passage in Plato's dialogue The Phaedo where Socrates rejects as ultimately unsatisfactory to the philosopher the various efficient-causal explanations of events in the world and insists that the only form of explanation of events which can satisfy the rationally inquiring mind is that in terms of final causes.[27]

In modern times, the term 'final causal' explanation has been dropped and we speak instead of teleological explanations – the explanation of events in terms of the goals or ends to whose realization they are directed, from the Greek *telos* meaning an end or goal. There can be no doubt at all that for the ancient Greeks there was a radical distinction between efficient-causal and teleological modes of explanation and indeed the Greeks regarded the teleological mode of explanation as much more ultimate and satisfying to reason than the efficient causal. It was for this reason that Aristotle sought to develop a whole system of teleological physics in which the events in the material world would be explained as elements in the divine plan of a supreme being, a supreme intelligence or spirit.[28]

While it is true that the attempt in recent times to conflate the efficient-causal and teleological modes of explanation has been associated with the work of some Anglo-American thinkers within the philosophical tradition of linguistic analysis, it is intriguing to find that the most detailed defence of the importance of maintaining a radical distinction between efficient-causal and teleological modes of explanation has also come from a number of other linguistic-analytic philosophers, most notably from Gilbert Ryle and Peter Winch.[29] Indeed in the case of Ryle and Winch as well as of certain other linguistic philosophers this insistence on the radical distinction of efficient-causal and teleological explanations is part of a wider conviction that the human sciences must adopt an interpretive methodology if they are ever to succeed in genuinely understanding and explaining human action. Given the long-standing and often vitriolic opposition between Anglo-American philosophy within the empiricist tradition of which linguistic philosophy is a contemporary expression and existentialist phenomenology which lies within the continental European rationalist tradition, it is surprising to find that these otherwise implacably opposed philosophers should agree so closely on the appropriate methodology of human science. That such a finding as that the basic principles of a subjectivist-interpretive methodology can be arrived at from so sharply contrasting points of philosophical departure can only buttress strongly the central argument of the book in defence of such a methodology. Since however I would regard existentialist phenomenology as alone providing a conclusive philosophical grounding of the subjectivist methodology (see my argument in Chapter 12) I shall only mention briefly here the character of the parallel deduction of an interpretive methodology within linguistic analysis before passing on to look at what I would regard as by far the most important contribution of linguistic analysts to an interpretive approach: namely the painstaking clarification of the radical distinction between efficient-causal and strictly teleological explanations.

There are quite a number of linguistic analysts who in recent times have argued for an interpretive methodology but I shall confine myself to an eclectic illustrative summary of their typical line of argument. The central feature of the linguistic-analytic argumentation is the analysis of our everyday concepts of action, intention, purposive activity and rule following, and the everyday explanations which we adopt for any intentional activity of ourselves or others. For this examination it is concluded that action is always goal-directed or intentional and that to explain an action will be to grasp the intention/goal (in other words, the Schutzian in-order-to motive) or the action. Such explanation of action in terms of the goals or (as many linguistic analysts say) the *reasons* for action of an agent is then sharply contrasted with the efficient-causal mode of explanation of the natural sciences. This is the sort of argument which pervades Winch's book and we have also already encountered instances of it in my discussion of von Mises' defence of a subjectivist methodology for economics (see Chapter 10, p. 153) and of H. L. A. Hart's analysis of rule-following activity (in Chapter 4, pp. 57–59).

Passing on then to what from the point of view of this book is the most significant contribution of the linguistic analysts to an interpretive methodology, we find that their extensive discussion of the distinction between efficient-causal and teleological explanations re-echoes the ancient Greek distinction and treatment, but the modern discussion has taken place in a rather different and more specific context. To be precise, the modern discussion has been very largely concerned with the nature of explanation of action which is involved in an interpretive human science while the role, if any, of teleological explanation of natural sciences has been discussed to a far lesser extent. The arguments in defence of a radical distinction between efficient-causal and teleological explanations in the case of human actions are scattered throughout the works of those linguistic analysts who in various ways have upheld the imperative of an interpretive approach to explanation of human actions. Hence rather than surveying these scattered remarks I shall now seek to present my own systematic account of the distinction, drawing mainly on these linguistic analysts and also to a lesser extent on certain themes from existentialist phenomenology.

There are, I believe, three fundamental arguments which demonstrate that a teleological explanation of human action in terms of the goals/ intentions/motives of the agent is radically distinct from the efficient-causal mode of explanation of the natural sciences.

In the first place the goal to which action is directed will be realized only *after* the action takes place – it is the end at whose realization the action is directed. Since an efficient cause must be an *antecedent* and independently identifiable event of which the action is the effect, the actual realization of the goal of the action cannot be regarded as an efficient cause thereof. However, most defenders of the notion that teleological explanations of human action are merely a species of efficient causal explanation would readily concede that the goal is not an efficient cause. Rather they cite the conscious state or activity of intention – what Schutz called the 'action fantasied in the future perfect tense' – as the efficient cause since the intention is held to precede the action which brings it to fruition.

Against the argument that the intention may be construed as an efficient cause of action I would point out that the relationship of intention to action is not one of efficient cause to effect but rather an 'internal logical' relation as Winch put it. To be precise, the intention is logically constitutive of the action *qua* action of a certain type. Following Ryle, we may recognize in the first place that to construe the intention as an efficient cause of action must be involved in either the category mistake of the paramechanical Cartesian theory of mind, or the even cruder mistake of materialist reductionism.[30] When we speak of the intention of action we are referring rather to some aspect of an action which is inseparable from it. To be precise, action is self-conscious goal-directed behaviour and when we refer to the intention of action we are referring to its self-conscious purposive and hence meaningful aspect. Indeed the intention is *logically constitutive* of the action not only *qua* action (as opposed to merely passive behaviour) but also *qua* action of a certain type (as opposed to of some other type). Thus the very same piece of observable behaviour could be an instance of two completely different actions if the associated intentions were different. We must contrast this logical interconnection of action and intention with the contingency of the efficient-causal nexus. For there is no suggestion that efficient causes are somehow logically constitutive of the effects to which they give rise; indeed, the very same observable effect could be produced by a variety of different causes and we would not want to say that the effect was a different effect simply because it arose from a different cause. (For example, if the road is wet this is the same effect whether produced by a recent shower or by somebody having washed their car on the roadside.)

The above discussion suggests that an action cannot be identified apart from the intention which underpins it and is its self-conscious aspect. I now wish to argue the converse that the intention is strictly speaking not separately identifiable from the action which gives it effect either. For in order that a person should be said to have an intention that person must have *begun to take at least some practical action towards actual realization* of the intended goal. To profess to having an intention but to have taken no steps towards its practical realization is to be in *bad faith*,[31] it is to be involved in a piece of hypocrisy. One may indeed be thinking about carrying out some project and weighing up its pros and cons, that is to say, one may deliberate *ad nauseam* about carrying out a project without ever taking any practical steps towards actually carrying it out. But once an intention is formed, that is to say, once a decision to act has been taken then unless at least some preliminary steps towards realizing the project are taken one is in bad faith; one cannot be said, strictly speaking, to have formed the intention. To have all manner of supposed good intentions but to do nothing about carrying them out is simply hypocrisy or bad faith.[32] Consequently, I would suggest that intentions are not separable from the actions which bring them to realization any more than the action is identifiable separately from the intention which underpins it. Furthermore, it follows from these discussions that the intention must always be simultaneous with or contemporaneous with the action which brings it to fruition: it cannot be temporally prior to the action.[33]

In the light of these three basic lines of argument which draw both on linguistic analysis and on some existentialist philosophical themes we may conclude that the relationship between intention and action is an internal, logical one which is clearly distinct from the contingent and temporally prior relationship of efficient cause to effect; and hence that the teleological mode of explanation of human action in terms of the intention of the agent is radically distinct from, and certainly not a sub-species of, the efficient-causal mode of explanation of the natural sciences.

The discussion above is a systematic presentation of the fundamental arguments for a radical differentiation of teleological explanations of human action from the efficient-causal mode of explanation of the natural sciences. There are a number of points in the basic line of argument which deserve some further clarification but which I did not introduce because I wanted to present the essential outlines of the argument in the first place. I shall now pause to comment briefly on a number of points in clarification and forestalling of objections to the above discussion.

First, I should emphasize that I am not seeking to deny the independent actual existence of conscious states and activities (as might an extreme empiricist). It is only in the case of intentions that I have argued that intention is not identifiable separately from the action which gives it effect; and even in that case I made the argument *not* on the empiricist ground that intentions are not empirically observable but rather on the *existentialist* ground that to profess an intention but to do nothing at all about carrying it out in practice is to be in bad faith, that is, not to have the intention at all but to be a lying hyprocrite in pretending to have it. There are a variety of other conscious states and activities which, although they can never be observed empirically may none the less be said actually to exist quite independently of any observable activity. Thinking, feeling, deliberation, and so on, would all be examples of such independently existing conscious states.[34]

It has been suggested by Davidson[35] that at least in the case of practically rational actions the antecedent and independently identifiable conscious processes of deliberation could be regarded as efficient causes of the subsequent actions. He speaks of the 'onset of a set of pro-attitudes' towards actions with certain properties as an efficient cause of those actions. Now the first reply to such a suggestion is that it is directly involved in the Rylean category mistake for Davidson is citing purely spiritual activities as the efficient cause of observable bodily behaviour patterns. Even if (as is quite likely) Davidson envisages an eventual reduction of the 'onset of pro-attitudes' in the deliberative process to neurophysiological states of the organism, that would involve an even more crude version of the Rylean category mistake. In any case as far as the proponents of a subjectivist-interpretive methodology are concerned it is the intention of an action which is sought when we seek to understand and explain human action and not the prior deliberative process. Indeed, it is difficult to see how the deliberative process could even be construed as an efficient cause of subsequent action since many of our deliberations do not culminate in any practical activity at all and it is only when an intention is formed in the moment of choice that any linkage between thought and action emerges. (I have already shown that the relationship of intention to action is an internal logical one and so cannot be construed as one of efficient cause to effect.) Hence the whole attempt to construe the prior deliberative processes of the agent in the case of practically rational actions as efficient cause of the action is seriously mistaken.

Before leaving this topic I should also like to forestall three possible and commonly encountered objections to the tough existentialist line which I adopted when arguing that to be said to have an intention an agent must at least have taken some practical steps towards realizing that intention.

Most commonly it is urged that it is possible for an agent genuinely to have formed an intention to act in a certain way but not to have done anything at all as yet because the time is not yet ripe. Thus, for example, I may have decided in December that in the subsequent August I shall visit Italy for a sundrenched holiday but I may well have done nothing at all as yet about carrying out the necessary steps for getting there. My reply in that case is that I have not yet strictly speaking formed the intention; I am still at the stage of musing, fantasizing, deliberating but I have *not* yet *committed* myself and so cannot strictly speaking be said to have formed the intention.

Closely related to this first sort of objection is that which argued that it is, possible for me to form an intention and then to 'change my mind', that is to change my plans before I ever get a chance to carry out the original intention. Again my reply here is straightforward: in the absence of any practical actions to bring the supposed intention to fruition the agent could not genuinely be said to have had the intention in the first place, but was still rather at the stage of deliberation. Indeed, in this sort of case my argument that an agent who has failed to take any practical steps to realize his goals is still at the deliberative stage is quite powerful, for surely if a person supposedly decides one thing and then before ever doing anything about it, changes his mind and decides to do something else we should say that such an agent was still deliberating as to how he or she should act.

Finally, given the imperfection of human knowledge it often happens that human agents make (bona fide) mistakes in the execution of their intentions and projects. It might be said that in such cases the agent somehow acted 'contrary to his intention' and so that the intention and the action carrying it out are separable after all. The point is, however, that as far as the agent was concerned he was not acting contrary to intention and the mistaken or failed practical activity was his attempt to carry his intentions into practice. Thus in the case of the agent the intention stands in an 'internal logical' relation to the mistaken project; and in giving an interpretive explanation of such an action in the human sciences we should have to explain the action in terms of the agent's own intentions (the subjective meaning of action for the agent) even though the action failed in the end to realize the agent's goals.[36]

The conclusion which may be drawn from this detailed discussion of the nature of interpretive explanation of human action in terms of the intentions of the agents is that there is a radical distinction between such strictly teleological explanations of human action as put forward by a subjectivist-interpretive human science and the efficient-causal mode of explanation of the natural sciences. I have established this clear-cut distinction by drawing at once on the age-old Aristotelian classification of causes and modes of explanation, on some themes of modern existentialist thought, and above all on the painstaking demonstration by certain linguistic analysis philosophers that the relationship of intention to action is radically different from the relationship of efficient cause to effect.

In thus establishing quite clearly the radical distinction of teleological explanation of human actions from the efficient-causal explanation as used in the natural sciences I have both supported the contention repeatedly upheld throughout this book that a subjectivist-interpretive human science is radically distinct from the natural sciences in virtue of the teleological mode of explanation of the human sciences; and I have also shown that there can be no hope of salvaging the superficial methodological monist position so popular among economists, by conceding the substance of an interpretive methodology but arguing that its teleological mode of explanation is only a sub-species of efficient-causal explanation such as is used in the natural sciences.

15.4   Are There Any Natural Sciences That Adopt a Teleological Mode of Explanation?

Throughout the above discussion I have drawn a sharp contrast between the natural sciences with their efficient-causal mode of explanation and the subjectivist-interpretive human sciences which are characterized by a strictly teleological mode of explanation. It could and has been suggested, however, that I have drawn up too sharp a dichotomy here since there are some modern natural sciences in which elements of teleological explanations appear to be present; hence that although the human sciences may adopt a teleological mode of explanation they are not in the end so radically distinct in their methods from the natural sciences as I have been suggesting.

In the concluding section of this chapter I wish to examine this line of argument briefly. As well as for the above reasons it is also important to examine this argument because it could be used as a last-ditch stand to salvage superficial methodological monism by arguing that human sciences even with a teleological mode of explanation are not so different from natural sciences since in some of the latter, such as biology and zoology, elements of teleological explanation are also present.[37]

I certainly cannot claim to be anything like an expert on the fields of biology, zoology and other natural sciences in which teleological notions may be found. Accordingly, what follows is rather more of an impressionistic sketch than an exhaustive discussion, although I do suspect that the sketch is sufficiently accurate for the methodological purposes in hand. What I wish to argue is that although there are certainly some elements of apparently teleological explanation present in a number of modern natural sciences these do not amount to teleological explanations, strictly so-called. In fact upon a closer examination they turn out to be nothing more than a loosely analogical and misleading use of a teleological terminology to describe, in a convenient shorthand, processes which are being explained in efficient-causal terms.

Teleological explanation involves the explanation of some event or activity in terms of the goals towards whose realization the event or activity is directed; it always involves the notion of purpose or the execution of a project. But any reference to purposes, goals and projects necessarily involves a reference to some *self-conscious* and purposively acting agent. It is sheer nonsense to speak of inanimate or non-conscious objects as having their own goals or as acting purposively to achieve their goals. It is only in the case of a being who can upon reflection know what he is doing and why he is doing it that we can ever strictly speak of such a being having goals or purposes. Hence a *strict* teleological explanation of an event or activity always involves the explanation of the event or activity in terms of the goals or intentions of the self-conscious subject of whose projects the event or activity is the practical execution. Whenever we have a strictly teleological explanation there must always be at least an implicit reference to some self-conscious subject and the intentions or projects of that subject. Non-conscious passive objects cannot have goals or be said to act purposively.

In the ancient natural sciences, typified by Aristotelian physics, teleological explanations abounded and since the goals towards which physical objects were supposed to tend were regarded as part of the overall plan of God for the universe, such explanations were in fact teleological in the strict sense as just defined. Despite the fact that the modern natural sciences have since the time of Bacon and Descartes completely abandoned the framework of Aristotelian teleology some apparently teleological conceptions remain in some modern natural sciences. These notions are mainly found in biology and zoology and I shall now examine them briefly with a view to showing that they do not involve any kind of *strict* teleological explanation at all but are rather thinly disguised efficient-causal explanations.

In biology, for example, the evolutionary process is often conceived in teleological terms, while in genetic theory genes are often spoken of in functionalist terms as having the function of bringing about this or that end state of an organism. Although functionalist explanations need not be strictly teleological in character they lend themselves readily to a teleological interpretation and may easily be expressed in the language of teleology.[38] In zoology various types of animal behaviour are described in clearly teleological language as economizing, learning, etc. It should be clear, however, that despite the teleological language none of these sciences are employing teleological explanation in the strict sense such as is found in the interpretive human sciences. For in none of these sciences is there any question of citing or referring to the goals of some self-conscious subject towards which the phenomena in question are practical steps to realization. There is, in the first place, no question of regarding genes or even animal organisms (at least not yet) as self-conscious purposively acting agents who know what they are doing and why they are doing it. Equally, there is no longer any question of regarding the natural processes of phenomena described in teleological terms as being parts of a divine plan for the universe (after the manner of Aristotelian physics). Since there is no reference to the ends of any self-conscious purposively acting agent there is no teleological explanation strictly so-called present in these natural sciences.

In fact upon a closer examination it will be clear that in all of these cases of apparently teleological concepts or explanations the phenomena in question are quite definitely being explained in *efficient-causal* terms and the functionalist or teleological language is being used very loosely for convenience. In the case of the theory of evolution for example the notion of the survival of the fittest organisms is simply a statement that organisms ill equipped to defend themselves will naturally tend to become extinct: it is not as if organisms reasoned out how best to defend themselves. In the field of genetic theory the key to understanding genes and the effects they produce is chemical interaction, not any kind of self-conscious process. Finally, in the field of animal behaviour where certain patterns of behaviour are described as 'learning tricks', etc., upon a closer examination it will become evident that this 'learning' process is being conceived in the crudest of stimulus response terms and certainly not as a process of self-conscious reflection and practical reasoning regarding appropriate courses of action by the animal. The very manner in which animals are taught tricks by persistently following up a certain behaviour with a reward (or punishment) of a physical variety proves that nothing more is involved in such 'learning' than the efficient-causal nexus of stimulus and response.[39]

Thus despite the veneer of teleological language it is clear that those modern natural sciences in which teleological conceptions appear to be present are certainly not adopting a strict teleological mode of explanation of any natural phenomenon; and indeed upon a closer examination it will be found that at root they are employing exactly the same efficient-causal mode of explanation as all of the other natural sciences. It would appear, therefore, that the teleological notions and language are being used in a loosely analogical manner to make a convenient and often suggestive shorthand reference to certain processes which at root are being under-stood, not in a strictly teleological but rather in a clearly efficient-causal manner. Natural scientists are, of course, perfectly entitled to choose to use teleological language as a convenient shorthand when referring to certain biological processes or patterns of animal behaviour. I would suggest, however, that this particular usage is seriously misleading and for that reason might better be dropped altogether.[40] It is misleading not only because, strictly speaking, teleotelical explanation must involve a reference to the goals or purposes of some self-conscious agent; but also because it has led to the seriously mistaken suggestion that those natural sciences such as biology and zoology in which some teleological conceptions occur are quite similar to the subjectivist-interpretive human sciences with their strictly teleological mode of explanation.

Since I have shown earlier in this chapter that a *strictly* teleological mode of explanation is radically distinct from an efficient-causal mode of explanation (of any given phenomenon or activity) it follows that the radical dichotomy between on the one hand the subjectivist-interpretive human sciences with their strictly teleological mode of explanation and, on the other hand, the natural sciences with their efficient-causal mode of explanation still stands.[41]

Notes

1 I have encountered these objections not only in textbook discussions but also in discussion seminars at the European University Institute of Florence in Italy.

2 The spirit of the nation, sometimes personified in the form of a god or goddess for example.

3 F. Hayek (1957), *Studies in Philosophy, Politics and Economics* (London: Routledge & Kegan Paul). A whole essay in the volume is devoted to precisely this theme (pp. 96–105).

4 R. Boudon (1979), *La Logique du Social* (Hatchette: Paris), ch. 4 for a large number of such examples.

5 R. Boudon, *La Logique du Social*, ch. 12.

6 Following on my proposed demarcation of the fields of sociology and economics in Chapter 14 it should not be surprising to find that sociology has paid a great deal of attention to the study of social wholes in the very broad sense of macro-level social phenomena.

7 R. Boudon, *La Logique du Social*, *passim*, but especially ch. 1.

8 R. Boudon, *La Logique du Social*, p. 33.

9 S. Lukes (1973), 'Methodological individualism reconsidered', in A. Ryan (ed.), *The Philosophy of Social Explanation* (Oxford: Oxford University Press).

10 Lukes calls this further step 'epistemological individualism'. It occurs only in the case of crude positivist thinkers.

11 This was in fact one of Kant's formulations of the categorical imperative, the fundamental principle of all ethical theory for Kant, cf. I. Kant (1969), *The Moral Law*, H. J. Paton (trans.) (London: Hutchinson).

12 J. S. Mill (1962), 'On Liberty', in M. Warnock (ed.), *Utilitarianism* (London: Fontana), ch. 1.

13 Hayek is an example of a political individualist who adopts a subjectivist approach to human science: Sartre is a counter-example, perhaps, at least in his later works where he espouses Marxian politics.

14 Automatic condemnation would follow indeed only if it were shown to involve 'ontological individualism', which I have shown to be a wholly implausible position.

15 S. Benn and G. Mortimore (eds.) (1976), *Rationality in Social Science* (London: Routledge & Kegan Paul). See in particular their introductory chapter.

16 I have already argued in Chapter 7 that such a postulate of 'adequacy of relevant information' is also highly plausible and so is not a difficulty for interpretive methodology.

17 On all of this, see Chapter 7, pp. 114–15.

18 Cf. behaviourist theories of emotions and emotional activities epitomize such an efficient-causal approach to explanation of impulsive actions such as fits of anger.

19 J.-P. Sartre (1971), *A Sketch for a Theory of the Emotions* (London: Methuen).

20 Cf. Chapter 12, p. 182, where I show how existentialist phenomenology can make a direct *a priori* contribution to the human sciences by elucidating the real essence of various conscious states or activities.

21 A. Schutz (1972), *The Phenomenology of the Social World* (London: Heinemann), p. 240.

22 It may be remarked that while economics focuses exclusively on cases of practically rational actions this does not preclude other human sciences from dealing with other aspects of practically rational actions. In other words the demarcation line between economics and other human sciences has nothing to do with practical rationality of action. Rather, as I have suggested in Chapter 14, for example, the demarcation between economics and sociology hinges on their respective focus on 'in-order-to' and on 'because' motives of action.

23 Cf. Chapter 7, p. 116 where I show that in the face of imperfect information rational agents will engage in a process of optimal search, collecting information up to the point where the expected gain from it just equals the marginal cost of collecting it.

24 There are, of course, the cases of drug and alcohol addiction, and so on, but it is doubtful that these belong to the sphere of practically rational actions in any case.

25 D. Davidson (1963), 'Actions, reasons and causes', *Journal of Philosophy*, vol. 60, pp. 690–700; also by Davidson (1971) 'Agency', in R. Binkely (ed.) *Agent Action and Reason* (Toronto: University of Toronto Press).

26 B. Aune (1977), *Reason and Action* (Dordrecht: Reidel), pp. 61–84.

27 Plato (1982) 'The Phaedo', in *The Last Days of Socrates* (Harmondsworth: Penguin), p. 157.

28 This illustrates an important point. There is no question of seeing non-conscious beings as having purposes or goals in Aristotelian physics. Rather natural events are seen as elements of the (universal) purposive activity of God as supreme self-conscious agent carrying out a divine plan.

29 See G. Ryle (1949), *The Concept of Mind* (London: Hutchinson) and P. Winch (1958), *The Idea of a Social Science and its Relation to Philosophy* (London: Routledge & Kegan Paul).

30 See. G. Ryle, *The Concept of Mind*. Chapter 1 of the book outlines with admirable clarity the Cartesian dualist theory of the mind and the fundamental category mistake which Ryle believes both the Cartesian theory and materialist reductionism of any sort involve.

31 This is the famous Sartrean notion of *mauvaise foi*, where one's actions contradict one's alleged values, goals and ideals.

32 An interesting reflection suggests itself here. The existentialist-Sartrean approach to intention which I am suggesting here involves a very hard-headed approach to practical action, one in which theory must be translated into practice or else to 'hold the theory is to be in bad faith'. To be in good faith requires that one should act on one's ideals/theories: may it then be the case that the 'practical man' who constantly and boringly insists that 'theory is fine, but in practice . . .' is persistently in bad faith. He is really saying, 'I like your theory but I won't act on it'.

33 Cf. G. O'Driscoll and M. Rizzo (1985), *The Economics of Time and Ignorance* (Oxford: Basil Blackwell), pp. 28–9. They rely heavily on showing that the relationship of intention to action is not one of temporal priority and hence not of efficient cause to effect in their rejection of deterministic theories of choice.

34 It is perhaps worth mentioning that it is never quite clear what Ryle's position is in regard to such conscious activities in *The Concept of Mind*. While definitively opposed to a materialist reductionism it is not clear whether he wants to see them as independently existing activities which are not observable or as aspects of activities which are observable. Thus Ryle seeks to say that knowledge and intelligence are dispositions to act in certain ways rather than mysterious psychic states or faculties. This is somewhat ambiguous and is symptomatic of a general defect in Ryle's work – that he is much stronger in the critique of Cartesian dualism than in the outline of a superior alternative theory.

35 D. Davidson, *'Actions, Reasons and Causes'*.

36 This re-echoes a point which I made repeatedly in Chapters 5 and 7 that in the case of practically rational actions human agents optimize in the light of information available to them. The fact that such information is imperfect does not mean that agents cannot attempt to optimize.

37 I mentioned this last ditch stratagem for rescuing a methodological monism only very briefly in footnote 12 of Chapter 13, rather than in the main text. This is because it is undoubtedly the weakest of any of the stratagems of desperation which might be adopted by positivist-leaning thinkers to defend a monism of method once they have conceded the imperative of teleological explanation in human science as the implication of human subjectivity.

38 H. L. A. Hart, *The Concept of Law*, pp. 186–7, argues that the prevalence of functionalist language and explanation in both biology and medical science testifies to the continuing influence of old Aristotelian teleology in some modern natural sciences.

39 Indeed, behaviourists have sought to understand human learning processes on a direct analogy with the stimulus response 'learning' process of animals. This ignores the self-conscious or reflective aspect of human learning and is in my view a serious 'objectivist' mistake (cf. P. Winch, *The Idea of a Social Science*, p. 60).

40 The same sort of misleading usages of teleological notions in the modern field of computers and high technology has been a source of widespread misconceptions and false hopes for the potential of such technology.

41 And, I may add, the last desperate defensive stratagem for superficial methodological monism is shown to fail.

16

A Conclusion and Some Open Questions

In the course of this work I have been roaming far and wide in the realms of philosophy and of the human sciences and so it will be appropriate in this final chapter to provide a retrospective sketch of my long itinerary, focussing now on the main stations en route and indicating the main conclusions at which I have arrived. Since such a wide-ranging work also raises a variety of difficult issues with which I have not been able to deal here for reasons of space and scope, I shall also indicate, in the spirit of critical rationalism which I have invoked throughout, a number of important questions which I have left open and outstanding.

16.1   The Argument of the Book in Brief

The central aim of this book was to make a decisive contribution to the debate in the methodology of human science between the objectivist-behaviourist approach with its efficient-causal mode of explanation and its insistence on a unity of method between natural and human sciences, and the subjectivist-interpretive approach with its teleological mode of explanation and consequent insistence on a radical distinction between the methods of the natural and human sciences. Having carried out a sustained critical appraisal of the claims of these two competing approaches, I have sought to resolve the debate decisively, in favour of the subjectivist-interpretive approach.

It should be added straight away that there are of course certain other methodological possibilities for the human sciences besides the objectivist-behaviourist and subjectivist-interpretive approaches which have been the terms of the debate and discussion in this work. There are, for example, various types of holistic or structuralist approaches, of which the neo-Marxist Frankfurt school of 'critical social theory' is a leading example, and these holistic approaches are explicitly opposed both to the objectivist-behaviourist and the subjectivist-interpretive approaches.[1] It was quite simply beyond the scope of this book to consider also the claims of this third major methodological alternative for the human sciences in relation to the claims of both the objectivist and subjectivist approaches, and a proper treatment thereof would merit a separate book. None the less, it will probably be evident enough from certain remarks and hints which I have made at various points in the work, notably in regard to the freedom of choice and the principle of methodological individualism, why I would regard the subjectivist approach as superior to any of the holistic approaches to methodology of human sciences.

My central concern, therefore, was to carry out a defence of the claims of the subjectivist-interpretive approach to the methodology of the human sciences against the objectivist-behaviourist approach, thereby seeking to achieve a decisive resolution of at least one of the areas of heated controversy and debate in human science methodology. I sought to carry out this defence by adopting two main lines of attack. First, by presenting a critical philosophical examination of the claims of both of these approaches to methodology. As the argument of Chapter 1 made quite clear it is only on this plane of philosophical argument that any methodological issue can be conclusively settled, so I regard the philosophical line of my argumentation as the decisive line of attack.

Secondly, I have supported the abstract philosophical argument with an illustrative case study of the methods used in practice by a leading human science: economics. Since this case study is no more than a description of methods actually used by economists, then again in the light of the arguments of Chapters 1 and 2, it cannot be a decisive argument in defence of any (critical) methodological position and served *purely* an illustrative function in the work.

The philosophical argument was carried out in Parts 1 and 3 of the book. Part 1 dealt with certain basic philosophical prolegomena and its central theme was a dialectical strategy of argument in defence of the notion of a critical philosophically based methodology of science guided by the regulative criterion of truth or quest for truth. This notion of methodology pervades the book from beginning to end, whence the importance I attached to establishing it firmly at the outset. I began in Chapter 1 by invoking the spirit of critical rationalism, arguing that the critical activity of reason in submitting all received opinion to critical questioning in the search for truth is not only the spirit which has made the most spectacular advances of European thought and civilization possible: it is the *only* spirit in which any academic inquiry or reasoned discussion can be carried out. Hence the critical activity of reason lies at the very basis of all human knowledge and is the inexorable starting point of all human inquiry.

This critical rational spirit will require *inter alia* that the methods of the sciences should not be taken for granted but should themselves be submitted to a critical scrutiny before the court of reason (guided by the regulative criterion of truth which is the *telos* of reason). Since none of the specific sciences can be used to develop such critique without becoming involved in a vicious circularity, and since any such critique raises ultimate questions concerning the conditions of the possibility of valid knowledge, etc., we must turn to the field of philosophy in order to develop a critical methodology of science. But in thus turning to philosophy as source for methodological critique a very special requirement for philosophy is stipulated in advance. In order to avoid the same sort of vicious circularity in which the sciences become involved if they seek to carry out a critique of their own methods, philosophy must be capable of providing its *own grounding*. This it can achieve only if it can build itself up from a set of first principles which are reflexively self-justifying (and so absolutely true).

In Chapter 2 I went on to consider and to refute those positions which have been opposed to the notion of a critical philosophically-based methodology of science (the antithesis phase of the dialectical argument in Part 1). I examined and sought to refute decisively the 'anti-philosophies' of positivism and relativism both of which argue (for various reasons) that philosophy is impossible and hence, *a fortiori*, that the methodology of science cannot be based on philosophy. I paid particular attention to the refutation of epistemological relativism and also to the refutation of one of its progeny in the field of scientific method – the instrumentalist notion of scientific theories – precisely because the refutation of these two positions was not only important in relation to the defence of a critical philosophically based approach to methodology but is also of further significance in the work. For later on, at a number of crucial junctures in the argument, I have drawn upon and presumed the decisive refutation of both relativism and instrumentalism.

Having rejected the relativist-inspired instrumentalist conception of scientific theory I went on in Chapter 3 to introduce an alternative conception of scientific theory which is directly in accord with the critical rational spirit in its quest for truth which I have held to lie at the basis of all science and all human cognition. This is the so-called 'realist' conception of scientific theory and explanation according to which the task of science is to achieve a true insight into the generative processes and mechanisms which underlie and give rise to natural phenomena or into the motivations which underlie human actions. This realist conception of theory as true insight contrasts sharply with the instrumentalist conception of theory as fiction and again it is a notion which I have invoked repeatedly later in the book.

Although vitally important to the argument of the work as a whole the discussions in Part 1 are really in the nature of philosophical prolegomena. The main philosophical discussion is carried out in Part 3 where I attempt to give the subjectivist-interpretive methodology of human science a fully rigorous philosophical foundation, and once again in developing this argument I adopt a dialectical strategy.

Following from the tough requirements for an adequate critical methodology which were laid down in principle in Part 1, I turned to the field of existentialist phenomenology as a starting point in my philosophical deduction and grounding of the subjectivist-interpretive approach. In Chapter 12 I showed how Husserl's method of pure phenomenology and its later descendent, existentialist phenomenology, offer a way in which philosophy can achieve a set of reflexively self-justifying propositions which can serve as its starting point – as the core of absolute truths at the basis of all human cognition. Among the propositions which can be laid down with certainty (because reflexively self-justifying) by existentialist phenomenology is a set of propositions which are of direct relevance to the methods of the human sciences. Phenomenology involves a turn by a consciousness to reflect upon itself – on its own activities and contents – as a field in which absolute certainties can be achieved on pain of performative self-contradiction. In this field of self-consciousness we can know with certainty not only that we are thinking and that we actually exist (the Cartesian *cogito*). We can also in reflection come to know with certainty that we are doing something or other, what we are doing, why we are doing it, and above all that we are always free (albeit within constraints) to do otherwise. In other words existentialist phenomenology allows us to establish as a reflexively self-justifying proposition that (each) man is a self-conscious and freely choosing being, in a word human *subjectivity*. From this it follows immediately that if we are to seek in human science a true insight into human action we cannot possibly offer an efficient-causal account of it since in the moment of freely choosing all antecedent determination is transcended and cancelled. Rather to understand the action of a freely choosing agent will require that we grasp the intention or goal of the agent, that we interpret the meaning or purpose of action for the agent. Hence from an analysis of the notion of human subjectivity, which was laid down with absolute certainty by existentialist phenomenology, we have arrived at the fundamental principles of a subjectivist-interpretive methodology of human science with its teleological mode of explanation.

Following the dialectical strategy of argumentation I go on in Chapter 13 to show how the same set of philosophical first principles laid down with absolute certainty by existentialist phenomenology also leads to a decisive refutation of the objectivist-behaviourist approach to the human sciences. We have just seen how the notion of man as a freely choosing and self-conscious being rules out any possibility of adopting efficient-causal explanations of human action in a human science which seeks true insights, and even more clearly indeed, the existentialist notion of human subjectivity definitively rules out any notion of man as object as a serious mistake or misconception. Hence once we have established man's subjectivity with absolute certainty in existentialist phenomenology it will follow immediately that the reductionist variant of the objectivist-behaviourist approach to human science is definitively refuted. I then proceeded to show that the other two variants of the objectivist-behaviourist approach, the instrumentalist version and the superficial methodological monist version, are equally decisively ruled out by existentialist phenomenology.

Having thus derived the fundamental elements of a subjectivist-interpretive methodology from a foundation of absolute certainty in existentialist phenomenology, in Chapter 14 I outlined the central principles of such a methodology. I emphasized that among the various possible variations on the theme of a subjectivist approach I was following very closely the most mature and sophisticated version of such an approach which was put forward by Alfred Schutz. Thus, for example, against the more extreme early versions of the subjectivist-approach as found in the historical and hermeneutical schools of the last century, I emphasized that the theories of interpretive human sciences are conjectures (since we cannot know for sure the contents of other people's conscious states); and hence stand in need of empirical testing against actual patterns of human activity in the world. At the same time, I followed Schutz in also arguing that since the teleological mode of explanation of action which is central to the subjectivist-interpretive methodology is radically distinct from the efficient-causal mode of explanation of the natural sciences, there is a radical differentiation of method between the natural and human sciences.[2]

I then followed Schutz further in outlining in somewhat more detail some of the more important principles of a subjectivist-interpretive methodology of human science. I dealt with the important distinction between the objective meaning and the deeper subjective meaning of actions, arguing that the latter is the *quaesitum* of an interpretive methodology. I examined the notion of motivation, introducing Schutz's interesting distinction of 'in-order-to' and (genuine) 'because' motives and I sought to clarify the role of 'because motivation' in an interpretive human science.

Then, in Chapter 15, I turned to look at a miscellany of standard criticisms or misapprehensions regarding a subjectivist-interpretive methodology in order to strike pre-emptively against them. I clarified the precise and minimal sense in which a subjectivist-interpretive methodology involves a principle of (methodological) individualism and also the precise role and meaning of rationality postulates in interpretive human sciences. Finally, I drew both on existentialist phenomenology and also in particular on the works of certain modern linguistic-analysis philosophers in order to examine the nature of a strictly teleological explanation and to establish definitively that such explanations are radically distinct from the efficient-causal mode of explanation. From this demonstration it will follow conclusively that the Schutzian subjectivist human sciences which follow a strictly teleological mode of explanation are radically distinct from the natural sciences with their efficient-causal mode of explanation[3]: in other words a 'methodological dualism' as between the natural and human sciences.

Sandwiched in between the philosophical arguments in Parts I and 3 of the work is the exhaustive methodological case study of economic science. My main reason for introducing such a case study was to bring to life the highly abstract categories and distinctions of the purely philosophical plane of discussion, thereby hopefully affording the reader a better grasp of what is involved in the philosophical discussion. It should be emphasized again that this case study is purely illustrative and could not constitute a rational ground for favouring or adopting a subjectivist-interpretive (or any other) methodology of human science. For the case study simply presents a description of the methods actually used by economists and unless one were to adopt the crudely uncritical 'descriptivist' attitude to methodology (which I have refuted in Chapter 2) the case study can be no more than illustrative.

My reasons for choosing economics as the topic of my illustrative case study are banal: it is a leading and well-established human science with which I have a deep familiarity.

In Chapters 5 and 6 I carried out a quick survey of the methodological character of mainstream microeconomic and macroeconomic theory. I began by noting the definition of economics as a science of choice in the face of scarcity and by showing that economists have adopted a single formal and universal principle for explanation of any deliberate choice, the optimization principle. Precisely because the optimization principle is purely formal and makes no reference whatever to any specific goals or constraints of agents I suggested that it could be derived as an *a priori* principle for explanation of any deliberate choice from an existentialist phenomenological elucidation of the essence of any such choice. Certainly, that is the way that the optimization principle has been treated by economists for I go on to show that over the whole field of microeconomic theory the optimization principle provides the basic key to explanation. The purely formal optimization principle is being effectively presumed to be true *a priori* and economists in the various branches of micro theory have been simply fleshing out its content by making various conjectures as to the specific goals of agents and as to the constraints they face in various kinds of situations. Thus, for example, in the perfectly competitive theory of the firm it is assumed that economic profits are the goal of the firm and that it faces constraints given by cost curves and a horizontal demand curve: it is then automatic for the economist to explain the activity of firms in perfect competition as profit maximisation, that is to say, in terms of the optimization principle.

I also argued that much of the more advanced work in the field of macroeconomics which aims to be compatible with microeconomic theory and in particular modern macro-theorizing that is conducted within the broad framework of general equilibrium analysis will also be based upon the optimization principle as a basic key to explanation. Since the optimization principle involves explanation of human action (in cases of deliberate choice such as are the sole focus of economic theory) as the attempt by agents to realize their goals or intentions in practice to the greatest possible extent in the light of the information available to them it will be clear that any explanation of action in terms of the optimization principle will be a clear-cut and unmistakable instance of the subjectivist-interpretive approach to the human sciences and of its strictly teleological mode of explanation of action (in terms of the goals of agents). Therefore, since I have shown how the optimization principle underpins the whole of microeconomic theory and all of the more satisfactory advanced macroeconomic theories of the present day, I concluded that mainstream economic theory is a shining and clear-cut exemplification of the subjectivist-interpretive methodology with its teleological mode of explanation at work in the actual practice of a leading human science.

Chapter 7 went on to consider in what precise sense mainstream economic theory based on the optimization principle as its basic key to explanation of human action could be said to involve postulates of 'rationality' of human agents. I have included this discussion, which is somewhat of a digression from my main line of argument in Part 2, simply because a great deal of unnecessary confusion has surrounded the precise sense in which rationality of agents is presumed by the optimization principle, and the discussion here may be linked up with the wider question of rationality postulates involved in any subjectivist-interpretive human science which is raised in Chapter 15 of Part 3.

That mainstream economics is a shining exemplification of a Schutzian subjectivist-interpretive methodology and so radically distinct in its methods from the natural sciences will come as a shock to most economists. In Chapters 8 and 9 I examine the methodological sayings of a long succession of leading mainstream economists from the last century up to the present day. In what little they have had to say on methodology almost all mainstream economists (the only exception being the small Austrian School mentioned below) have upheld an objectivist-behaviourist position and have insisted that there should be a strict unity of method between the natural and the human sciences. Most often economists have adopted the particularly unsatisfactory 'superficial methodological monist' version of objectivism or in some instances the instrumentalist variant. Given what we have discovered about the unmistakably subjectivist-interpretive character of mainstream economic theory it is really quite astonishing to find not a single mention of either Schutz or Weber in the methodological comments of so many leading mainstream economists. It follows that mainstream economists have been involved in a very serious misconception regarding the character of the methods they use in practice and that there is a serious gap between their objectivist behaviourist *precepts* and their actual subjectivist-interpretive methodological *practice*.

Given the philosophical argument of the work as a whole which has defended the Schutzian subjectivist-interpretive methodology as the only appropriate approach to the human sciences I concluded Part 2 by arguing (in Chapter 11) that this gap between methodological precepts and practice (on the question of the subjectivist versus objectivist approach to economics) should be closed off by bringing methodological precepts into line with practice. In Chapter 11 I also noted, following Blaug, that there is a second significant gap between economists' precepts and practice on the matter of empirical testing of theories. While urging rigorous testing in their precepts economists have been rather lax about carrying out that precept as Blaug has shown at some length. Hence given that in a Schutzian version of the subjectivist-interpretive methodology which I have defended in Part 3 empirical testing of interpretive theories is of vital importance for the human sciences, I conclude that Blaug's methodological gap between precept and practice on the matter of empirical testing ought to be closed off by bringing practice into line with methodological precepts.

I have mentioned that there is one sub-group on the fringes of economic mainstream which has not been involved in the misconception of urging an objectivist-behaviourist precept while practising a subjectivist-interpretive approach to economics, the so-called Austrian School. In Chapter 10 I have examined the methodological position of this interesting exceptional school at some length. All of the Austrian economists have urged that economics should adopt a subjectivist-interpretive approach and they have rightly regarded mainstream economic theory as the epitome of such an approach. However, most Austrian economists, possibly reflecting a residual influence from the historical and hermeneutical schools of the last century, have also held that the interpretive theories of mainstream economics will be true *a priori* and will not need to be submitted to empirical tests. Von Mises has been the foremost exponent of this '*a priorist*' tenet of the Austrian position. He would defend this position, it would seem, by arguing that when framing interpretive theories regarding the goals or intentions of human agents we can have 'empathetic intuitions' of their goals which will be true *a priori* and in no need of empirical testing.

I have argued in Part 3 that the requirement of empirical testing is an integral part of a subjectivist-interpretive methodology because (following Schutz) I have shown that since we cannot know with certainty the contents of other persons' conscious states, interpretive theories in human science are always conjectures in need of testing, so that there can be no question of *a priori* empathetic intuitions. Hence I conclude that although the Austrian School mark a definite improvement over most mainstream commentators by dint of their defence of a subjectivist-interpretive methodology, their methodological precepts are still seriously defective because of their *a priorism* and rejection of the need for empirical testing. Indeed, not only is their methodological precept defective on philosophical grounds, it does not square well even with the practice of economists who although decidedly lax in the matter of empirical testing of their interpretive theories (as Blaug has shown) have none the less done some empirical work with a view to testing their theories.

It will be noticed that I have said that *most* Austrian economists have adopted the extreme *a priorist* position regarding empirical testing; for not all of them have adopted it. I pointed out briefly in Chapter 10 that it is possible to identify a small sub-group within the Austrian sub-group of mainstream economists which would concede a role for empirical testing in establishing the applicability or inapplicability of theories to actual situations in the world (although not their truth/falsity). Although this view which I have labelled as the 'applicability thesis' could turn out to be very interesting it has not been expounded systematically or consistently by any of the Austrians.[4] There are at most only hints or vague adumbrations of such a thesis and since these are in any case confined to a sub-group within the school, they constitute only a very minor qualification to my overall characterization of the methodology of the Austrian School as being unsatisfactory because of its espousal of an extreme *a priorism*.

The above is summary of the main line of argument of the book. Along the way there have been many stops for brief excursions up branch-lines, excursions which often led into highly exotic and rarefied countryside. These branch-line sorties or digressions were necessary in order to deal with some of the manifold tricky issues which inevitably crop up in a work which seeks to carry out a thorough critical appraisal of the methodology of the human sciences, although I would by no means claim to have dealt with anything like all of the side issues which emerged and demand some kind of answer in the course of the work.

To take some examples of side issues with which I have sought to deal, I have examined the Popperian logic of falsification in some detail, and I have looked at such diverse topics as the theory of emotion and the appropriate line of demarcation between economic *qua* science of deliberate human choice and certain other disciplines (notably sociology).

These are all side issues which arose in the course of the argument and with which I have sought to deal briefly. There are inevitably many more issues which are raised in the course of such a work but with which I have not been able to deal for reasons of space and scope. In the next section of this chapter I shall review some of these.

16.2   Some Issues Left Outstanding

From the very outset, I have invoked the spirit of critical rationalism which I have shown in Chapter 1 to be the necessary foundation of all human knowledge. This spirit requires us to call every received opinion or convention into question in a relentless and open-minded critical probing guided by the overall regulative criterion of pursuit of truth, the *telos* of Reason. In thus pursuing the truth in an open-minded critical spirit one must be ever mindful of Socrates' vital maxim: that one of the only propositions of whose truth he could be absolutely certain was the severe limitation of his own knowledge, or put another way the wide extent of his own ignorance. Thus while the inexorable *telos* of the activity of critical reasoning is absolute truth, we must always bear in mind that the achievement of such truths is an extremely difficult activity and that the number of such truths which have been attained by philosophy or other disciplines is very limited indeed.

It is with considerations such as these above in mind that after the forceful presentation of my proposed defence of a subjectivist-interpretive methodology of the human sciences in the course of the book I have thought it important in this final chapter to emphasize that there is also a variety of issues which have been left unsettled and thus outstanding in the book. By drawing attention to these outstanding issues which require much further research and discussion I have sought to dispel any air of dogmatic finality which my rigorous presentation of the main argument may have given. The spirit of my argument was rather one of a hard hitting but openminded dialogue or debate and it is precisely in order to bring out its critical rational character that I shall end the work by outlining openly some of the main problems raised but not dealt with by the work and which point the way towards further discussion, debate and critical research.

There is of course a variety of such issues left outstanding in the course of the work and I shall only indicate here what I believe to be the more important of these. In each case I shall first outline the unsettled question or issue left outstanding and I shall then make some suggestive comments regarding the sort of problems which each opens up.

At the beginning of this chapter I pointed out that my overall aim was to make a contribution to the debates in the methodology of human science by examining at some length the claims of the objectivist-behaviourist and subjectivist-interpretive approaches and by attempting to resolve that controversy definitively in favour of the subjectivist-interpretive approach. But I noted that it would be possible to identify other possible approaches to the methodology of the human sciences than the two just mentioned. The most important of these alternatives is that which we may call the 'social holistic' approach to human science which comes in a number of distinct versions, but perhaps the leading proponents in recent years have been the neo-Marxist Frankfurt School of so-called 'critical social theory'.[5]

The social holistic approach, and in particular its Frankfurt School variant is explicitly opposed to the subjectivist-interpretive approach to methodology of human science. Following Marx and Durkheim, it argues that there are certain social 'facts', forces or structures which an individual is powerless to control and which exert a determining influence on his various activities. Hence the key to explanation of human actions in society will lie in a holistic determinism, whereby individual behaviour is seen as the efficient-causal product of inexorable social forces. It will be readily clear why this third major methodological alternative is implacably opposed to the subjectivist-interpretive approach which embodies an explicit principle of methodological individualism (Chapter 15 pp. 217–22) and which holds that in the moment of free choice all antecedent determination of action of whatever kind is transcended and cancelled so that human actions must be explained teleologically in terms of the agents' own goals (Chapter 12, p. 186). Indeed, given the philosophical argument drawing on existentialist phenomenology which I have deployed in Chapters 12 to 14 in defence of the subjectivist-interpretive approach to the human sciences there is already a fair indication of why I would regard that approach as preferable also to the 'social holistic' approach in any of its versions (neo-Marxist, or otherwise).

It was, however, quite beyond the scope of this book to carry out an exhaustive examination of the claims of the social holistic alternative in its various versions in relation to the subjectivist-interpretive approach to the human sciences. Accordingly, we may rate as the first important issue left outstanding by the work the need to assess the claims of this third leading alternative in the methodology of human sciences in relation to the subjectivist-interpretive approach.

A second issue which may be said to have been left outstanding in the course of the book and which would merit considerably more research and discussion is the practical implications of adopting a subjectivist-interpretive methodology in the day-to-day practice of the various human sciences. I have of course indicated at some length how a subjectivist-interpretive methodology has worked out in the practice of economic science, that being the central theme of Part 2. But apart from a few fleeting references to some of the implications of a subjectivist-interpretive approach for psychological therapy and for social policy, I have said nothing at all about the practical implications for human sciences other than economics.

In developing and fleshing out these implications there are two important and closely related issues which will be illuminated. First, what will be the line of demarcation between the various human sciences if and when they have all adopted a subjectivist-interpretive approach? I have already made one brief suggestion in Chapter 14 showing how within the principles of a Schutzian subjectivist-interpretive approach to human science a most illuminating line of demarcation between economics and sociology may be drawn (Chapter 14, pp. 209–11). Sociology focuses on the 'because motives' of action taking the 'in-order-to motives' largely for granted; while the focus of economics is the converse. There is, however, clearly a great deal more to be said on the question of demarcation lines among subjectivist-interpretive human sciences. Secondly, arising out of this study of demarcation lines there is also the whole question of interdisciplinarity among human sciences if and when they all adopt a subjectivist-interpretive methodology. There are difficult questions to be answered concerning the merits of narrow specialization in developing theories in specific human sciences while ignoring others, and even more tricky still is the issue of whether sound policy prescriptions should be based on the theories of any one human science or should be interdisciplinary in character. All of these issues and more besides would have to be tackled in a full examination of the implications of the subjectivist-interpretive methodology for the detailed practice of the various sciences and so once again for reasons of scope and space I have not sought to carry out such an examination in this work. I have confined illustration of the subjectivist-interpretive methodology in practice to the case study of economics which was carried out in Part 2.

A third major issue which has been left outstanding in the book is the question of what precisely can be achieved by empirical tests of scientific theories. I have, of course, tried to establish a number of points firmly on the question of empirical testing, as for example in Chapters 2 and 3 where I defended the Popperian logic of falsification which shows that empirical evidence can only show a theory to be false but can never show it to be true (because of the fallacy of induction). Also in Chapter 14 I argued that the theories of a subjectivist-interpretive human science are conjectural and stand in need of empirical testing just as much as do the theories of natural science. Although these points are fairly clearly established in the work, there is another point about empirical testing which I have left very much as an open question. In the course of Chapter 10 where I considered the views of the Austrian economists on empirical testing I noted a 'moderate *a priorist*' position which holds that empirical testing in economics (or other subjectivist human sciences) can only establish whether or not a theory is applicable/inapplicable in some real world situation: it cannot pronounce the theory to be simply false.[6] (The fallacy of induction already rules out pronouncing a theory true on the basis of empirical tests.) I called this view of empirical testing the 'applicability thesis' and I suggested in Chapter 10 that at the very least it seemed to be a correct view of what precisely can be achieved by empirical testing in the human sciences. But beyond this brief suggestion I did not venture.

I should now like to suggest that the applicability thesis is as relevant to testing of theories in natural science as in human science and hence that it opens up a whole array of tricky philosophical issues which call for further critical discussion. Let us consider the sort of empirical test of an economic theory which illustrates very clearly what is involved in the applicability thesis. When empirical tests of the theory of perfect competition are made in real-world market structures which have significant elements of monopoly power the theory will apparently be 'falsified' in various of its predictions (although not in all of them). However, an economist would be very reluctant to say, therefore, that perfect competition theory is simply false because its predictions are not (or are never) being realized in (monopolistic) market structures. Rather, the economist would hold that the theory is *inapplicable* to those situations, but may very well be applicable to certain other market situations. Drawing out the full implications of this point we may say that even if there is no market in today's world to which perfect competition theory applies still the theory cannot be pronounced simply false because there have been perfectly competitive market situations in the past of which the theory was true, i.e. to which it was fully applicable, and there may again be such market situations in the future. All we can say is that perfect competition theory is inapplicable today, that it is false in the actual world. But as long as the theory is logically consistent, that is to say as long as the theory could conceivably be 'true of some possible world' (that is applicable in some situation) we cannot pronounce it to be simply false (or absolutely false).

I believe that this new conception of what can be achieved by empirical testing in the human sciences is on the right track and I now wish to emphasize that exactly the same drift of argument applies to testing in the natural sciences. For as in the case of theories in human science each natural science theory has a more or less clearly defined field of applicability and if the predictions of the theory are found to be false in areas beyond that defined field of applicability we would not pronounce the theory false, but only say that it was inapplicable to that situation. Popper himself has admitted this point in passing. He holds that if there were a huge cosmic accident, such as an explosion of the sun, we would *not* say that various of our scientific theories of today's world had been falsified but only that they are inapplicable in the new cosmic situation.[7]

From these considerations we arrive at the notion that *every* scientific theory will have a well-defined field of applicability; and any empirical test of the theory on the basis of evidence drawn (perforce) from some *actual* situation in the world can *only* establish the inapplicability of the theory to that actual situation.[8] It cannot lead to a pronouncement that a theory is simply true (which would in any case involve the fallacy of induction), or simply false. It would, however, be very far beyond the scope of this book even to start indicating the tricky philosophical problems in the theory of truth and in the logic and epistemology of possible worlds to which the above reflections on the applicability thesis must, I suspect, lead. Accordingly, having given some hint of how far-reaching may be the problems left outstanding in regard to empirical testing, I shall say no more on these matters here, leaving them as an open question requiring much further critical discussion and research.

Perhaps the most difficult of all the issues left outstanding in the book is the question of what constitutes a genuine explanation in science. I have already said something on this question in Chapter 3 when I suggested that scientific explanation of a phenomenon involves subsumption of the phenomenon under an insightful generalization of which it is an instance. I did not defend this notion of explanation there, rather I simply derived it from a view of explanation as generalization which is widely held among contemporary philosophers of science and is sometimes known as the Hempel – Popper covering law notion of explanation; and from the so-called realist conception of scientific theory as true insight. As I noted in Chapter 3, this hybrid notion of explanation was very much a provisional one, for there is a veritable Pandora's box of difficulties which is opened up when we begin to probe the question of what constitutes a genuine explanation in science.

Almost all philosophers and scientists would agree that it involves something more than mere elaborate description of the phenomena to be explained. With the exception of a small group of thinkers who uphold a 'descriptivist' conception of theories according to which scientific theories can be no more than mere redescription of complex data in succinct, often mathematical language,[9] philosophers and scientists have been agreed that explanation involves offering a rationally satisfactory account of how or why a certain phenomenon comes to be as it is. However, when philosophers of science (or even practising scientists) have gone on to try to specify what would be a 'rationally satisfactory' account of a phenomenon, wide, complex and often seemingly intractable differences emerge; and the attempt to deal with and resolve these often leads one back to a consideration of the very fundamentals of human cognition and what it can hope to achieve. To give a brief sampling of the sorts of issues that arise. Are covering laws merely elaborate descriptions after all? Is it the attainment of insight which is the essence of explanation and if so why should explanations have to be general in character? Have we explained anything unless we have given an account not only of *how* a phenomenon comes to be but also of *why* it should be so? And so on.

It goes without saying that it would have been beyond the scope of this work to have sought to grapple with these involved issues concerning the nature of genuine explanation in science. Accordingly I shall content myself with simply signalling them here as a final important set of issues left open and outstanding in the book.

16.3   My Three Main Conclusions

Since the discussions in the course of this book have been so wide-ranging it may be useful to finish off by stating clearly the main conclusions which I have sought to achieve therein.[10] Reflecting the interdisciplinary character of the work, of the three main conclusions which I seek to draw one is drawn from pure philosophy, another pertains largely to economic science, while the major conclusion is concerned with the appropriate methodology of the human sciences.

These three main results which I have attempted to achieve are as follows: *the purely philosophical result*, that is the spirit of critical rationalism and its corollary that any genuinely critical methodology of science must be based on philosophy. In Part 1 I argued at some length that the critical activity of Reason in its relentless pursuit of truth lies at the very basis of all human inquiry and knowledge, and indeed that it provides the only possible foundation for reasoned discussion or for academic work of any sort. Invoking this spirit of critical rationalism which demands that every received opinion should be submitted to critical scrutiny, I showed that *inter alia* the methods of the sciences cannot be simply taken for granted but must also be subjected to a critical appraisal. Such a critical methodology of science cannot be developed by any one of the specific sciences without becoming involved in a vicious circularity and so I argued that we must turn to *philosophy* to develop our methodology of science. In order that a critical philosophically based methodology should avoid the same sort of vicious circularity as specific sciences encounter if they try to provide a methodological critique of scientific method I argued further that philosophy must be capable of providing its own justification or ground by basing itself on a set of reflexively self-justifying propositions as its first principles. Thus we arrived at a conception which together with the spirit of critical rationalism (and of which it is a corollary) has pervaded the whole of the book: the notion of a critical philosophically based methodology of science guided by the goal of (pursuit of) truth (the inexorable *telos* of Reason) and which will stand in a normative relation to the actual practices of science.

The *conclusion in methodology* of the *human sciences*, that is the decisive defence of a subjectivist – interpretive methodology and rejection of the objectivist – behaviourist approach. The attempted establishment of this second conclusion was in fact the major aim of the book and the other key results have emerged in the course of moving towards it. Following the demonstration in Part I that methodological issues can only be dealt with adequately and resolved decisively on the plane of philosophy I sought in Part 3 to show how the subjectivist-interpretive methodology can be deduced from a foundation of absolute certainty in a philosophy built up from reflexively self-justifying propositions. In order to reach such a philosophical foundation of absolute certainty for the methodology of human science I turned to existentialist phenomenology showing how it can establish a core of reflexively self-justifying propositions regarding human subjectivity. I then used them as the philosophical basis from which the central principles of a subjectivist-interpretive methodology of human science, with its teleological mode of explanation and in particular the mature Schutzian version of such a methodology, can be directly deduced. I also showed how these same set of philosophical propositions and considerations refute decisively the objectivist-behaviourist approach to the human sciences with its efficient-causal mode of explanation. Finally, since the teleological mode of explanation of the subjectivist approach is radically distinct from the efficient-causal mode of explanation which pervades the natural sciences I concluded that there ought to be a radical differentiation of methods between the natural and human sciences: a thesis known as methodological dualism.

The *result* in economics, that is that mainstream economic theory is the shining exemplification of a Schutzian subjectivist-interpretive methodology with its teleological mode of explanation at work in the practices of a human science. I sought to establish this result by the methodological case study of Part 2, in which I examined at length the methodological character of the corpus of mainstream economic theory and found it to be unmistakably subjectivist-interpretive in character in virtue of the centrality to all economic theorizing of the optimization principle. But I also found, rather surprisingly, that the bulk of mainstream economists have not been apprised of the subjectivist-interpretive character of their theorizing. In what little they have said on methodological matters most economists have urged a 'superficial' methodological monist' (or sometimes an instrumentalist) version of the objectivist-behaviourist approach as the appropriate methodology of economics. In the light of what my own examination of the corpus of mainstream theory has shown, this widespread objectivist-behaviourist methodological precept of most economists is entirely at variance with the manner in which they practise their science. Accordingly, in the light of the second major conclusion of the book – the decisive philosophical defence of a subjectivist-interpretive methodology of human science – I concluded that this 'methodological gap' or inconsistency between an objectivist-behaviourist precept and a subjectivist-interpretive practice should be eliminated by bringing precept into line with practice in the methodology of economics.

Notes

1   To the former, because of its positivism, to the latter, because of its
    methodological individualist principle. For a good survey of this approach and

its opposition to both objectivist and subjectivist approaches, see for example, R. Bernstein (1978), *The Restructuring of Social and Political Theory* (Oxford: Basil Blackwell) and J. Habermas (1972), *Knowledge and Human Interests* (London: Heinemann).

2 In other words, one does not need to have recourse to the extremes of the Historical School to prove a radical difference of method between natural and human science.

3 I show in Chapter 15 that even apparently teleological explanations in the natural sciences turn out upon examination to be efficient-causal explanations expressed in teleological language as a convenient shorthand.

4 Even in the case of Hayek, probably the clearest exponent of such a view, we find that he has changed his view on the question of *a priorism* in the course of his (long) career. See for example T. Hutchison (1981), *The Politics and Philosophy of Economics* (Oxford: Basil Blackwell), pp. 210–19.

5 Cf. footnote 1 of Chapter 16 for reference to the principal exponents of this approach.

6 Cf. Chapter 10, p. 157.

7 Cf. K. Popper (1972), *Objective Knowledge* (Oxford: Oxford University Press), p. 22.

8 When we adopt the applicability thesis the Popperian logic still applies. For it is still the case that any finite set of data could be consistent with the predictions of a large range of different theories; hence that finite sets of evidence cannot possibly establish the applicability to the actual situation any more than they can establish the truth of any one of the theories which predicts correctly (cf. Chapter 2, p. 33 and Chapter 3, p. 44).

9 The position descriptivism has already been discussed briefly in Chapter 9, Note 30, p. 149.

10 A detailed summary of the argument leading towards these conclusions has already been given in the first section of this chapter.

Bibliography

Ackley, G. (1978), *Macro-economics: Theory and Policy* (London: Macmillan).

Archibald, G. (1961), 'Chamberlin v. Chicago', *Review of Economic Studies*, vol. 29, no. 1, pp. 2–28.

Aune, B. (1977), *Reason and Action* (Dordrecht: Reidel).

Ayer, A. J. (1972), *Language, Truth and Logic* (London: Pelican).

Barnes, B. (1982), *T. S. Kuhn and Social Science* (London: Macmillan).

Barthes, R. (1973), *Mythologies* (St Albans: Paladin).

Baumol, W. (1952), 'The transactions demand for cash', *Quarterly Journal of Economics*, vol. 66, no. 4, pp. 545–56.

Becker, G. (1977), 'The economics of marital instability', *Journal of Political Economy*, vol. 85, no. 6, pp. 1141–87.

Benn, S. and G. Mortimore (eds) (1976), *Rationality in Social Science* (London: Routledge & Kegan Paul).

Bernstein, R. (1976), *The Restructuring of Social and Political Theory* (Oxford: Basil Blackwell).

Bhaskar, R. (1975), *A Realist Theory of Science* (London: Leeds).

Blaug, M. (1968), *Economic Theory in Retrospect* (Cambridge: Cambridge University Press).

Boland, L. (1979), 'A critique of Friedman's critics', *Journal of Economic Literature*, vol. 17, pp. 503–22.

Boudon, R. (1977), *Effets Pervers et Ordre Social* (Paris: PUF).

Boudon, R. (1979), *La Logique du Social* (Paris: Hachette).

Breit, W. and H. Hochman (eds) (1971), *Readings in Micro-economics* (New York: Holt Rinehart & Winston).

Brentano, F. (1966), *The True and the Evident* (London: Routledge & Kegan Paul).

Buchler, J. (ed.) (1939), *Philosophical Writings of C. Peirce* (London: International Library of Psychology, Philosophy and Scientific Method).

Butler, E. (1983), *Hayek* (London: Temple Smith).

Caldwell, B. (1982), *Beyond Positivism* (London: Allen & Unwin).

Camus, A. (1957), *L'etranger* (Paris: Gallimard).

Cicourel, A. (1964), *Method and Measurement in Sociology* (New York: Free Press).

Clower, R. (1965) 'The Keynesian counter-revolution: a theoretical appraisal', in F. Hahn (ed.), *Theory of Interest Rates* (London: Macmillan).

Comte, A. (1877), *Cours de Philosophie Positivie* (Paris: Ballière).

Cornford, F. (1970), *Plato's Theory of Knowledge* (London: Routledge & Kegan Paul).

Craib, I. (1976), *Existentialism and Sociology: a Study of Sartre* (Cambridge: Cambridge University Press).

Descartes, R. (1979), *Discourse on Method and the Meditations* (Harmondsworth: Penguin).

Dilthey, W. (1961), *Meaning in History*, H. Rickman (ed.) (London: Allen & Unwin).

Dolan, E. (ed.) (1976), *The Foundations of Modern Austrian Economics* (Kansas City: Sheed & Ward).

Downs, A. (1957), *An Economic Theory of Democracy* (New York: Harper).

Farber, M. (1943), *The Foundation of Phenomenology* (New York: University of New York Press).

Fergusion, C. (1972), *Micro-economic Theory*, 3rd ed. (Homewood, Ill.: Richard Irwin).

Findlay, J. N. (1958), *Hegel: a Re-examination* (London: Allen & Unwin).

Ford, J. (1975), *Paradigms and Fairy-Tales*, Book 1 (London: Routledge & Kegan Paul).

Friedman, Maurice (1953), *The Worlds of Existentialism* (Chicago: Chicago University Press).

Friedman, Milton (1953), *Essays in Positive Economics* (Chicago: Chicago University Press).

Friedman, Milton and L. Savage (1948), Utility analysis and behaviour towards risk', Journal of Political Economy, vol. 56, no. 4, pp. 279–304.

Galbraith, J. K. (1967), *The New Industrial State* (London: Hamish Hamilton).

Garfinkel, H. (1967), *Studies in Ethno-Methodology* (Englewood-Cliffs, N. J.: Prentice-Hall).

Goffman, E. (1968), *Asylums* (Harmondsworth: Penguin).

Hanbermas, J. (1972), *Knowledge and Human Interests* (London: Heinemann).

Hahn, F. (ed.) (1965), *The Theory of Interest Rates* (London: Macmillan).

Hahn, F. (1977), 'Keynesian economics and equilibrium theory', in Harcourt, G. C. (ed.), *The Micro Foundations of Macro-economics* (London: Macmillan).

Hahn, F. and M. Hollis (eds.) (1979), *Philosophy and Economic Theory* (Oxford: Oxford University Press).

Hampshire, S. (1959), *Thought and Action* (London: Chatto & Windus).

Harcourt, G. C. (ed.) (1977), *The Micro Foundations of Maco-economics* (London: Macmillan).

Hart, H. L. A. (1970), *The Concept of Law* (Oxford: Clarendon Press).

Hayek, F. (1955), *The Counter-Revolution of Science* (Glencoe: The Free Press).

Hayek, F. (1967), *Studies in Philosophy, Politics and Economics* (London: Routledge & Kegan Paul).

Hayek, F. (1978), *New Studies in Philosophy, Politics and Economics* (London: Routledge & Kegan Paul).

Hegel, G. W. F. (1971), *The Phenomenology of Mind* (London: Allen & Unwin).

Hempel, C. (1965), *Aspects of Scientific Explanation* (New York: Free Press).

Hollis, M. (1977), *Models of Man* (Cambridge: Cambridge University Press).

Hollis, M. and S. Lukes (eds) (1982), *Rationality and Relativism* (Oxford: Basil Blackwell).

Hollis, M. and E. Nell (1975), *Rational Economic Man* (Cambridge: Cambridge University Press).

Hookway, C. and P. Pettit (1978), *Action and Interpretation* (Cambridge: Cambridge University Press).

Hume, D. (1969), *A Treatise on Human Nature* (London: Pelican).

Husserl, E. (1960), *Cartesian Meditations* (The Hague: Martinus Nijhoff).

Husserl, E. (1964), *The Idea of Phenomenology* (The Hague: Martinus Nijhoff).

Husserl, E. (1965), *Phenomenology and the Crisis of Philosophy*, Q. Lauer (New York: Harper).

Husserl, E. (1970), *Logical Investigations*, Vol. 1 (London: Routledge & Kegan Paul).

Husserl, E. (1970), *The Crisis of European Science and Transcendental Phenomenology* (Evanston, Ill.: North Western University Press).

Hutchison, T. (1977), *Knowledge and Ignorance in Economics* (Oxford: Basil Blackwell).

Hutchison, T. (1982), *The Politics and Philosophy of Economics* (Oxford: Basil Blackwell).

Jaspers, K. (1969), *Nietzsche* (Chicago: Gateway).

Kaldor, N. (1972), The irrelevance of equilibrium analysis', *Economic Journal*, vol. 82, no. 4, pp. 1237–55.

Kant, I. (1969), *Critique of Pure Reason* (London: Macmillan).

Katouzian, H. (1980), *Ideology and Method in Economics* (London: Macmillan).

Kenny, A. (1963), *Action, Emotion and Will* (London: Routledge & Kegan Paul).

Keynes, J. N. (1936), *The Scope and Method of Political Economy* (New York: Augustus Kelley).

Knight, F. (1956), *On the History and Method of Economics* (Chicago: Chicago University Press).

Kolakowski, L. (1972), *Postivist Philosophy* (Harmondsworth: Pelican).

Kolakowski, L. (1975), *Husserl and the Search for Certitude* (London: University Press).

Koutsoyiannis, A. (1979), *Modern Micro-economics* (London: Macmillan).

Kuhn, T. S. (1970), *The Structure of Scientific Revolutions* (Chicago: Chicago University Press).

Laing, R. D. (1965), *The Divided Self: an Existentialist Study in Sanity and Madness* (London: Penguin).

Laing, R. D. (1969), *Self and Others* (London: Tavistock).

Lakatos, I. (1976), *Proofs and Refutations* (Cambridge: Cambridge University Press).

Lakatos, I. and A. Musgrave (eds) (1970), *Criticism and the Growth of Knowledge* (Cambridge: Cambridge University Press).

Latsis, S. (ed.) (1976), *Method and Appraisal in Economics* (Cambridge: Cambridge University Press).

Leijonhufvud, A. (1968), *On Keynesian Economics and the Economics of Keynes* (Oxford: Oxford University Press).

Leijonhufvud, A. (1969), *Keynes and the Classics* (London: Institute of Economic Affairs).

Levinson, P. (ed.) (1982), *In Pursuit of Truth; essays in honour of Sir Karl Popper's 80th birthday* (Brighton: Harvester Press).

Lipsey, R. (1983), *Introduction to Positive Economics*, 6th ed. (London: Weidenfeld & Nicolson).

Lipsey, R. and K. Lancaster (1956), *The general theory of second best*, *Review of Economic Studies*, vol. 24, no. 1, pp. 11–32.

Littlechild, S. (1978), *The fallacy of the mixed economy. An Austrian critique of economic thinking and policy* (London: Institute of Economic Affairs).

Locke, J. (1960), *An Essay Concerning Human Understanding*, ed. by P. Laslett (Cambridge: Cambridge University Press).

Lukes, S. (1973), *Individualism* (Oxford: Basil Blackwell).

Lukes, S. (1973), 'Methodological individualism reconsidered', in A. Ryan (ed.), *The Philosophy of Social Explanation* (Oxford: Oxford University Press).

Machlup, F. (1978), *Methodology of Economics and Other Human Sciences* (New York: Academic Press).

McIntyre, A. (1971), *Against the Self-Images of Man* (London: Duckworth).

Marcel, C. (1951), *Being and Having* (Boston, Mass.: Beacon Press).

Marcuse, H. (1964), *One-dimensional Man* (London: Routledge & Kegan Paul).

Marshall, A. (1962), *Principles of Economics* (London: Macmillan; 8th ed.).

Merleau-Ponty, M. (1962), *The Phenomenology of Perception* (London: Routledge & Kegan Paul).

Mill, J. S. (1962), *Utilitarianism and Other Essays*, ed. M. Warnock (London: Fontana).

Mill, J. S. (1963–69), *Collected Works*, Vols 2, 3, 7 and 8 (Toronto: University of Toronto Press).

Mises, L. von (1949), *Human Action* (London: Hodge).

Myrdal, G. (1958), *Value in Social Theory* (London: Routledge & Kegan Paul).

Nagel, E. (1963), 'Assumptions in economic theory', *American Economic Review Supplement*, vol. 53, no. 2, pp. 211–19.

Nietzsche, F. (1968), *Twilight of the Idols* (Harmondsworth: Penguin).

Nietzsche, F. (1977), *Thus Spake Zarathustra* (Harmondsworth: Penguin).

O'Driscoll, G. and M. Rizzo (1985), *The Economics of Time and Ignorance* (Oxford: Basil Blackwell).

O'Sullivan, P. J. (1984), 'Friedman's methodology revisited: a proposal for a decisive refutation of the F-twist', *Explorations in Knowledge*, vol. 1, no. 2, pp. 32–49.

O'Sullivan, P. J. (1985), 'Review of "In pursuit of truth"', *Explorations in Knowledge*, vol. 2, no. 2, pp. 54–60.

Pareto, V. (1972), *Manual of Political Economy* (London: Macmillan).

Passmore, J. (1968), *Hume's Intentions* (London: Duckworth).

Patinkin, D. (1965), *Money, Interest and Prices* (New York: Harper & Row).

Phelps, E. (1970), *Micro-economic Foundation of Unemployment and Inflation Theory* (New York: Norton).

Plato (1970), *The Republic*, trans. H. Lee (Harmondsworth: Penguin).

Plato (1970), 'The Theaetus', 'The Sophist', in F. Cornford *Plato's Theory of Knowledge* (London: Routledge & Kegan Paul).

Plato (1974), *The Symposium*, trans. W. Hamilton (London: Penguin).

Plato (1982), *The Last Days of Socrates*, trans. H. Tredennick (Harmondsworth: Penguin).

Popper, K. (1957), *The Poverty of Historicism* (London: Routledge & Kegan Paul).

Popper, K. (1959), *The Logic of Scientific Discovery* (London: Hutchinson).

Popper, K. (1963), *Conjectures and Refutations* (London: Routledge & Kegan Paul).

Popper, K. (1972), *Objective Knowledge* (Oxford: Clarendon Press).

Popper, K. (1976), *Unended Quest* (London: Fontana).

Ricoeur, P. (1967), *Husserl: an Analysis of his Phenomenology* (Evanston, Ill.: North Western University Press).

Robbins, L. (1935), *An Essay on the Nature and Significance of Economic Science* (London: Macmillan).

Robinson, J. (1982), *Economic Philosophy* (London: Watts).

Roche, M. (1973), *Phenomenology, Language and the Social Science* (London: Routledge & Kegan Paul).

Rosenberg, A. (1981), *Sociobiology and the Preemption of Social Sciences* (London: Routledge & Kegan Paul).

Runciman, W. (1972), *A Critique of Max Weber's Philosophy of Social Science* (Cambridge: Cambridge University Press).

Russell, B. (1972), 'Russell's logical atomism', D. Pears (ed.) (London: Fontana).

Ryan, A. (ed.) (1973), *The Philosophy of Social Explanation* (Oxford: Oxford University Press).

Ryle, G. (1963), *The Concept of Mind* (Harmondsworth: Penguin).

Samuelson, P. (1967), *Economics* (New York: McGraw-Hill).

Samuelson, P. (1972), *Collected Works*, Vol. 3 (Cambridge, Mass.: MIT Press).

Sartre, J.-P. (1948), *Existentialism and Humanism* (London: Methuen).

Sartre, J.-P. (1963), *Les Mains Sales* (London: Methuen).

Sartre, J.-P. (1966) *La Nausée* (Paris: Gallimard).

Sartre, J.-P. (1969), *Being and Nothingness* (London: Methuen).

Sartre, J.-P. (1971), *A Sketch for a Theory of the Emotions* (London: Methuen).

Sartre, J.-P. (1972), *The Psychology of Imagination* (London: Methuen).

Schumpeter, J. (1972) *History of Economic Analysis* (London: Allen & Unwin).

Schutz, A. (1962–66), *Collected Papers*, Vols 1–3 (The Hague: Martinus Nijhoff).

Schutz, A. (1972), *The Phenomenology of the Social World* (London: Heinemann).

Shackle, G. L. (1972), *Epistemics and Economics* (Cambridge: Cambridge University Press).

Steiner, G. (1975), *After Babel* (Oxford: Oxford University Press).

Stewart, I. (1979), *Reasoning and Method in Economics* (London: McGraw-Hill).

Strasser, S. (1963), *Phenomenology and the Human Sciences* (Pittsburgh: Duquesne University Press).

Tobin, J. (1958), 'Liquidity preference as behaviour towards risk', *Review of Economic Studies*, vol. 25, no. 2, pp. 65–86.

Trigg, R. (1973), *Reason and Commitment* (Cambridge: Cambridge University Press).

Ward, B. (1972), *What's Wrong with Economics?* (London: Macmillan).

Weber, M. (1970), *The Protestant Ethic and the Spirit of Capitalism* (London: Allen & Unwin).

Weber, M. (1978), *Economy and Society*, G. Roth and C. Wittich (eds), (New York: Bedminster Press).

Winch, P. (1958), *The Idea of a Social Science and its Relation to Philosophy* (London: Routledge & Kegan Paul).

Wittgenstein, L. von (1958), *Philosophical Investigations* (Oxford: Basil Blackwell).

Wittgenstein, L. von (1961), *Tractatus Logico-Philosophicas* (London: Routledge & Kegan Paul).

Wong, S. (1973), 'The F-twist and Samuelson's Methodology', *American Economic Review*, vol, 63, no. 3, pp. 312–25.

Index